S0-AVO-367

To be with him, or to read him, is a great experience, as he has the power of making one feel one could do all he has done. I don't know whether this is a mark of genius, certainly few people have it.

E. M. FORSTER, LETTER TO FLORENCE BARGER, 1926

Lawrence, an odd gnome, half cad – with a touch of genius.

HON. AUBREY HERBERT, NOTE IN PRIVATE DIARY, 1914

A TOUCH OF GENIUS

A TOUCH OF GENIUS
The Life of T. E. Lawrence

MALCOLM BROWN

Julia Cave

PARAGON HOUSE
New York

First American edition, 1989

Published in the United States by

Paragon House
90 Fifth Avenue
New York, NY 10011

Copyright © 1988 by Malcolm Brown and Julia Cave.

All rights reserved. No part of this book may be
reproduced, in any form, without written permission
from the publishers, unless by a reviewer who wishes
to quote brief passages.

Reprinted by arrangement with J. M. Dent & Sons Ltd.,
London

Library of Congress Cataloging-in-Publication Data

Brown, Malcolm.
A touch of genius : the life of T.E. Lawrence / Malcolm Brown,
Julia Cave.—1st American ed.
p.   cm.
Reprint. Originally published: London : J.M. Dent, 1988.
Bibliography: p.
Includes index.
ISBN 1-55778-203-2
1. Lawrence, T. E. (Thomas Edward), 1888-1935.   2. World War,
1914-1918—Campaigns—Middle East.   3. Great Britain.   Army—
Biography.   4. Soldiers—Great Britain—Biography.   I. Cave,
Julia.   II. Title.
D568.4.L45B74 1989
940.4'15'0924—dc19
[B]   88-30127
                                                                                          CIP

Manufactured in the United States of America

CONTENTS

PREFACE

We should like to express our gratitude to the many people who have contributed in various ways to the making of this book. Our thanks must go to the staffs of the numerous libraries from which we have drawn material, but especially honourable mention should be made of the Department of Western Manuscripts of the Bodleian Library, Oxford, and in particular of Dennis Porter, Senior Assistant Librarian, and of Colin Harris and the staff of Room 132. We should also like to thank the staffs of the Public Record Office, London; of the Houghton Library at Harvard (particularly Vicki Denby); and of the Harry Ransom Humanities Research Center at Austin, Texas (particularly Cathy Henderson). Other individual librarians, archivists or keepers whom we are pleased to thank are Dr D. A. Rees of Jesus College, Oxford; Dr Michael Halls of Kings College, Cambridge; Michael Bott of the Reading University Library; Roderick Suddaby and Jane Carmichael of the Imperial War Museum, London; and Peter Murton of the Royal Air Force Museum, Hendon.

In regard to illustrations we should particularly like to thank the Imperial War Museum, who have supplied us with many excellent photographs from Lawrence's own wartime collection, which he deposited with the Museum in the 1930s. He severely discouraged any publication of them in his lifetime and regretted their being even shown to enquirers; by contrast this remarkable collection, along with the rest of the War Museum's huge store of photographs, is now available not only to the professional historian but also to members of the public, who are encouraged, by appointment, to visit, browse and even buy their own copies. We are very grateful also to the Bodleian Library, which supplied us with many important stills of high quality, its especially strong suit being family photographs and photographs of Lawrence himself, including some rare glimpses of him during the war years. Other sources we are pleased to acknowledge are the British Library, the BBC Hulton Picture Library, the BBC's Design Department (for photographs taken in 1962 by the late Roynon Raikes), the Oxford City Library, the Palestine Exploration Fund (special gratitude to R. L. Chapman), the Royal Geographical Society and the Audio-Visual Centre of the University of Newcastle-upon-Tyne. One other photograph which proved difficult to trace finally came to us by courtesy of Messrs Christie. Our thanks also to Paul J. Marriott for permission to republish from his book on Lawrence's Oxford years his map of the 1908 bicycle journey through France; Hugh Leach who lent us his photograph of a wrecked engine of the Hejaz Railway; and Mrs D. K. O'Conor of New Jersey, U.S.A., who gave us special permission to publish two photographs taken by her father, Herbert Garland, like Lawrence a notable destroyer of Turkish trains during the Arabian campaign. Details of the source of each individual illustration are given below.

The reference to a book supposed by one misinformed bookseller of the 1920s to be entitled *Seven Pillows of Wisdom* (see the footnote on page 178) emerged from a friendly letter from Professor Stanley Weintraub of the Pennsylvania State University, whom we thank not only for this but for his other more notable contributions to Lawrence scholarship. Our thanks also go to Betty Brown who meticulously scrutinized the text for errors both at the typing and the proof-reading stage.

We are pleased to thank the BBC for support and sustenance during the production of the television documentaries *T. E. Lawrence 1888–1935* (1962) and *Lawrence and Arabia* (1986), and for permission to quote from them. We would also like to pay special tribute to David Lytton and Philip Donnellan whose knowledge and professional skill during the making of the 1962 programme helped to produce some of the most valuable interview material included in the following pages. Joy Curtiss was a researcher on both these programmes, and her expertise in finding suitable stills has much enriched the corpus of illustrations from which we have been able to make a selection. An important consequence of working on these films was that of meeting so many people who knew T. E. Lawrence or had made serious studies of him. Many of these are referred to in the Introduction but we should like to single out for special mention a number of people whose interest and friendship have been of particular value to us: Arthur Russell formerly of the Tank Corps; Laurence 'Rory' Moore formerly of the Imperial Camel Corps; Suleiman Mousa, Lawrence's Arab biographer; Michael Yardley, himself an author of a recent biography of Lawrence; and Christopher Matheson of San Francisco, a longtime Lawrence enthusiast. We also wish to express our warm gratitude for the helpfulness and friendship of Jeremy Wilson, Lawrence's authorized biographer; of H. St. John Armitage C.B.E., who subjected our narrative chapters to rigorous scrutiny and offered much valued advice; and, most importantly of all, of A. W. Lawrence and his late wife Barbara.

Lastly we should like to thank the Trustees of the *Seven Pillars of Wisdom* Trust, of whom A. W. Lawrence is one, for permission to publish material within their copyright, and the Keeper of the Public Records at the Public Records Office for permission to publish material which is the copyright of the Crown.

M.B.   J.C.

SOURCES OF ILLUSTRATIONS

The authors and publishers also wish to acknowledge permission to quote from copyright material as follows:
Bodleian Library, Oxford: 6, 9, 31, 39, 57, 63b, 86, 113, 123, 149, 151a, 154a, 155, 160, 162, 163, 173, 175, 182, 183a, 183b, 191, 192, 194, 203, 204a, 204b, 208 212. BBC: 5, 21. British Library Newspaper Library, Colindale: 168, 217a, 217b. British Museum: 36, 41, 42. Christie's, London: 138b. Golden Cockerel Press: 24a, 25. Hugh Leach: 99b. Hulton Picture Library: 56, 139b, 141, 221a, 221b. Imperial War Museum: iv, 1, 63a, 69, 71a, 71b, 71c, 72a, 76–7, 77, 80–81, 87, 89, 92, 92–3, 96, 99a, 108, 110, 114–5, 118, 132, 133, 134, 139, 151b, 222. Jonathan Cape: 172a, 172b. Lowell Thomas Collection: 64b. National Portrait Gallery: 209a. Mrs R. O'Conor: 72, 73. Oxford County Libraries: 13b, 14a, 14b, 17. Paul J. Marriott: 24b. Palestine Exploration Fund: 47. Public Record Office: 138a. Reading University, Dept. of Archives and Manuscripts: 189a, 214a, 214b. Royal Geographical Society: 98. Arthur Russell: 170. St Nicholas Church, Moreton: 220a. Squadron-Leader J. R. Sims Retd.: 4, 209b. University of Newcastle upon Tyne: 158–9. University of Texas: 64a. Photographs by Malcolm Brown: 13a, 51a, 51b, 111, 154b, 171, 188, 189b, 220b.

Of the above the following are photographs by T. E. Lawrence: 14b, 36, 39, 69, 71a, 71b, 71c, 76, 77, 86, 87, 89, 96, 110, 118.

NOTE ON SOURCES

Among the Public Record Office sources referred to in the Introduction the following were found to be of value:

for the war years:
FO 882 series, particularly 882/5, 6, 7, 8, 9, 12, 13, 16, 17, 18, 25, 26, 27 (the last three consist of issues of the *Arab Bulletin* for 1916, 1917 and 1918 respectively); 882/1 is an Index to the series but an incomplete one.
FO 371/6237
WO 95/4403 and 4415
WO 158/603, 604, 605, 606, 620, 640B

for the political years:
CAB 27/24 and 37
FO 608/92 and 93
FO 371/4182 and 4183
FO 686/93
FO 882/13

The Spelling of Arabic Names

When *Revolt in the Desert*, the abridged version of Lawrence's account of the Arabian campaign *Seven Pillars of Wisdom*, was being prepared for its publication in 1927, the publisher took up with Lawrence the matter of his inconsistency in the spelling of Arabic proper names. 'Arabic names won't go into English, exactly,' Lawrence replied, 'for their consonants are not the same as ours, and their vowels, like ours, vary from district to district. There are some "scientific systems" of transliteration, helpful to people who know enough Arabic not to need helping, but a washout for the world. I spell my names anyhow, to show what rot the systems are.' However, he was reasonably consistent in spelling such names as occurred most frequently in his narrative and we have therefore followed his general usage, which is also on the whole the usage of his wartime reports: thus for example Akaba not Aqaba, Abdulla not Abdullah, Feisal not Feisul. When quoting other writers we have adopted the style of the person quoted: Ronald Storrs for example wrote Abdulla as Abdallah and Feisal as Faisal. Any confusion should be easily dispelled by reference to the Index, in which all such variations are collated.

INTRODUCTION

In October 1917, roughly a year after Lawrence had become involved in the Arabian campaign, his Oxford friend and mentor, D. G. Hogarth, at that time a senior member of British Military Intelligence in Cairo, wrote home to his sister:

> [Lawrence] is going out again for a spell and [his family] must not expect letters from him; but whenever I have news of him I'll let them know the facts whether through you or direct. But the intervals will be long. Tell his mother he has now five decorations including the C.B. (to qualify for which he had to be promoted to major) and despises and ignores the lot.... [H]is reputation has become overpowering.

It was not, however, his reputation in the war which transmuted T. E. Lawrence, Oxonian, archaeologist and brilliant amateur soldier, into 'Lawrence of Arabia'; that was the product of the post-war publicity machine devised by the American Lowell Thomas, which made him into a kind of matinée idol in the film star mode. Thereafter, however much he might twist and turn or change his name, celebrity lay permanently about him, and the popular press pursued him with the single-mindedness with which it now pursues royalty. Partly liking, but mostly hating his fame, he became the stuff of fiction in his own lifetime. As his brother, A. W. Lawrence, put it in 1962:

> Fantastic legends started to appear about him soon after Lowell Thomas's show. The French had evidence at one time, they thought, that he was stirring up a rebellion and leading it in Morocco, and he had to be dragged out of an Air Force camp in England and shown to the French ambassador. And that sort of thing continued all the

time. He could have no reasonable private life. Such legends even
went on after he was dead. Now he has become the subject of extreme
adulation or equally extreme denigration, the process having gradually
gained strength as the witnesses to his actions died off. In neither of
these two over-dramatized figures, the saint and the charlatan, can I
really recognize more than a trace of the brother whom I knew and
liked.

It was perhaps inevitable that a man who was so universally admired in his
lifetime should raise intense controversy after his death. One generation's heroes
are frequently the next one's rejects, but in his case the adulation and media
myth-making had been such that there was no chance of avoiding a veritable
dam-burst of criticism sooner or later. When he died in self-sought obscurity
at the age of 46, he was as ill served by the press's obituary writers in death as
he had been by its investigative reporters when he was alive. The *Montreal Daily
Herald*, for example, wrote: 'Lawrence belonged to the era of chain-mail and
broadswords, when men broke their lances in impossible quests, and to the age
of the troubadours when men boasted of their deeds under one moon and under
the next covered their vanity with sackcloth. . . . One cannot dictate to posterity,
but we hope that a few generations will remember him, if only as a baffling and
arresting figure – a knight in shining armor in an age of colored shirts.'

The unintentional result of such excess, which Lawrence himself would have
genuinely loathed, was positively to invite subsequent denigration. In fact it was
not until twenty years later that his reputation met its supreme critic, in a writer,
novelist and poet who had himself fought in the First World War, though in a
grimmer theatre than that in which Lawrence had performed. Richard Aldington
had served on the Western Front, and had subsequently attacked conventional
romantic assumptions in his bitterly satirical novel *Death of a Hero*. That people
should reimpose worn-out ideas of heroism on Lawrence, who had fought in
one of the war's minor, if colourful sideshows, was plainly too much for
Aldington; and when, having decided to write his life, he found certain inconsist-
encies and oddities about Lawrence's story, he turned his book from a biography
into a 'biographical enquiry' in which he began as prosecutor and ended virtually
as hanging judge. Thereafter other notable books chipped at the legend. In 1962
the Arab historian Suleiman Mousa produced a biography presenting an 'Arab
view' (published in English in 1966), which argued that Lawrence's role in the
desert war was much smaller than had been thought in the West and that the
main credit belonged to Feisal and other Arab leaders. In 1968 Phillip Knightley
and Colin Simpson revealed in the *Sunday Times*, and in the following year in
a best-selling book, that Lawrence had submitted himself at various times
between 1923 and 1935 to severe beatings, which have been variously interpreted
as a form of mediaeval flagellation or, in more twentieth-century terms, as

masochism; knowledge of this aspect of him would surely have stunned his admirers of the twenties and thirties. It could also be said that the Robert Bolt/ David Lean/Sam Spiegel film *Lawrence of Arabia* could scarcely have happened as it did, had not Aldington made Lawrence seem a much less sacred, more sinister – and therefore more fascinating – figure than the crusader saint he was once taken to be.

When Aldington's book appeared in 1955 there was much controversy in the review and letter columns. Many Lawrence admirers were enraged and certain aspects of it proved deeply hurtful to those close to him. Contrary to general belief, Aldington was not the first to publish the fact of Lawrence's illegitimacy but he made such play of it – for example describing it as 'obviously the clue to Lawrence's abortive career and tortuous character' – that he caused not merely embarrassment but also offence. However, in a long and balanced review of the book in the *Daily Telegraph* Lord Vansittart stated his belief that Aldington had 'done good service by writing it. For it will provoke not only interest but anger, and in the clang a balance may be struck'.

Enough mud clings to the image for it to be still mildly fashionable to use adjectives such as 'sham' or 'bogus' when referring to Lawrence, but the general assumption is that Aldington belaboured his subject too fiercely and that if he gained a victory it was to some extent a short-lived one.[1] And generally, though there have been notable exceptions, there has been an increasing tendency among his biographers to arrive at an interpretation of him which makes him a credible, but still very remarkable, T. E. Lawrence rather than an incredible Lawrence of Arabia. A. W. Lawrence's view is beginning to prevail, and Vansittart's 'balance', as he hoped, is being struck.

This book aims to portray a Lawrence in line with this centrist view, and it does so out of a conviction that comes from much research and from the experience of having met and talked to many people who knew the man himself. I owe the latter advantage to the fact that in the course of my long career as a Producer of historical documentaries for BBC Television I was twice privileged to work on major programmes about Lawrence, once as co-producer and once as adviser and associate. Both were seen by very large audiences and were very favourably reviewed, and I am convinced that both helped to move opinion towards a more realistic assessment of their subject. If this is so it is, I believe, largely because in making such programmes one turns automatically to people

---

1 See for example Martin Seymour-Smith's recent biography of Robert Graves, *Robert Graves, His Life and Work* (1982), which refers dismissively to Aldington's book as 'now only a curiosity piece, with little bearing on Lawrence.' Graves himself, notwithstanding certain disagreements with Lawrence and his reluctance to be aligned with what he called 'the ageing members of the Lawrence Bureau', continued to 'believe' firmly in him in spite of Aldington's strictures.

who knew the man in question personally rather than those with theories about him; and overwhelmingly the witnesses we included on both occasions supported and substantiated a balanced, middle-of-the-road interpretation. If anything mystified them it was the absurd lengths to which some people went to idolize or denigrate him. If anything angered them it was the assumption, implicit in the writings of Lawrence's denigrators, that his friends must all have been dupes or fools. (Such an assumption, incidentally, would have to include among those allegedly taken in by him people of the calibre of Winston Churchill, Lord Allenby, Lady Astor and Thomas Hardy.)

Between them the two films assembled a cast-list which included Sir Alec Kirkbride, Siegfried Sassoon, Henry Williamson, David Garnett, E. M. Forster, Mrs Eric Kennington, Air Commodore and Mrs Sydney Smith, his friend and Arabic teacher from pre-war days Fareedah el Akle, even the founder of the Lawrence legend, Lowell Thomas, together with numerous others who had been with him at school, at university, in the war, or had known him during his Tank Corps and R.A.F. years, including A. H. G. Kerry, C. F. C. Beeson, Canon E. F. Hall, S. C. Rolls, Laurence 'Rory' Moore, Jock Chambers, Arthur Russell and Pat Knowles. In addition Sir Basil Liddell Hart acted as adviser and senior friend in the making of the earlier programme. The clear-sighted reminiscence of these witnesses gave Lawrence an actuality, a solidity indeed, easily lost in books arguing some special case. The first of these programmes was made in 1962, and its keynote speech was the statement by A. W. Lawrence quoted at the beginning of this Preface. The second of these programmes was made in 1985–6, again with A. W. Lawrence participating, this time as a veteran in his middle eighties. After carefully considering and assessing the finished programme he wrote to its producer, my colleague and co-author Julia Cave: 'It is impeccable, a splendid achievement. I can't thank you enough, not only as an individual but on behalf of historic truth.'

This book has also been produced, its authors believe, on behalf of historic truth. It has grown out of the two programmes referred to, the second of which offered the extra advantage of visiting, photographing and filming in some of the key places with which Lawrence was associated during the Arab Revolt – such as Akaba, Azrak and the magnificent and unforgettable Wadi Rumm. To sense the atmosphere of such places is a considerable aid to understanding. Visiting Jordan also allowed us to meet and talk with a number of notable Arabs about this vital period of their history, among them Suleiman Mousa, most benign and friendly of scholars, who while sticking loyally to his 'Arab view' nevertheless acknowledges that Lawrence was an important figure in the Revolt and indeed, thanks to his best-selling *Seven Pillars of Wisdom*, a remarkable international publicist for it! However, though the programmes paved the way to the book, the latter, as already implied, is much more than simply a collage of transcriptions of our recorded interviews (though we have quoted from a considerable number of them) interlaced with the most easily available photographs.

On the visual side great attention has been paid to the organization of the illustrative material, much of which has been assembled in special sections on specific subjects, so that it complements rather than merely accompanies the central narrative. Moreover, the illustrations include not only a wide range of high-quality photographs, many of them rare and many by Lawrence, but also such items as one of his contributions to the Oxford High School Magazine published in facsimile or, also in facsimile, pages from his books, including the rare subscribers' edition of *Seven Pillars of Wisdom* produced in 1926.

As for the narrative, this has been much enriched by quotations from hitherto unpublished letters and, in respect of the war years, by important documentary evidence which deserves wider currency than it has been given so far. I refer to the mass of papers preserved in the files of the Arab Bureau and the Egyptian Expeditionary Force and now housed at the Public Record Office at Kew, London; material which was not released into the public domain until fifty years after the end of the First World War – and was therefore unavailable to both Lawrence's most admiring and his most critical biographers. The letters, reports and assessments in these files help, we believe, to define Lawrence's role in a new and important way; and do so to the improvement rather than the diminution of his present reputation. Indeed, while generally it is true that the principal Arab participants in the desert campaign have been given less than their due in the West, the new material makes it difficult to concede that Lawrence's part in it was simply that of a mere also-ran liaison officer with a fluent pen and a talent for public relations. As we quote in full in Chapter 7, in 1927 Lawrence wrote to Robert Graves that he expected that when all the documents of the Revolt were finally revealed to students, the latter would find small errors in his account in *Seven Pillars of Wisdom*, but would 'agree generally with the main current of [his] narrative.' There is much more evidence yet to be published than can be included here, but our overall conclusion is that Lawrence was quite right in his assertion to Graves. *Seven Pillars of Wisdom* is, we believe, much more of a precise military memoir than has usually been thought. Sometimes seen as though it were primarily a work of literature (and it is that, undoubtedly) it is predominantly a work of history as well.

That it has also been possible to inject into the narrative, particularly that covering the post-war years, valuable insights from some of Lawrence's unpublished correspondence stems from the fact that, having now left the BBC to become a full-time author, I have undertaken as a parallel task to working on this biography the production of a new one-volume selection of his letters to mark the centenary of his birth. This project is being carried out at the request of A. W. Lawrence and his fellow Trustees of the *Seven Pillars of Wisdom* Trust, who have given me privileged access to the very large reserve collection of Lawrence material in the Bodleian Library, Oxford. In addition, material has been assembled from a wide range of other sources in Britain and the United States. The only previous comprehensive selection was published in 1938, edited by the writer and critic David Garnett, who produced an impressive and highly readable book despite his frequently expressed frustration at being unable to use many letters of whose existence he was well aware but which for various reasons were denied to him. Most of these barriers have now been withdrawn and in addition a vast amount of new material has become available, so that the publication of a major new selection is long overdue. The Trustees have kindly allowed the use of extracts from some of these letters in this present book. We have thus been able to use quotations from so far unpublished letters to Mrs George Bernard Shaw, Lady Astor, Lord Trenchard, Lord Lloyd, Robert Graves, E. M. Forster, and numerous others. Many of these letters will be published in the new volume.

The original intention when the book was commissioned was that Julia Cave and I should be joint authors. However as the book grew in scale and, we believe, in the quality and scope of its material, the fact that I was now a freelance author while Julia Cave was continuing her career as a senior Producer of the Music and Arts Department of BBC Television meant that much of the burden of the narrative and the organization of the visual material fell on me. Nevertheless the book represents our joint view.

We have both come to appreciate that something important has happened as a result of the demotion of Lawrence from the pedestal required by his hero-worshippers and his elevation from the pit demanded by his detractors. Lawrence has become available to people who see him neither as saint nor charlatan but as a man of great intelligence and vulnerability trying to cope with the pressures of the modern age. Someone who was drawn to him for this reason (and who has made an important contribution to the understanding of him) is the American Professor John E. Mack, whose biography of him *A Prince of our Disorder*, published in 1976, won the Pulitzer Prize. Having spoken to virtually every witness he could find, both Arab and British, and spent several years combing through the relevant documentation, he stated his conclusion thus: 'I unabashedly regard [Lawrence] as a great man and an important historical figure.' What is perhaps even more worthy of note is that Mack also wrote: 'Lawrence's struggles have been consistently important and moving to me. I have found it easy, though disturbing, to identify with his hopes, his actions and his pain. He has enabled me, as he did so many others, to see possibilities that were not dreamed of before.'

This points, surely, to a fascinating paradox. The more that Lawrence has been brought down to ground level, the more interesting he has become. To a generation like the present, not remotely concerned with troubadours or knights in armour, the modern version of Lawrence is the only one we want to know. Just as we accept almost with relief the newly discovered facts that Livingstone could be ruthless and fell short of his high hopes as a missionary; that Kingsley lived in a manner far removed from the *mores* implied by *The Water Babies*; or that Captain Scott was a naval officer of his times and not quite the simplistic hero of popular imagination, so we have no difficulty in accepting that Lawrence had his weaknesses and his failures too. Indeed, it could be said that he has survived well the contemporary practice of turning the searchlight on to the secret lives of notable people, whether it be a Lloyd George, a Franklin D. Roosevelt, a John F. Kennedy, a Marilyn Monroe, or a T. E. Lawrence. For it is his humanity which is the core of his appeal now. Not being called on to admire or despise him, we can relate to him. His books continue, in the modern phrase, to run and run but there is also something about his odd and rarely happy life that draws people to him, particularly in that at the height of a quite extraordinary fame he turned his back on what most people assume to be greatly desirable – status, privilege, the prospect of a comfortable future – and became an ordinary underpaid serviceman. In his 'Author's Preface' to *Seven Pillars of Wisdom* he acknowledged the contribution to the Arabian campaign of many to whom his 'self-regardant picture' was 'not fair', adding: 'It is still less fair, of course, like all war-stories, to the unnamed rank and file, who miss their share of credit, as they must do, until they can write the despatches.' By the time he wrote that preface, on 15 August 1926, he had himself been for four years a member of the 'unnamed rank and file'. Since most people are rank and file, he had, as it were, joined the general crowd. Which is why the second half of the story, the adventures of Aircraftman J. H. Ross and Private T. E. Shaw, is arguably quite as interesting as the earlier part, the rise of Captain, Major and Colonel Lawrence of, to quote Hogarth's description, the 'overpowering' reputation.

Lawrence, replying in 1933 to Liddell Hart, at that time writing a biography of him, told him: 'I can be on terms with scholars, or writing people, or painters or politicians: but equally I am happy with bus conductors, fitters or plain workmen: anybody with a trade or calling. And all such classes are at home with me, though I fancy none of them would call me "one of them". Probably my upbringing and adventures – and way of thinking – have bereft me of class. Only the leisured classes make me acutely uncomfortable. I cannot play or pass time.' But he then added a cautionary word, of which we, also his biographers, should take due note. 'Lots of people go about saying that they alone understand me. They do not know how little they see, each of them separately. My name is Legion.' If we have brought into focus just some of the more important aspects of the personality and achievements of T. E. Lawrence we shall be well content.

Malcolm Brown
October 1987

A TOUCH OF GENIUS

1

OXFORD SCHOOLBOY

In the mid-1880s an Anglo-Irish landowner living in County Westmeath not far from Dublin abandoned his home and family to live with the governess whom he had appointed to the care of his four young daughters. He was approaching forty, she was fifteen years his junior. His wife, a severe and obsessively religious lady, was totally opposed to divorce, so the runaways had no prospect of legitimizing their union. They nevertheless proceeded to raise a family and over the next fifteen years had five sons; one born in Ireland, one in Wales, one in Scotland, one in the Channel Islands, and the youngest born in Oxford, the city in which they eventually settled, and where they set up their home in a gaunt semi-detached house, 2 Polstead Road, which was distinctly less grand than the country mansion where their lifelong love-affair began.

Thomas Robert Tighe Chapman was the legal name of the boys' father: Sarah Maden or Jenner or Junner was their mother – the confusion arises from the fact that she was herself illegitimate. In their new life they assumed the name Lawrence, a choice for which there appears to be no wholly satisfactory explanation. Their famous son T. E. Lawrence thought, wrongly, that it was the name of Sarah's supposed father; alternatively it has been suggested that she used the name 'Miss Lawrence' when practising as a governess. In 1914 the father inherited the family's baronetcy, being listed thereafter in Burke's *Peerage* as Sir Thomas Chapman while continuing to live in Oxford as Mr T. R. Lawrence, gentleman of independent means.

Though the parents had broken the moral code of their day they had not done so lightly for they were both deeply convinced Christians – the mother being particularly committed – and they were always to carry with them an acute sense of guilt. Yet they understandably kept their dilemma to themselves and in

consequence were able to fit without difficulty into their chosen social background. The Lawrences were to all intents and purposes a normal middle-class
family of suburban north Oxford.

Thomas Edward was the second of the sons, born in Tremadoc in Caernarvon-
shire, North Wales, in 1888. Throughout his boyhood he was usually known as
Ned. The eldest son, Montague Robert (Bob), was born in 1885; William
George (Will) followed Ned in 1889; Frank Helier (named after his Channel
Islands birthplace, St Helier) arrived in 1893, and the youngest, Arnold Walter
(Arnie), was born in 1900. On the whole the parents were not particularly

*Lawrence's birthplace at Tremadoc, North Wales. The accepted date of
Lawrence's birth is 16 August – he was apparently born in the early hours
of that day – but his birth certificate distinctly assigns it to the 15th, a date
which Lawrence himself was proud to claim, it being the birthday of Napoleon.*

No.2 Polstead Road, Oxford; semi-detached, brick-built, with four floors, including basement. Date of construction, about 1890. It stood in a newly established neighbourhood, just to the north of the university area, largely populated by professional men and their families, including many university dons taking advantage of the relatively recent abolition of the ancient regulations forbidding Fellows of colleges to marry.

gregarious and few adult visitors came to Polstead Road, but there was usually a welcome for the boys' school friends. A. H. G. Kerry, for example:

> I remember the family very well because we lived in the same road. The atmosphere in the house was very like that of an ordinary suburban North Oxford home. Father was a tall slender man, very distinguished looking, rather like Bernard Shaw, I should say. He was a very courtly gentleman. He had a red beard and whiskers, and he always went about in a Norfolk jacket and breeches, and was always waving when we passed him – very friendly looking. Mother I didn't quite see so much of, but I thought she was a bit frightening when I was young.

| T.E. (Ned) | W.G. (Will) | F.H. (Frank) | M.R. (Bob) |
| born 1888 | born 1889 | born 1893 | born 1885 |

'Mrs Lawrence' and her first four sons, photographed at Langley Lodge, Fawley, Southampton, about 1895. The youngest son, A.W. (Arnold) was not born until 1900.

E. F. Hall, however, retained a gentler image of Mrs Lawrence, seeing her as 'a very motherly person and nice and comfortable and kind'. Often in their house as a young boy of fourteen or fifteen he became very fond of her. Yet it is generally agreed that she was the more forceful and dominant parent and she administered the family discipline in the event of any misbehaviour, usually with beatings on the bare buttocks. Bob was never beaten, Ned frequently, Arnold only once. She was always to retain her wish to dominate and T.E. had consciously to keep her at a distance throughout his life. 'Mother is rather wonderful: but very exciting,' he wrote to Mrs George Bernard Shaw many years later, but added, 'I always felt that she was laying siege to me, and would conquer, if I left a chink unguarded.' Arnold too was aware of this urge on his mother's part to swallow, absorb or smother her sons. In his view her hope was that she would redeem herself from her sins vicariously through them; to this end she tried to steer them towards a lifelong commitment to God and Christianity, an aspiration which was realized in Bob's case but certainly not in that of Arnold or T.E.

Their father, however, though less forceful than their mother, was neither weak nor aloof. He could be firm when occasion required, could be decisive at times of crisis and had the capacity to make peace or to ease family tensions with a well chosen word. As befitted a gentleman, if one in reduced circumstances, he followed no practical profession, but he gave his sons practical benefits. He was perhaps particularly instrumental in developing Ned's interests; he taught him carpentry and photography, introduced him to the study of castles and churches, and passed on his own special enthusiasm for the bicycle. He was, it appears, a hard rider in both his lives; on horseback in the first, on the pedal-cycle in the second. In Arnold Lawrence's words, 'Father was a great bicyclist. He often did a hundred miles a day. He was always buying next year's model.'

But while the boys could take or leave their father's offerings, there was no refusing the religious discipline imposed on them by their mother. Three times each Sunday they walked to St Aldates Church in downtown Oxford, where the rector was the veteran Canon A. M. W. Christopher, for several decades an influential figure in the religious life of the city. Anglo-Catholicism was predominant in Oxford, but the Lawrence family preferred Canon Christopher's low church, evangelical brand of Christianity, which was concerned less with high ritual than with personal redemption. He had convinced the guilt-ridden parents that they were not beyond the hope of divine forgiveness, and they and their sons sat at his feet faithfully for many years. Thomas Lawrence became a member of the church committee. Bob underwent conversion there and, to his mother's profound satisfaction, embarked on the road which was eventually to take him as a medical missionary to China. Ned himself became a Sunday School teacher and a member of the Church Lads' Brigade: many years later

A. H. G. Kerry recalled him in 'that funny little hat' the Brigade boys used to wear. Though eventually he ceased to believe in conventional Christianity, he was to be permanently affected by religious concepts and sanctions.

Parallel with their religious went the boys' secular education, but this, by contrast, followed a mainstream, conventional course. All five brothers went to the Oxford City High School, a newly opened grammar school low in fees but high in reputation, which provided a sound classical education and which already had excellent connections with the adjacent university. The number of boys in attendance at this period was never much higher than 160 or 170, so it was natural that the Lawrence brothers stood out. Lawrence II, or ii – as Ned was formally known in the school – seems to have made no great mark in his junior years, but as he grew older he began to establish himself as a character, clever, forceful, unpredictable, even eccentric. He was short – just under 5′ 6″ when fully grown – but he was far from puny; toughened by bicycle rides and other athletic pursuits he was eventually to make himself, in his own phrase, 'a pocket Hercules'. If he chose to exert himself he was not to be ignored, as a schoolfriend, H. F. Matthews, remembered:

> My first vivid impression of him was of going down the school corridor together one day when the head boy, who was swanking somewhat, put on his straw hat before he got out of school. And Ned Lawrence, always in those days objecting to swank, crept up behind him and tipped his straw hat down over his nose. Of course he was captured and taken out into the playground, and was asked if he would apologize and with his typical giggle he said, 'No, of course not.' So the head boy said, 'Well, I'll have to thrash you.' He proceeded to do this and Ned got on his back on the floor with his two arms round the head boy's legs, and while he was being thrashed he was kicking the head boy up the behind very hard. And the head boy's spectacles came off, and I think Ned won that round.

Lawrence tended later to dismiss his schooldays as being a waste of time and a period of misery, by contrast with which his university days offered 'so noble a freedom'. No doubt he chafed at the restrictions and the wearisome routines of the classroom, but nevertheless, at least in his senior years, he appears to have contributed much more than the expected minimum to school life. This is evident from the Oxford High School Magazine, which offers a fascinating and entertaining insight into his developing career. Unfortunately it did not commence publication until 1903, by which time he had been there for seven years, but the glimpses it provides of him between 1903 and 1907 are many and rewarding.

It has generally been assumed that he took no part in team games; indeed, his mother is on record as saying that 'cricket and football had no attraction –

The four senior Lawrence brothers: Ned, Frank, Bob (standing), Will, dressed
in a style appropriate to middle class North Oxford.

he was too deeply engrossed in other things'. According to the magazine, however, he played at least once for the school junior cricket team in 1904 when he caught out a member of the opposing side off the bowling of his friend Kerry. Again, his mother stated that he was 'keen on cross-country paper chases', but he also seems to have excelled in more formal athletics. In 1906 he was third in the Gymnasium competition, which included performance on 'Bars, Horizontal Bars, Rings, Horse, Rope and Ladder'; his friends Hall and Kerry were second and fourth respectively. The previous year at the annual sports he narrowly missed being second in the mile. In 1907, however, he had his revenge, winning in five minutes thirteen seconds; Kerry was third. On the academic side he was consistently successful; in 1904 he won the Fifth Form prize in Divinity, while a year later he took the Greek prize. He was placed in the First Class in the Oxford Local Examinations in 1906; in order of merit he was 13th, Hall being 6th and another close friend, C. F. C. ('Scroggs') Beeson being 39th. He also attempted one of the school's most distinguished awards, the Earl of Jersey's Prize for an English Essay, in both of his last two years. In 1906 he was joint runner-up, but in 1907 he took the prize; the subject – *Our Colonies*.

In addition he contributed to the literary pages of the magazine three pieces which all bear the distinctive hallmarks of the Lawrence style. (One is printed on page 14.) In particular, perhaps, his contribution to the symposium compiled by 'Scroggs' Beeson *How to Win a Scholarship* is highly characteristic. He was asked to discuss History, the subject in which he had just gained a minor scholarship at Jesus College. 'Dates disgust,' he writes, 'facts undigested nauseate, encyclopaedic information aggravates. One must write a nice style.' It might almost be an apologia for *Seven Pillars*. The piece also makes clear a crucial commitment to archaeology. 'In all my *vivas* [college interviews] antiquities have been the most important topic: in the last, especially, the merits of pottery and brass-rubbings engrossed the attention of the examiners.'

By this time his enthusiasm for the mediaeval past was firmly established. His mother has recorded that he was about nine and a half when he rubbed his first brass in Witney Church; he was soon decorating his bedroom with the figures of magnificently armoured knights. He became an adept and zealous brass-rubber, travelling far and wide, often with an invited companion of whom the most regular was 'Scroggs' Beeson, who also joined him in frequenting the excavations that were being carried out at that time in the centre of Oxford as a preliminary to rebuilding. 'We found that pottery of various ages was being dug up,' Beeson recalled later, 'and by offering threepence or sixpence to the workmen they kept the specimens which they found and we collected them later on.'

All this was highly laudable, except that Lawrence acquired the reputation of at times pursuing his passion for the past somewhat too vigorously. Another friend, T. W. Chaundy, recalled an expedition which took them to Waterperry Church in rural Oxfordshire, where there were brasses inaccessible behind some pews. 'Lawrence, already ruthless, made short work of the obstruction, and I still hear the splintering woodwork and his short laugh, almost sinister to my timorous ears.' Beeson, on the other hand, has defended Lawrence's methods.

> I know there have been all sorts of stories about damage done to churches when Lawrence visited them but that isn't really true. If you had to rub a brass, you had to clean it up, get the dust out of the engravings and from round the edges, perhaps shift the carpet or even

the furniture, but no damage was done so far as I know, although certain irate incumbents wrote to the newspapers and said vandals had appeared.

However, Warren Ault, an American Rhodes Scholar and subsequent Professor of History at Boston, who was a friend of Lawrence in his undergraduate years and took part in later brass-rubbing excursions, noted that Lawrence carried a screw-driver in his back pocket to remove a brass he suspected might have an earlier portrait on the other side; Ault was posted at the lych-gate to give the alarm in case anyone appeared. And Beeson has admitted that during their schooltime outings 'many a trespass was committed in Lawrence's company'. But then the work Lawrence and he were about was not youthful skylarking, nor, as he put it, 'a mere collector's hobby'. This was serious research, followed by visits to the Tower of London or the Wallace Collection; and in the case of the pottery, glass, coins and other archaeological relics collected from the Oxford workings, there was the city's own Ashmolean Museum where they became regular visitants, bearing their finds and seeking advice and information. The boys soon became experts on such related subjects as mediaeval armour and heraldry. In Beeson's words, 'A herald's jargon was permanently acquired, which, with many another special terminology, eventually enriched the vocabulary of *Seven Pillars*.'

It was with Beeson that Lawrence shared what was to become a long-standing enthusiasm, the concept of 'ideal book-making'. They dreamed, for example, of producing a Froissart's *Chronicles* illustrated only by contemporary art. In the O.H.S. magazine, Beeson mocked their joint craze with an advertisement for a new *High School Hysterical History of the World*, to be produced in 170 volumes in a whole range of bizarre bindings and to include 'thousands of articles from the pens of competent historians both contemporaneous and cosmopolitan.' One promised article – *The development of pottery in Western Oxford*, by 'Prof. Lawrence'.

About this time, apparently, an episode occurred which has much puzzled students of Lawrence's early career. He left home and enlisted as an ordinary soldier in the Artillery, being eventually bought out by his father. In later references to this odd interlude, the length of time he allegedly served is variously given as 'a while', 'three or four months' and even '8 months' – the last of which is plainly absurd, in that no suitable gap exists in his known biographical data into which so long an absence from Oxford could be fitted. However, a biographer of his Oxford years, Paul Marriott, has pointed out that the period between Christmas and Easter 1906 is not otherwise accounted for, so that his first experience of life in the ranks might possibly have taken place then.[1] Marriott has discovered

1 Paul J. Marriott, *Oxford's Legendary Son – Lawrence of Arabia*, privately published.

what might perhaps be a confirming detail in the minute book of the City High School, in which it is recorded that at a meeting held on 30 April 1906 the Governing Body of the school gave Thomas Edward Lawrence permission to stay on as a pupil for another year.

Why he should thus run away to enlist has never been adequately explained. He himself suggested the following addition to the manuscript of Liddell Hart's biography, '*T. E. Lawrence' in Arabia and After*, published in 1934: 'In his teens he took a sudden turn for military experience at the urge of some private difficulty, and served for a while in the ranks.' One much favoured speculation is that the 'private difficulty' was his discovery that he was illegitimate, though he himself dated this far earlier. But no one knows; he himself once described the subject as 'hush hush' and in any case the episode only briefly interrupted his education. He was now ready to move, in Oxford parlance, from town to gown, from city school to city university. He tried for a History Scholarship at St John's College, which had accepted Bob and would later accept Will, but he failed; so he invoked his Caernarvonshire birth and turned to Jesus College, which had special awards open only to men with Welsh connections. In January 1907 he was elected to a Meyricke Exhibition there with an annual value of £40. It was his acceptance at Jesus which prompted him to comment in his contribution to Beeson's symposium on winning scholarships: 'Unkind critics laud the virtue of a birth in Wales, or of any of the other countries that have conquered England.'

LAWRENCE AT THE CITY OF OXFORD HIGH SCHOOL

(Left) The School Facade. In 1881 *the Oxford Corporation noted: 'It has long been felt a reproach to the City of Oxford, that being the site of one of the most ancient and famous of the Universities of Europe, it has yet been absolutely without any recognized Grammar School for the sons of its citizens.' The gap was filled by the Oxford High School, which was opened in* 1881. *T.E. Lawrence was at the school from* 1896 *to* 1907.

(Below) Ned Lawrence in 1901, *from a school photograph.*

'At school the Lawrences first began to impress my awakening consciousness by the regularity with which new members of the family appeared: each in a dark blue-and-white striped jersey that became almost a uniform, the softness of the wool matching a certain gentleness of speech and fairness of face. Out of this rising family Lawrence II gradually became distinct by a spareness of body and a pithy energy of speech.'

(T.W. Chaundy, Oxford High School 1896–1906, *from* T.E. Lawrence by His Friends)

One of Lawrence's contributions to the school magazine. published in the edition of July 1904 when he was fifteen.

Playground Cricket.

PLAYGROUND cricket has no handbook, so I think that some hints to youngsters who aspire to gain honours in this subject will be acceptable. The game runs on slightly the same ground as Playground Football, so that there must be some likeness between their respective implements. A playground is again indispensable, but a cap will not do for the ball. It can however be a stone, or a piece of wood: I have even seen a potato used with success. One man bats, another forty or so bowl. There are generally two balls, which are committed to the safe keeping of the Captain during school hours. The forty boys scrimmage for the balls, and a game of Rugby football is played, till one gets hold of it and bowls at the stumps. The stumps deserve mention. A wooden wall was improvised for wicket-keeper, and 3 stumps were chalked upon it, in white and blue. These having slightly faded a second pair in white was applied to the first, coinciding in width but not in height ; consequently six inches of blue overtop the white bails. The profound wisdom which dictated this may not appear at first sight, but the fact is that when big boys are bowling the blue is counted as the top; when big boys are batting the stumps do not extend beyond the white. That shows our wisdom. Unfortunately some facetious individual (we would duck him if we could find him) has added four more white stumps, and four more bails, which slightly disconcert the batsmen, but greatly improve the chances of the bowler.

The block is the next matter of importance. It can be located anywhere within the four mile radius, but on this occasion is about three feet away from the stumps, and bears about 45" E. of N. from a straight line drawn at right angles to the stumps. The block itself is an irregular shaped opening resembling the Isle of Wight, 26·3 centimetres in length, and from 8 to 5 centimetres in width, in depth about 10 centimetres. The bat is indescribable. A mass of willow, slightly rotten in places, and resembling a mop at the bottom. The handle is said to be cane, but one player who has had a most extensive and varied acquaintance with canes, both at home and abroad, declares that no cane *ever* stung like this bat, so it must be of some foreign substance. The balls go, some into the side windows of the school, some through those of the factory, others again attach themselves to the windows opposite.

LAWRENCE ii.

(Above) Lawrence's Sixth Form. T.E. Lawrence stands extreme right; his raised right hand is in fact taking the photograph, as was made clear in an account of the occasion contributed by one of the group, T.O. Balk (seated, extreme left) to the school magazine in April 1966.

'The photograph of the VI Form 1906–07 was taken in July 1907 on the small lawn in front of the school. Ned Lawrence was the prime mover in making the record of a very pleasant year. He persuaded the Head to give his consent and also the time needed to arrange the group and photograph it. He used his own (box – I think) camera fixed on a tripod and was able to take the photograph himself by connecting the camera by means of a length of rubber tubing to his cycle pump which he kept carefully out of sight as he stood in the group. He also made the prints and presented them to the members of the VIth.

P.S. I always think when I look at the group that the Head's expression reveals his considerable doubts of the likelihood of success of T.E.'s scheme.'

2

YOUNG MAN ON A BICYCLE

Lawrence later claimed to have been aware of his illegitimacy from the age of ten, but – unless this is taken to be the cause of the Artillery interlude mentioned in the previous chapter – it can be reasonably assumed that in his childhood and youth he was not overly obsessed by his family situation, nor unduly disturbed at the deception which his parents had to practise in presenting themselves to the world as Mr and Mrs Lawrence of Polstead Road. The best argument for this conclusion is the stream of eloquent and affectionate letters he sent home, first as schoolboy and then as undergraduate, as he bicycled at home and abroad pursuing his historical interests. Most of the letters are addressed to his mother, and though they are plainly meant to be read by the rest of the family he frequently seems to be addressing her alone. These do not seem to be the outpourings of a secretly embittered son.

> Kindly take heaps of love from me to yourself, and when you've had enough, divide the remainder into three portions, and give them to the worms [his usual name for other members of the family] you have with you. . . . Loud snores to all. Love to yourself.   Ned
> [From Colchester, 13 August 1905]

> I am so delighted to hear you are so much better, go on and improve: I think we must take a cottage on Boar's hill for you: mountain (!) air seems to set you up at once. . . . If possible, you must come to Carnac next year with me: it is quite cheap: rail to Vannes, and ride only about 30 miles in the week when we are there. I am planning a trip.
> [From Dinard, 24 August 1906]

Lawrence's bicycle was a specially built machine, with dropped handlebars and, reputedly, the first 3-speed gear at the Oxford High School. On it he made a series of ambitious journeys which took him first to various parts of England, and afterwards to Wales and France. Sometimes he was accompanied by his father or one of his brothers, sometimes by 'Scroggs' Beeson, but mostly he rode alone. The declared object of his travels was the study of mediaeval castles, about which he was evolving ideas which would eventually coalesce in his university thesis on the castles of the crusaders. But there was a parallel purpose – to challenge himself, extend his powers, prove that he could reach and go beyond the punishing standards he set himself. Relish in his achievements frequently shows in his letters:

> At Erquy, when returning from bathing, I rode a measured half-kilo on the sand in 40 seconds exactly. There was a gale behind me, and the sands were perfectly level and very fast, but still 30 miles per hour is distinctly good. I have never gone faster; of course my high gear was the one I rode. [14 August 1906]

> From Le Puy I rode up for 10 miles more, (oh dear 'twas hot!) consoling myself with the idea that my sufferings were beyond the conception of antiquity, since they were a combination (in a similar climate) of those of Sysiphus [sic] who pushed a great weight up hill, of Tantalus who couldn't get anything to drink, or any fruit, and of Theseus who was doomed ever to remain sitting: – I got to the top at last, had 15 miles of up and down to St. Somebody-I-don't-want-to-meet-again, and then a rush down 4,000 feet to the Rhone. [2 August 1908]

It was the urge to devise almost impossible challenges which was responsible for what was to become a famous Lawrentian achievement in Oxford – the nocturnal navigation of an underground waterway called the Trill Mill Stream; though again there was a reason for this in that he had discovered the existence of the stream in the works of the seventeenth-century historian Anthony Wood. This particular escapade was undertaken by Lawrence with his schoolfriend E. F. Hall. Hall was also with him at Jesus College, where on one occasion Lawrence (who unlike Hall did not, apart from one term, live in college) came to visit him in his rooms.

> He turned up one morning mad as a hatter; I thought he was quite out of his head. He had a revolver in his hand and he walked in and said: 'I've been trying to see how long I could go without food and without sleep.' And he'd done it for forty five hours or so. I said, 'Well, let's get rid of this revolver.' And he fired a shot down the Turl [Turl Street, in which Jesus College stands]. It was fortunately a blank

*Jesus College, Oxford, where Lawrence was an undergraduate from 1907–10,
viewed from Turl Street – known in Oxford as 'the Turl'.*

cartridge, but I was quite glad to get it out of the way. I was quite frightened of him. That was the kind of thing he did.

Hall has always been convinced that this was all part of 'a sort of hardening process as if he were preparing for something big to come'.

> As part of this process he slept in a coffin. I don't know whether he bought it or made it but he slept in it on hard boards without any pillows.... There was an intensity in his eyes which is very difficult to describe. You could feel that he was going to be something exceptional. But what I don't know. He was sort of groping after it.

Hall, older than Lawrence by just one day, was 98 (and a Canon of the Church of England still taking services) when he recorded the interview from which these extracts were taken. Four decades earlier he had contributed to the symposium *T. E. Lawrence by His Friends* which was published shortly after Lawrence's death. In his piece he had described another of Lawrence's 'inexplicable vagaries' at this time, namely that of lying in wait as some of the more athletic members of the college, of whom Hall was one, emerged from the porter's lodge changed for the river or the football field; he would then 'follow us through the streets, solemnly walking a few paces in the rear, and afterwards explain to us our merits or deficiencies judged by the Greek standard of physical excellence'. Hall was never certain if this was sheer affectation 'or if it originated in leg-pulling, of which we could never tell where it began or ended'.

From time to time over the years his college has collected reminiscences by Lawrence's contemporaries, each of whom has added another feature to the portrait of Lawrence the undergraduate. The following, by Rev. H. D. Littler, from an account printed in the *Jesus College Magazine* of June 1935, refers to the one term which he spent living in college, the Summer or Trinity Term of 1908:

> I remember the first time I called on him: it was dusk, and as I opened the door I was petrified to see what looked like a ghost – in reality it was a life-size brass rubbing from a knight's tomb, which Lawrence had hung on his wall, as his idea of a jolly bit of decoration. I usually read late, till 3 a.m. or 4 a.m., and as he went to bed after lunch and slept till about 11 p.m. and read all night, he often dropped in on me. Even in those early days I remember thinking that he had the mind of a mediaeval monk: his values were quite different from ours, the games of the average undergraduate meant little to him and of ambitions or dreams in the worldly sense he had none. To be self-sufficient in the Platonic or perhaps the Stoic sense was his ideal, though I felt even at Oxford that he deprived himself unnecessarily of many pleasant contacts in his deliberate aim at avoiding the possibility of unhappiness and disappointments by holding aloof from men.

It was a constant source of argument between us, I being temperamentally at the opposite pole.

The following is from the *Jesus College Record* of 1986, from a contribution by a veteran Honorary Fellow of the college, A. G. Prys-Jones, one year junior to Lawrence, who met him first in the rooms of a mutual friend. He invited him to pay a visit, which Lawrence did soon after:

A minute or two after he had left, a very normal, intimate friend of mine dropped in. He was a typical rowing and rugger man of the old school, a stalwart upholder of tradition and correctness in all things, superlatively honest, dependable and loyal. In his blunt Anglo-Saxon way he said 'I've just passed that lunatic Lawrence on the staircase. What's he been doing on our territory?' 'Seeing me' I replied. 'My God, Prys, the man's barmy. Don't you know that?' 'Well' I said 'either that or some kind of genius. I can't tell yet. Give me time, old man: I've only just met him.'

'You Welshmen do seem to have the knack of picking the queerest fish. I know he's barmy. He doesn't run with the boats, he doesn't play anything. He just messes about on that awful drop-handled bicycle. And if he ever wore a bowler hat he'd wear it with brown boots.' 'Well, well,' I said, 'that of course is perfectly dreadful. But he's got the most charming manners, probably a first-class brain, and he's most refreshingly out of the ordinary. . . .' After that I got to know Lawrence pretty well, he would drop into my rooms casually at any time. . . . During the time of our friendship I never saw him eat a single solid meal. The utmost he seemed capable of in the food line was to nibble at a few biscuits, a piece of chocolate or a handful of raisins. I never understood how he retained his extraordinary physical vitality on such meagre rations . . . .

Somewhat to the surprise of his fellow undergraduates Lawrence was conformist enough to join the University Officers' Training Corps, though, as Prys-Jones recalls, he was not its smartest member. 'He never seemed able to get his puttees wound correctly, and the hang of his uniform showed considerable eccentricity. This was suitably commented upon on one occasion by our Company Sergeant-Major, a meticulous Grenadier Guardsman. "Damned disgrace the way some of you gentlemen come on parade." ("Gentlemen" was uttered with withering sarcasm!)' Prys-Jones also noted that Lawrence was guilty of minor indiscipline at camp in preferring to take his slumber outside rather than inside the tent. On the other hand he was an excellent marksman and scout, and showed no exhaustion after any route-march.

All this raises an interesting speculation: how exceptional was Lawrence in the Oxford of his time? There has perhaps been a tendency among his admirers to assume that he was a unique high-flyer among a host of lesser beings. Yet his Oxford generation was the one whose lost brilliance is usually mourned when people think of the casualty lists of the Western Front in the First World War. Edwardian Oxford was a gathering ground of many outstanding and, inevitably, not a few eccentric young men. It is surely not entirely coincidental that Max Beerbohm's celebration of Oxford eccentricity, *Zuleika Dobson*, appeared in 1911. Certainly there were as many Sebastian Flytes and Anthony Blanches on hand as there were in Evelyn Waugh's Brideshead generation of the 1920s. Moreover, this tradition of flamboyant eccentricity was well established before Lawrence's time. A decade earlier, John Buchan's Oxford generation, which included men of the calibre of Raymond Asquith and the Hon. Aubrey Herbert (later to become Lawrence's own close friend), had excelled in the kind of bizarre activity which also appealed to the young Lawrence. Janet Adam Smith lists some of them in her biography of Buchan: 'canoeing as far as they could between a winter's dawn and dusk; walking to London or Cambridge in twenty-four hours; riding across country on a compass course, regardless of back gardens or flooded rivers; sleeping out of doors; scrambling over Oxford roofs (once the short-sighted Aubrey Herbert fell through into a bank, and was held up by a manager with a gun), and never giving a damn for authority, or thinking of the consequences.'[1]

Yet on the smaller stage of Jesus College, which was not among the leading colleges academically or socially, Lawrence undoubtedly stood out, as a highly intelligent and unusual young man of whom people took notice. Vyvyan Richards, two years his senior, first heard of him as 'a queer stranger among us, who walked solitary in the still quadrangles of the college at all hours of the night'. He resolved to call on him.

> An invitation brought him up, at about 10 or 11 in the evening, to my room . . . a quietly moving, slight figure with longish flaxen hair and an unforgettable grin. And there we sat by the night – the first of many such memorable nights in Oxford. . . . As we talked and talked . . . some quick and deep affection took hold of me whose vividness stirs me still after thirty years have passed away. The rest of my life at Oxford, rather more than a year, was spent in a golden atmosphere of almost daily companionship with my new exciting friend.

The above is taken from Vyvyan Richards' *Portrait of T. E. Lawrence*, published in 1936, shortly after Lawrence's death. In Knightley and Simpson's *Secret Lives*

---

1 *John Buchan*, by Janet Adam Smith, 1969, p. 62.

Lawrence's private retreat at Polstead Road; a custom-built two-room bungalow put up for him by his parents during his university years. It was once widely thought he built it himself, a claim now entirely discredited.

'I would hunt him out in the Bodleian and find him squatting on the floor in a remote corner with some large mediaeval volume on his knees, or in his own small cottage of two rooms which his father had given him at the end of their home garden. . . There he would be on the hearth-rug by a peat fire, sometimes face down over a book, or sometimes sitting naked and placidly drawing his own foot and leg. That room was austere and simple as his own life was to be to the end.'

(Vyvyan Richards, Portrait of T.E. Lawrence)

of Lawrence of Arabia, published in 1969, Richards is quoted as admitting that when he met the young undergraduate with the flaxen hair 'it was love at first sight'. But he met with no response from Lawrence. 'He had neither flesh nor carnality of any kind; he just did not understand. . . . He never gave the slightest hint that he understood my motives or fathomed my desire. . . . I realize now that he was sexless – at least that he was unaware of sex.'[1]

What of his attitude to the opposite sex, as it appeared to his Oxford contemporaries? C. F. C. Beeson recalled that 'when one talked about the normal interests of boys – in adolescence girls came into it quite a lot – he just closed up, he wasn't interested in that kind of thing at all. He didn't seem to be interested in the theatres or the St Giles's annual fair, which was a great occasion for roistering.'

But one girl did attract him, Janet Laurie, a family friend from their brief time at Fawley in the New Forest, where they had lived before moving to Oxford. Sent to Oxford to a boarding school, she was a frequent visitor to Polstead Road – a rare female admission to so male a household – and on at least one occasion she and her sister were given breakfast, strictly against regulations, in Lawrence's rooms in Jesus College. The relationship was mainly a bantering one; Janet was something of a tomboy – indeed, with her close-cropped hair, she had been taken for a boy by the young Lawrences when they saw her for the first time from several rows behind in church. But suddenly Ned became serious, though to begin with he seems to have offered himself more as admiring troubadour than actual suitor. E. F. Hall, invited by Lawrence, took part in a somewhat unusual outing on the river.

> He asked would I come with him and Janet Laurie, and would I get the punt, which I did; and I got Janet on board and I was at the other end ready to punt. I looked for Lawrence, and he was nowhere to be seen. Then I looked again and he was about fifty yards behind upstream, following in a canoe. So I was left with the beautiful Janet and he just worshipped from a distance. Extraordinary. I saw Janet [many years] later in the cathedral in Exeter; she said she was married and lived in such and such a place and did I remember that occasion? 'Oh yes,' I said. 'He was very keen on you.' 'Oh I knew that,' she said.
>
> I don't think he would have married. If he did it wouldn't have lasted six weeks. It couldn't. He was a true unorthodox.

---

1 A. G. Prys-Jones, quoted earlier in this chapter, ends his memoir of Lawrence in the *Jesus College Record* of 1986 with the following comment: 'I ought to add in conclusion that never once during the period of our friendship did I detect any trace of the homosexuality attributed to him later: and I never heard him swear or tell a risqué story, though most of us occasionally did both.'

However, it appears that Lawrence did actually consider marriage to her. Late in life Mrs Janet Laurie Hallsmith, as she then was, told Lawrence's American biographer Professor Mack of an occasion following dinner at Polstead Road when Ned suddenly bolted the door and proposed.[1] Her response was to laugh – partly due to sheer astonishment, but partly because she had by then become attracted to the third brother, the tall and handsome Will. Indeed, the relationship with Will apparently developed to the point where they hoped to marry, despite the disapproval of Mrs Lawrence, whose opposition to any of her sons' taking such a step was as passionate as it was instinctive. Will's death in 1915 brought that possibility to an end. In one of T.E.'s war letters home he asked for Janet Laurie's address, but it is not known whether or not he wrote. He later became godfather of her first child.

Perhaps his brief wooing of Janet was an impulse, as surprising to him as to her, or perhaps it was one of his rare gestures towards conventionality. The essential Lawrence of this time was not the romantic canoeist offering courtly love from afar, but the energetic bicyclist counting the miles or the kilometres of his strenuous journeys; or the embryo historian climbing with sketch book and camera to often dangerous heights on the castles of England, Wales and France, and describing his discoveries and experiences in his long letters home.

Side by side with his passion for mediaevalism ran his interest in the Greek and Roman world. When he rode on his remarkable two-month journey through France in 1908 he was aware, as he cycled steadily south, that he was approaching a prospect he had long dreamed about: his first sight of the Mediterranean Sea.

1 *A Prince of our Disorder*, John E. Mack, 1976, p. 65.

LAWRENCE'S 2000 MILE BICYCLE RIDE

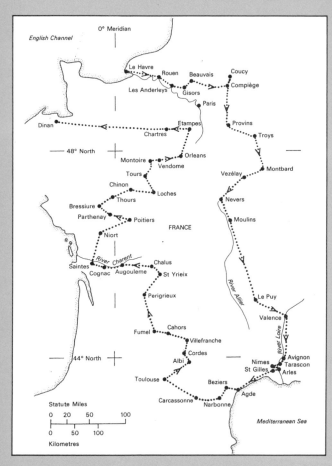

Lawrence's drawing of the thirteenth-century chateau at Coucy, near Compiègne.

'Its keep is 200 odd feet high (it used to be vaulted, when it must have been overpowering: the revolutionaries wanted to destroy it, so they exploded half a ton of powder in the basement. The tower didn't break (walls 20–30 feet high) but it acted like the barrel of a gun, & sent the vaults into Mars and Jupiter) – and there are splendid remains of 4 other towers, a great hall with two tiers of cellars beneath, and domestic buildings:– besides the town has almost complete walls around it. On the whole I made a note of Coucy as a glorious place.'

(From a letter to his mother, 23 July) The keep which Lawrence so much admired was blown up by the Germans in 1917.

The map of Lawrence's remarkable journey through France in 1908, which lasted from 16 July to 8 September, and during which he caught the malaria which was to affect him throughout his life. The trip was also notable for a stream of letters to his family and friends, and for the numerous drawings and photographs of considerable quality which he brought back.

(Map from Oxford's Legendary Son – The Young Lawrence of Arabia, *by Paul J. Marriott)*

THE CASTLE OF COUCY. (RESTORED)

V. LE DUC.

LE PONT VALENTRÉ
CAHORS.

T.E.'s sketch of the Pont de Valentré, over the River Lot at Cahors; it was both bridge and armed fortress, and successful defender of the city in mediaeval times.

'From Najac I rode x miles downhill Villefranche & then xxx splendid level miles to Cahors, the birthplace of Clement V, and other people. A bridge there is of the xiv cent. with archways & portcullises, machicoulis & loopholes: very interesting & very pretty.'
(To his mother, 16 August 1908)

Many years later he wrote to a correspondent living in Cahors:

'I envy you a residence in Cahors. It is so long since I followed the Lot from its hills down almost to Bordeaux, but I vividly recall the beauty of its swift reaches: and your bridge is superb. The place was full of interest to me as an archaeologist. It is unfortunate that I cannot come back.'
(Letter to Mlle Schnéegans, 26 November 1934)

3

STUDENT CRUSADER

On his diet of bread, milk and fruit Lawrence cycled through France, towards the castles on the Mediterranean coast. He had just ridden up from Arles to a 'queer little ruined & dying town' in the mountains, called Les Baux, when, as he recorded in a letter home from nearby Aigues–Mortes on 2 August 1908, he had 'a most delightful surprise', for 'suddenly the sun leaped from behind a cloud, & a sort of silver shiver passed over the grey: then I understood, & instinctively burst out with a cry of "θαλασσα, θαλασσα" ["Thalassa, Thalassa"][1] that echoed down the valley: it also startled two French tourists who came rushing up hoping to find another of the disgusting murders their papers make such a fuss about I suppose. They were disappointed when they heard it was "only the Mediterranean!" '

Aigues–Mortes itself had its own enchantment, and his romantic nature fell in love with this 'old, old town'. 'From it St Louis started for his crusades and it has seen innumerable events since.' But less romantic were the mosquitoes: 'I'm all one huge bite.' It was here that he was first infected with malaria, an illness that was to recur for the rest of his life. He wrote home:

> I bathed today in the sea, the great sea, the greatest in the world: you can imagine my feelings: . . . I felt that at last I had reached the way to the South, and all the glorious East; Greece, Carthage, Egypt, Tyre, Syria, Italy, Spain, Sicily, Crete . . . they were all there and all within reach. Oh, I must get down here, – farther out – again! Really

---

1 'The sea, the sea': the cry famous in ancient Greek history of Xenophon's army of the Ten Thousand when they caught their first glimpse of the Black Sea on their journey home from Mesopotamia.

this getting to the sea has almost overturned my mental balance: I
would accept a passage for Greece tomorrow.

But on the following day he turned inland. He was not to set foot in Greece
for more than two years – instead his first travels out of Europe were to be not
in the Classical but in the Holy lands of the East, the territory disputed between
Christianity and Islam in the twelfth and thirteenth centuries during the mediaeval crusades.

Lawrence was able to take advantage of a new university regulation allowing
him to submit a thesis in addition to taking the normal final examination for his
History degree. The subject he chose, one close to his already established
interests, was the influence of the crusades on the military architecture of
Western Europe. He had covered much of the European ground by his various
bicycle rides around the castles of England, Wales and France, but for the other
side of the coin he needed to visit Syria and Palestine. Early in 1909 he began
to make plans to devote the year's long vacation to this purpose. Towards the
end of his school days he had been introduced to Dr D. G. Hogarth, Keeper
of the Ashmolean Museum at Oxford. Hogarth, an archaeologist and classical
Middle Eastern scholar, encouraged Lawrence in his studies and was to become
his great friend and mentor and a major influence on his life. (Lawrence was
later to write of him: 'He is the man to whom I owe everything I have had since
I was seventeen.') Hogarth now suggested that he should write for advice to
Charles Doughty, the famous Arabian explorer and author of the legendary
Travels in Arabia Deserta. Lawrence, a great admirer of that classic work, took
up Hogarth's suggestion, only to receive a sternly discouraging reply. 'Long daily
marches on foot', wrote Doughty in his highly individual style, 'a prudent man
who knows the country would, I think, consider out of the question. The
populations only know their own wretched life and look upon any European
wandering in their country with at best a veiled illwill. . . . I should dissuade a
friend from such a voyage, which is too likely to be most wearisome, hazardous
to health and even disappointing. . . .'

In spite of Doughty's advice, Lawrence determined to go, to go alone and on
foot. He learned some conversational Arabic from an expatriate Syrian Protestant
clergyman, borrowed an annotated map of the area from an archaeologist friend,
and through Lord Curzon, then Chancellor of Oxford University, applied for
the necessary *Iradés* – letters of safe conduct to help travellers pass through the
Turkish-occupied lands of the Middle East. Hogarth acquired a suitable camera
for him at a reduced cost of £40 and his father contributed £100.

In June 1909 he sailed for the East on the S.S. *Mongolia* and travelling via
the Straits of Gibraltar and Port Said reached Beirut in July. This was to be his

point of departure. As on his previous journeys he wrote long and detailed letters home, which are part diary, part vivid description, part useful observations for his thesis.

Lawrence set off almost immediately to visit the castles south of Beirut.

> The country is fearfully hilly . . . so that walking any distance is hard work. My average is only about 20 miles a day, and the people here think that good. I have not been footsore at all, and my clothes and baggage have been quite satisfactory. . . . I sleep variously – one night at a Greek priest's, in native houses (or on top of them) and the rest in the open air. I like the latter best on the whole. . . . so far I have enjoyed myself greatly, except for 258 flea-bites on my right fore-arm. Remainder in proportion: fearfully dirty places.

He at once showed a remarkable ability to adapt to the customs and culture of the Arabs, though he found he had more affinity with the country people than with the town dwellers. The renunciation of civilization and a reliance on nature were attractive to him, although he never really came to terms with the dirt and the squalor – one of his great joys was a hot bath, and cleanliness, both physical and mental, was an essential element of his puritanical philosophy.

This southern journey took in a handful of castles but most lay ahead; in all he was to visit thirty-six out of a possible fifty. He returned briefly to Beirut, then on 6 August set off again, this time in a northerly direction through the highlands of western Syria towards Tripoli. He travelled with a minimum of clothing and equipment – a light-weight suit with many pockets, a pair of walking boots, two pairs of socks, two shirts, his map, his camera and tripod, and quantities of spare film. As a precaution against bandits and other dangers on the road he also carried a Mauser pistol. He was a crack shot and could fire with either hand.

On the journey north he passed through Jebail (ancient Byblos), which lays claim to being the first seaport in history and where a crusader castle dominated the bay. Here he called at the American Protestant Mission School and stayed for a few nights, meeting Miss Holmes, the school's director and Fareedah el Akle, a Syrian Christian school teacher six years older than himself. They were to become firm friends. Fareedah later wrote of his 1909 journey that 'the stories of his adventures and the hardships he endured on that trip, as he related them to us later, would make the most thrilling reading; they would sound like the Arabian Nights.'

On the road to Tripoli he visited several more castles. He wrote to his father:

> This is a glorious country for wandering in, for hospitality is something more than a name: setting aside the American and English mission-aries who take care of me in the most fatherly (or motherly) way – there are the common people each one ready to receive one for a

night, & allow me to share in their meals: & without a thought of payment from a traveller on foot. It is so pleasant, for they have a very attractive kind of native dignity.

From Tripoli he walked on towards Aleppo. This part of the journey was more dangerous than before – the country was very mountainous and the area had long associations with violence. The locals carried rifles and valued their firearms as a badge of manhood. He was put up for one night by an Arab nobleman:

> A young man very lively, & rather wild, living in a house like a fortress on top of a mountain: only approachable on one side, & then a difficult staircase. . . . He had just bought a Mauser & blazed at everything with it. His bullets must have caused terror to every villager within a mile around: I think he was a little cracked. Then I got to Hosn which is I think the finest castle in the world: certainly the most picturesque I have seen – quite marvellous.

The castle at Hosn was the most famous of crusader fortresses, Crac des Chevaliers. He spent three days photographing it and drawing his usual meticulous sketch-plans; then moved on to see and record several more castles, sleeping where he could.

> I will have such difficulty in becoming English again, here I am Arab in habits and slipping in talking from English to French and Arabic unnoticing . . . you may be happy now all my rough work is finished successfully: and my thesis is, I think, assured.

The castle at Sayhun drew more superlatives: 'it was, I think, the most sensational thing in castle-building I have seen'. From there he went on towards Aleppo, this time with a mounted escort for his protection. He took five days to walk 120 miles – 'stumbling & staggering' over 'ghastly roads' for thirteen hours a day. The escort had been provided because he had recently been shot at 'by an ass with an old gun': Lawrence fired back, probably grazing the man's horse as it bolted for about half a mile.

> At any rate he stopped about 800 yards away to contemplate the scenery, & wonder how on earth a person with nothing but a pistol could shoot so far: & when I put up my sights as high as they would go & plumped a bullet somewhere over his nut he made off like a steeple-chaser, such a distance was far beyond his old muzzle-loader. I'm rather glad that my perseverance in carrying the Mauser has been rewarded, it is rather a load but practically unknown out here.

On reaching Aleppo at last he booked into the best hotel, Baron's, and took a much needed hot bath. The third and final stage of the journey, begun in early September, took him north-eastwards across the River Euphrates to Urfa

– ancient Edessa. As a sideline on this leg of the journey he was looking for antiquities to take back to Hogarth and the Ashmolean, and managed to buy some thirty Hittite seals. It was on his way back from Urfa that he was set upon and nearly murdered by a local villager. Understandably he said nothing about this when writing home but in a letter to the Principal of Jesus College, Sir John Rhys, he explained that circumstances had prevented his return on time and briefly mentioned the incident:

> My excuse for outstaying my leave must be that I have had the delay of four attacks of malaria when I had only reckoned on two: even now I am exceedingly sorry to leave the two castles in the Moabite deserts unvisited. I would go to them certainly, only that last week I was robbed & rather smashed up. Before I could be fit for walking again (and it is very hard physically in this country) the season of rains would have begun. . . .

He also told the Principal that he had had 'a most delightful tour . . . on foot and alone all the time, so that I have perhaps, living as an Arab with the Arabs, got a better insight into the daily life of the people than those who travel with caravan and dragomen.' He hoped that his late return by a week would not be considered 'an unpardonable offence'.

By 22 September he was back in Aleppo, having finished his journey. He had walked eleven hundred miles. He was weak from his malaria bouts, very short of money, and, to add to his troubles, his camera had been stolen. His clothes were so worn out that, as he wrote home, 'I'd never get them past the sanitary inspection at P[ort] Said', and his boots were 'porous'.

> I've walked them to bits at any rate, & my feet lately have responded to it. They are all over cuts & chafes & blisters, & the smallest hole in this horrid climate rubs up in no time into a horrible sore. I can't imagine how many times I would have had blood poisoning already if it hadn't been for my boracic: but I want to rest the feet now or there will be something of the sort. To undertake further long walks would be imprudent, for even in new boots these holes would take long to heal.

He also told his family of 'an absurd canard in the Aleppo paper of a week ago: my murder near Aintab (where I didn't go). . . . The hotel people received me like a ghost.'

He arrived back in Oxford on 14 October. His experiences had taken their toll. Ernest Barker, history don and friend of the family, has described how one day that October 'at the end of a lecture a man came up to me whom I did not recognize – a man with a very fine face, which seemed thinned to the bone by privation. When he spoke to me in his low, quick voice I found that it was Lawrence.'

The five Lawrence brothers: (left to right) T.E., Frank, Arnold, Bob and Will in 1910; the year in which T.E. won his first-class honours degree and his Senior Demyship (i.e. senior scholarship) at Magdalen College; and in which – in November – he left for Syria.

He wrote to Hogarth's colleague, E.T. Leeds, from Rouen, on 2 November:

'Mr Hogarth is going digging: and I am going out to Syria in a fortnight to make plain the valleys and level the mountains for his feet.'

Sometime after his return Lawrence gave his friend and fellow-historian at Jesus College, A. G. Prys-Jones, a privileged private view of some of the many sketches, plans and photographs which he had brought back from his journey. 'As I sat fascinated,' Prys-Jones recalled, 'poring over these romantic treasures from the east, he said: "Now, you see, they'll have to give me a First. Nobody but myself has seen all these castles, and examiners can't admit their ignorance." '

In the summer of 1910, Lawrence duly gained a first-class degree in Modern History, mainly because of the brilliance and novelty of a thesis which was singled out as being 'very remarkable'. In line with what he called his 'rather knight-errant style of tilting against all comers in the subject', his thesis set out to prove that whereas the general view of historians was that the castle architects of Western Europe had followed and imitated their counterparts of the East, the precise opposite was the truth. Whatever the examiners may have thought of his conclusions, they could have no doubt as to the quality, style and originality of his material.

His first visit to the East had undoubtedly been a success, as he informed Doughty.

> You may remember my writing to you in the beginning of the year to ask your opinion on a walking tour in Northern Syria. This has ended happily (I reached Urfa Edessa, my goal) and the Crusading Fortresses I found are so intensely interesting that I hope to return to the East for some little time.

4

ARCHAEOLOGIST

The wish Lawrence had expressed in his letter to Charles Doughty was soon to come true. Only five months after gaining his degree he was off to the East again. This time his destination was the ancient Hittite city of Carchemish on the banks of the River Euphrates in northern Syria, on what is now the border between Iraq and Turkey. D. G. Hogarth was to direct an important excavation there under the patronage of the British Museum and at his suggestion, the Museum had offered Lawrence an appointment as one of the archaeologists. He had done his protégé the further favour of securing for him a Senior Demyship – a post-graduate scholarship – at Magdalen, the Oxford college of which he, Hogarth, was a fellow. The award carried an emolument of £100 a year.

Another wish was to be fulfilled on the journey. 'By extraordinary good fortune' the steamship *Saghalien* in which he was travelling had faulty engines and kept breaking down. After a day in Naples, 'wonderfully beautiful . . . quite as fine as Beyrout', the ship sailed through the Aegean to Athens, where the engines failed again, giving him his first chance to set foot on Greek soil. It was more than two years since he had written to his mother from Aigues-Mortes, after his first sight of the Mediterranean, that he would 'accept passage for Greece tomorrow'. Now that at last the long awaited moment had come he was not disappointed.

> Just as we entered the Piraeus [the port for Athens] the sun rose, &
> like magic turned the black bars to gold, a wonderfully vivid gold of
> pillar and architrave and pediment, against the shadowed slopes of
> Hymettus. That was the Acropolis from a distance: – a mixture of all
> the reds & yellows you can think of with white for the high-lights and

brown-gold in the shadows. Of course I got ashore at once.

After passing through 'the intolerable cesspit of the Piraeus' he eventually reached the legendary city, Athens itself. His enthusiasm for the architecture and sculpture of Ancient Greece had been fired by his study of classical literature, in particular of Homer, whose *Odyssey* (a work he was later to translate) was a constant companion.

> I walked through the doorway of the Parthenon, and on into the inner part of it, without really remembering where or who I was. A heaviness in the air made my eyes swim, & wrapped up my senses: I only knew that I, a stranger, was walking on the floor of the place I had most desired to see, the greatest temple of Athene, the palace of art, and that I was counting her columns, and finding them what I already knew. The building was familiar, not cold as in the drawings, but complex, irregular, alive with curve and subtlety, and perfectly preserved.

The ship broke down again, this time for a whole week, at Constantinople, capital of the Ottoman Empire – an opportunity to explore another legendary city. Constantinople was the bridge to the East which he had begun to know and understand, and where he was to live and work for the next seven critical years of his life.

On Christmas Eve 1910 he arrived at the American Mission school at Jebail, where he was welcomed as a long-lost friend. After two months' study there, according to Fareedah el Akle, he was 'able to read, write, and speak very simple Arabic'. At the end of February 1911, Hogarth and his Cypriot foreman, Gregori, arrived in Beirut to collect Lawrence, and to travel with him to Carchemish. It was the severest winter for forty years and the mountain road to Damascus, the Syrian capital, had been made impassable by snow, so the three men set off on a roundabout route, travelling by sea and rail and visiting some of the cities and sites of northern Palestine, including Mount Carmel and Nazareth. (Neither he nor Hogarth liked the latter place, though, if viewed from a certain hill-top, he told his mother, 'it is then no uglier than Basingstoke, or very little'.) Part of their journey by train was on the recently built Pilgrim Railway. This line, known as the Hejaz Railway – the Hejaz being the vast desert area to the east of the Red Sea which includes the holy cities of Mecca and Medina – ran from Damascus in the north to Medina in the south. The original plan had been to build it on to Mecca, but this was prevented by the forceful opposition of the camel caravans, which feared a curtailment of their lucrative business at the time of the annual Haj, or holy journey, to the birthplace of the prophet Mohammed. This was Lawrence's first contact with the railway that he would later help the Arabs to attack in time of war. On the way north to Damascus the three men stopped for lunch in the station buffet at Deraa – a town he was to revisit in far less propitious circumstances some years later.

> At Deraah [sic] all was sunny, and we had a French déjeuner in the Buffet, where Mr. Hogarth spoke Turkish & Greek, & French, & German, & Italian, & English all about the same as far as I could judge: it was a most weird feeling to be so far out of Europe: at Urfa and at Deraah I have felt myself at last away out of the Renaissance influence, for the buffet was flagrantly and evidently an exotic [sic], & only served to set off the distinctiveness of the Druses and their Turkish captors.

At the beginning of March they arrived at Aleppo – sixty miles south–west of Carchemish and the nearest large town. Here another archaeologist, R. Campbell Thompson, an expert in ancient inscriptions, was waiting to join the team. They took rooms in Baron's Hotel for nine days while they collected food and equipment for the expedition. While staying there they were entertained on most evenings by the British Consul, R. A. Fontana and his wife Winifred. Mrs Fontana became one of Lawrence's rare women friends, though her first meeting with him was not promising, for, as she wrote later, 'something uncouth in Lawrence's manner contrasting with a donnish manner of speech, chilled me'.[1] But then she saw from his anxious looks towards his archaeological chiefs that he had been constrained to pay this official visit and was longing for it to end. This aroused, as she put it, her 'freedom-worship', so that when later her husband invited him to dine the following evening and he refused because he had no dress clothes available, she backed him against the protests of the others. 'This was possibly the first brick in the foundations of our subsequent friendly relation, for he came to dine after all, and our mutual delight in the table-talk of David Hogarth – that prince of Learning and Worldly Wisdom – became in after years a happy subject of remembrance between us.'

Generally at dinner parties, according to Mrs Fontana, he would say very little but 'his silence was never dull. He listened with a lively intensity that could be extremely disconcerting, and when he put in a shot it was usually a good one, apt to leave some unlucky poser with a wrecked attitude'. She and Lawrence were also drawn together by a mutual love of literature. During the three years he was to spend at Carchemish he often visited the Consulate to borrow books. Commenting later on the general impression that 'Lawrence had no time for women' she wrote that at this time he 'spared no pains for this woman's comfort and happiness'.

Hogarth, who liked comfortable living, had already ordered from England, among other luxuries, nine sorts of jam and three kinds of tea. The men also

---

1 In *T. E. Lawrence by His Friends*, edited by A. W. Lawrence, 1937.

had with them a large collection of classical books, including Shakespeare, Dante and Spenser. Having assembled their stores the expedition set off on 9 March for the two-day journey to Jerablus, a village three-quarters of a mile from the site.

> Mr. Hogarth drove & walked & rode: Thompson rode & walked: I walked, except of course over the river. . . . We only got in about 4 o'clock: and have been unpacking since: eleven baggage horses, ten camels . . .

The site of Carchemish, an ancient Hittite city built around 1500 B.C., had first been excavated, under British Museum sponsorship, in 1878. Several important sculptures and reliefs had been recovered but progress had been slow and transporting the heavy blocks of stone unearthed had proved almost impossible, so, in 1881, excavation had been abandoned. However, when at the beginning of the century the importance of the Hittite civilization was fully realized in archaeological circles, Hogarth was asked to assess whether work should be resumed. He recommended that excavation should begin again immediately, but it was not until 1910 that a permit could be obtained from the Turkish authorities. By this time the site had become completely overgrown so

The living-room of Lawrence's house, Carchemish.

that Hogarth and his colleagues were confronted on arrival with an enormous mound dominating the landscape, presenting them with the daunting task of digging through the product of three decades' neglect plus various layers of occupation to reach the original Hittite city underneath. Labour was hired from among the local villagers and the dig began.

In 1911 when the British party arrived in Carchemish, Syria had been ruled by the Turks for almost four hundred years but now their power was in decline and they had only a tenuous hold over the Arabs and Kurds in the area, who were in constant feud, with much resort to murder and brigandage. The Germans, potential allies of the Turks, were building the Berlin to Baghdad railway which the British saw as a potential threat to their political and economic undertakings in the Orient. By now German engineers had reached the Euphrates and had started the long process of constructing a bridge across the river only a few hundred yards from the excavations. Such was the background against which the archaeologists went to work. The local headman lent them a low stone building which the team set about adapting to their needs, attempting to make it as comfortable as possible since the weather was still bitterly cold.

Lawrence's principal task was to record finds and direct the work force. He had a remarkable eye and was able to remember and connect fragments which other people would miss. His other major role was that of expedition photographer. Ever since becoming interested in photography as a boy he had managed to acquire the latest equipment, and as far back as his cycling tour of France in 1907 had succeeded in taking a picture of Mont St Michel with his telephoto lens from fifteen miles away. Now in Carchemish he again had the finest equipment available, having brought with him a specially designed archaeological camera, with a large selection of lenses, including a bronze telephoto attachment. This, combined with the volatile political situation and the fact that the excavations had been reopened at a time when the Germans were working so close to the site, has led some biographers to speculate that the expedition had another and more sinister purpose, that of spying on the movements of the Turkish and German work forces and the progress of the railway.

Interviewed on this subject in 1985, Lawrence's brother A.W., himself a distinguished archaeologist, strongly denied the allegations.

> Of course that is nonsense. They have also suggested that he had been trained as a spy by Hogarth and that all Hogarth's excavations were in fact concealed spying efforts as well as Carchemish. I happen to have been within a mile or two of all the sites Hogarth excavated, and except at Alexandria where there was a consul and presumably a trained staff who could do that sort of spying, there was absolutely no conceivable gain to be achieved, because there was nothing to spy upon. At Carchemish there was the building of the railway bridge

which took years and years and was visible to everybody and couldn't possibly be hidden. It is just journalistic invention.

A. W. Lawrence acknowledged that in times of impending war archaeologists and similar field workers might be asked to keep their eyes open, because 'they have been to places nobody has been to and it is natural that they should be asked about them', but his view on his brother's principal preoccupation at Carchemish was quite clear. 'I think T.E. was mainly enjoying himself.'

Lawrence took a particular interest in the local population and its customs, and this proved valuable in his working relationships with the men.

> Some of the workmen are rather fine-looking fellows: all of course are thin as sticks: and the majority small: there was no one within an inch of Mr. Hogarth's height: indeed the majority were hardly more than mine. Many shave their heads, others let their hair grow in long plaits, like Hittites. . . .

> Our people are very curious and very simple, and yet there is a fund of directness and child-humour about them that is very fine. I see much of this, for I sleep every day on the mound and start every day at sunrise, and so choosing of new men falls to my lot. I take care in the selection, utterly refusing all such as are solemn or over-polite, and yet [we] are continually bothered into blood-feuds, by getting into the same trench men who have killed each other's kin or run off with their wives. They at once prepare to settle up the score in kind, and we have to come down amid great shouting, and send one to another pit.

One friendship especially helped Lawrence to cross the gap between his western background and the local way of life. Selim Ahmed, nicknamed Dahoum, 'the little dark one' (probably because he was so fair), joined the excavation as a donkey boy and became Lawrence's constant companion and protégé.

> He talks of going into Aleppo to school with the money he has made out of us. I will try to keep an eye on him to see what happens. . . . Fortunately there is no foreign influence as yet in the district: if only you had seen the ruination caused by the French influence, & to a lesser degree by the American, you would never wish it extended. The perfectly hopeless vulgarity of the half-Europeanized Arab is appalling. Better a thousand times the Arab untouched. The foreigners come out here always to teach, whereas they had much better learn, for in everything but wits and knowledge the Arab is generally the better man of the two.

Lawrence taught Dahoum the use of the camera and the fifteen year old boy became quite adept. They went off on expeditions together across the Euphrates,

Photograph by Lawrence showing a relief reconstructed from pieces found in the excavations. The piecing together of sculptures in this way was mainly, though not entirely, his work, because, to quote A.W. Lawrence 'neither Campbell Thompson nor Woolley had an eye for style.' The Arab boy left is almost certainly the young Dahoum.

exploring the country, Lawrence frequently dressed like his companion in Arab clothes. The Arabs on the site – to quote Leonard Woolley, who succeeded Hogarth as director of the excavation in 1912 – were 'tolerantly scandalized' by the friendship, especially when in 1913 Lawrence, staying on when the season's dig was over, 'had Dahoum to live with him and got him to pose as a model for a queer crouching figure which he carved in the soft local limestone and set up on the edge of the house roof; to make an image was bad enough in its way, but to portray a naked figure was proof to them of evil of another sort.' However, Woolley had no doubt about the falsity of any such assumption. 'The charge was quite unfounded,' he wrote in his important contribution to *T. E. Lawrence by His Friends*. 'Lawrence had in his make-up a very strong vein of sentiment, but he was in no sense a pervert; in fact, he had a remarkably clean mind. He was tolerant, thanks to his classical reading, and Greek homosexuality interested him, but in a detached way, and the interest was not morbid but perfectly serious; I never heard him make a smutty remark and am sure he would have objected to one if it had been made for his benefit: but he would describe Arab abnormalities baldly and with a certain sardonic humour. He knew quite well what the Arabs said about himself and Dahoum and so far from resenting it was amused, and I think he courted misunderstanding rather than tried to avoid it; it appealed to his sense of humour, which was broad and schoolboyish. He liked to shock.'

In the summer of 1913 Lawrence took Dahoum and the site foreman Sheikh Hamoudi (a wild character with whom he had become friends, and who had once nursed him through a bad attack of dysentery) home to Oxford. The three stayed in the bungalow at the end of the garden at Polstead Road and his mother attempted to speak French with the visitors in their flowing desert robes. The Arabs created quite a sensation in Oxford, cycling around (on ladies' bicycles of course), and Lawrence even took them to London, where they were amazed by the underground railway. After Lawrence's death Hamoudi recalled the one time he was angry with his hero.

> When Dahoum and I went to Oxford many wished to photograph us as we sat with him in our customary Arab clothes. And after they took a picture they would come and speak to him, and always he would say 'No, No'. One day I asked him why he was always saying 'No, No,' and he laughed and said, 'I will tell you. These people wish to give you money. But for me you would now be rich.' And he smiled again. Then I grew angry. Indeed I could not believe I heard right. 'Do you call yourself my friend,' I cried to him, 'and say thus calmly that you keep me from riches?' And the angrier I grew the more he laughed and I was very wrath at this treachery. At last he said when I had turned away and would no longer look at him, 'Yes, you might have been rich, richer than any in Jerablus. And I – what should I have been?' and he paused watching my face with his eyes. 'I should have been the showman of two monkeys.' And suddenly all my anger died down within me.

By August the three were back at Carchemish. This was a happy time for Lawrence – plenty of good books to read and a healthy outdoor life. His Arabic was improving and he was becoming an expert on the local customs. He had a small boat with an outboard motor sent from Oxford and he enjoyed many adventurous trips on the Euphrates. He kept up a constant stream of letters enthusiastically describing his experiences:

> The most pleasing part of the day is when the breakfast hour gets near; from all the villages below us on the plain there come long

lines of red and blue women & children carrying bread in red-check handkerchiefs, and wooden measures full of leben on their heads. The men are not tired then, and the heat is just pleasant, and they chatter about and jest & sing in very delightful style. A few of them bring shepherd's pipes and make music of their sort.

This rather austere way of life in an all-male community suited Lawrence's puritanical nature. He did not smoke or drink and always ate sparingly. He grew to love the harshness of the desert landscape.

I feel very little lack of English scenery: we have too much greenery there, and one never feels the joy of a fertile place, as one does here when one finds a thorn-bush and green thistle. Here one learns an economy of beauty which is wonderful. England is fat – obese.

In his work Woolley found him curiously erratic. Everything depended on how far he was interested, and not everything in field archaeology sorted with

Lawrence as archaeologist at the British Museum 'dig' at Carchemish in Syria, 1913. Lawrence, centre, stands by one of the Hittite slabs excavated at the site, with Leonard Woolley. Woolley wrote later of Lawrence: 'From the outset he was excellent with the Arab workmen, in a way he was rather like them, for the fun of the thing appealed to him as much as did its scientific interest.'

his sense of values. Sometimes he took full notes, giving the gist of the matter but not always in an easily available form, while at other times he took no notes at all. But Woolley found his relationships with the Arab workmen excellent from the outset. 'In a way', he observed, 'he was rather like them, for the fun of the thing appealed to him as much as did its scientific interest. It was he who invented the system whereby a discovery was saluted by revolver shots carefully proportioned to its importance; the men competed together as to who should have the greatest number of shots to his credit in the course of the season, and the hope of a few more cartridges was the chief incitement to hard work. Or Lawrence and Hamoudi would suddenly turn the whole work into a game, the pick-men pitted against the basket-men or the entire gang against the wagon-boys, until with the two hundred men running and yelling half a day's output would be accomplished in an hour; and Lawrence would lead the yells.'

Mrs Fontana often visited Lawrence on the site, sometimes taking her children along, and she remembered his kindness to the family and the fun they had on their adventurous canoe trips across the Euphrates, when 'clad in shorts and a buttonless shirt held together with a gaudy Kurdish belt, [Lawrence] looked what he was: a young man of rare power and considerable physical beauty. The belt was fastened on the left hip with a huge bunch of many-coloured tassels,

Lawrence and Woolley (centre) photographed with the Carchemish work force.

symbol, plain to all arabs [*sic*] that he was seeking a wife. No doubt it was the soft water of the Euphrates in which he loved to swim and subsequent drying in fierce sunlight, that burnished his hair: it is the sober truth that I have not seen such gold hair, before nor since – nor such intensely blue eyes.' She noted that the local people also found him an object of admiration. 'The dark-eyed, richly coloured arabs who came to exhibit their finds on the "Dig" or to beg quinine for their fevered children (Lawrence seemed to know them all by name and their children's names too) watched him with fascinated affection.'

In September 1913 one of Lawrence's younger brothers, Will, called to see him in Carchemish. He was on his way to India to take up a teaching post, and he was much excited and impressed by what he found. He wrote home enthusiastically: 'I'm with Ned now, who's very well, and a great lord in this place.' Lawrence showed him around Aleppo and fired his mind with the romance and beauty of the place. He arranged for Will to go across country on horseback to meet a great chief, Busrawi, who gave them a traditional feast. Will was obviously delighted by this visit to his elder brother. 'When I saw him last as the train left the station,' he wrote as he continued his journey, 'he was wearing white flannels, socks and red slippers with a white Magdalen blazer and was talking to the governor of Biredjik in lordly fashion.'

Will's visit to his brother inspired a poem which he dedicated 'To T.E.L.':

> I've talked with counsellors and lords
> Where words were as no blunted swords
> Watched two Emperors and five Kings
> And three who had men's worshippings,
> Ridden with horsemen of the East
> And sat with scholars at their feast
> Known some the masters of their hours
> Some to whom years were as pressed flowers:
> Still as I go this thought endures
> No place too great to be made yours.

Lawrence was to remember his four years at Carchemish as the happiest in his life. His relationship with Dahoum – Selim Ahmed – was so strong that it provides the main argument for the claim that his dedicatory poem 'To S.A.' in *Seven Pillars of Wisdom* was written as a tribute to him. (Dahoum died of typhus in 1918).

> I loved you, so I drew these tides of men into my hands
>   and wrote my will across the sky in stars
> To earn you Freedom, that seven-pillared worthy house,
>   that your eyes might be shining for me
>   when we came. . . .

When Lawrence returned to the dig for the third season in 1913, the idyllic days at Carchemish were drawing to a close. In Europe it seemed that war with Germany was becoming inevitable, and a clash with the Ottoman Empire would almost certainly ensue. Lord Kitchener, who since 1911 had been British Agent in Egypt, realized that if war came it would be essential to protect the Suez Canal. The Sinai peninsula was a natural bastion against an invasion of Egypt, but the part under Turkish control was an almost uninhabited area, unmapped and almost unexplored. Kitchener decided that a geographical survey was essential, to draw up maps and provide useful topographical information. Surprisingly, the Turks gave permission for a limited survey. Captain S. F. Newcombe of the Royal Engineers was put in charge and to give the operation a plausible cover it was conducted under the auspices of a respectable archaeological organization – the Palestine Exploration Fund. Towards the end of 1913 Woolley and Lawrence were asked to join the project. Lawrence wrote to his mother, 'We are obviously only meant as red herrings, to give an archaeological colour to a political job.'

Accompanied by Dahoum, Lawrence and Woolley set off from Carchemish to join Newcombe at Beersheba, where Newcombe was pleasantly surprised to find that his companions were young and lively. In the weeks that followed the archaeologists and the professional soldier got on well together although frequently going their own ways. Their menus were somewhat limited, as Lawrence described to his Ashmolean friend E.T. Leeds:

> We have evolved rather a sporting dinner: Woolley you know likes a many storied edifice.
>
> Hors d'oeuvre
> The waiter (Dahoum) brings in on the lid of a petrol box half a dozen squares of Turkish delight.
> Soup.
> Bread soup.
> Then
> Turkish delight on toast
> Then until yesterday
> Eggs
> Then, sweet . . .
> Turkish delight
> Dessert
> Turkish delight
> Of course bread is ad lib

In six weeks they covered the Sinai desert, surveying the tracks and the water points while Woolley and Lawrence also collected the material on the archaeology of the region from which they were to compile a report to be published in due course by the Palestine Exploration Fund. In February 1914 Lawrence found himself at Akaba, a small fishing village at the northern end of the Gulf of Akaba and on the border between Egypt and the Ottoman Empire – a place which was to assume much strategic importance in the coming war.

5

INTELLIGENCE OFFICER

Lawrence was to return to Akaba some three years later in circumstances which would ensure that, in Western eyes at least, his name and Akaba's would be indissolubly linked. But even this first visit had its adventurous aspects. The Kaimakam of Akaba – the local Turkish governor – forbade him, as he put it to Leeds, 'to photograph or archaeologize. I photographed what I could, I archaeologized everywhere.' Denied the use of a boat, he and Dahoum improvised a raft out of two zinc tanks and with planks for paddles rowed to Faraoun, a tiny island in the bay on which stood the decayed ruins of a crusader fort. 'The whole squadron sailed across safely, saw, judged and condemned the ruins as uninteresting, and splashed homewards, very cold and very tired.' Eluding the attentions of a Turkish lieutenant and half a company of soldiers, they headed north to Petra where, being short of money, they were fortunate enough to meet a wealthy English traveller, Lady Evelyn Cobbold, who lent them the necessary funds for their journey back to Carchemish.

He resumed his archaeological work but this season of 1914 was to be no normal one. In June he left for London. Dahoum was appointed custodian of the site for what was meant to be a relatively brief absence but in fact Lawrence was never to see him or Carchemish again. Within weeks all Europe was at war and though at first Turkey remained on the sidelines it was generally assumed that if she came in she would do so on the side of Germany, which had been cultivating her friendship for years. The Turkish authorities were now, as Lawrence was later to put it to his biographer Liddell Hart, 'sore about the Sinai survey, which they felt had been a military game', so Kitchener insisted on the Palestine Exploration Fund's bringing out its archaeological report 'p.d.q. [pretty damn quick] as whitewash'. But it never had a chance to fulfil Kitchener's

A Byzantine cistern at Biz Birein, with Dahoum at the far side to set the scale. (Photograph taken by Lawrence in 1914.)

purpose; long before it could be printed Turkey, after a three-month hesitation, had joined the belligerents. Woolley and Lawrence hurried to conclude their joint work, which was published that winter under the title *The Wilderness of Zin*. 'It certainly was the filthiest manuscript made,' Lawrence wrote of it in a letter to Hogarth, while to Dr Cowley of the Bodleian Library he commented, 'parts of the book are frivolous, so don't call it a "serious contribution".' By contrast, the notable Middle Eastern archaeologist Sir Frederick Kenyon considered it a work of 'literary merit deserving wider publicity'.

As soon as they had finished *The Wilderness of Zin* both Lawrence and Woolley began casting about for suitable war work, hoping to use Newcombe as an ally. Growing impatient, Woolley 'wangled' (Lawrence's word) a commission in the Artillery, but Lawrence persevered in the direction which suited him most and finally found himself in the presence of Colonel Coote Hedley, who was in charge of the Geographical Section of the General Staff (Intelligence) of the War Office. Hedley knew of him and took him on immediately, unperturbed by the fact that Lawrence arrived hatless, in grey flannels and looking about eighteen. Beginning as a civilian he officially became a soldier in late October, being commissioned as a second lieutenant on the 'special list', a convenient category to cover officers with no regimental attachment. He was based in London where for some three months he worked on maps, particularly of the area over which he had just travelled, Sinai. 'Today has been an awful scramble,' he wrote one Sunday to Leeds, 'for some unit (report says K's [i.e. Kitchener's] private sec) asked for a complete map of Sinai, showing all roads and wells, with capacity of latter, and a rough outline of hills. As Sinai is in manuscript in 68 sheets it meant a little trouble. . . . I came up like St George in shining armour . . . and by night behold there was a map of Sinai eighteen feet each way in three colours. Some of it was accurate and the rest I invented.'

The capital, teeming with khaki, posters and patriotism, was not a congenial scene: 'I disapprove of London on eighteen counts,' he wrote to Dr Cowley. But he was finding the work stimulating and enjoyable. 'This month up here has been great sport,' he wrote to Leeds in November. 'I'm sure somebody will ask the W[ar] O[ffice] for an epic poem on Sinai about next Friday, and I'll be turned on to that.'

In mid-November he wrote to his brother Will, then teaching in India but showing increasing signs of the 'wild patriotism' (T.E.'s phrase) which would bring him to an airman's death on the Western Front within the year: 'I am going out to Egypt probably, at the end of this week, on special service. The Turks may do something in that direction . . . [However] nothing doing, I fancy either in the Caucasus or in Sinai till next spring . . . hope not, since I want time to look round and polish up my Bedouin dialects.'

Lawrence, travelling with Newcombe, reached Cairo on 14 December 1914; three days later Woolley, seconded from the Artillery, arrived in the company of George (later Lord) Lloyd M.P. and the Hon. Aubrey Herbert M.P. It was a gathering of the talents, as Lawrence made clear neatly to Leeds in a Christmas Eve letter datelined Intelligence Dept., War Office, Cairo: 'There wasn't an Intelligence Office, and so we set to, and are going to make them one: today we got the office, and we all have the Intelligence.' Aubrey Herbert came to a similar conclusion. 'My department', he wrote in a letter of February 1915, 'is made up of engineers, MPs, archaeologists and MPs.' It was almost a combination of Oxford Senior Common Room and London Club gathered for war; in modern terms, it was a 'think tank'. There was also a French Dominican monk, Père Jaussen, fluent in Arabic, an expert on Sinai, 'very witty, amusing and clever and very useful as an interpreter'. Then there was *The Times* correspondent Philip Graves – 'very learned in the Turkish army organization', said

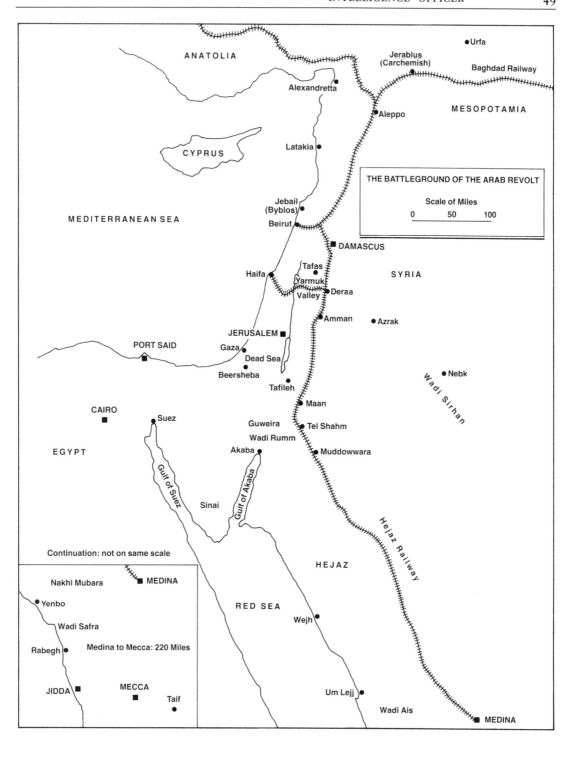

THE BATTLEGROUND OF THE ARAB REVOLT

Scale of Miles

0   50   100

ANATOLIA

Urfa

Jerablus
(Carchemish)

Baghdad Railway

Alexandretta

Aleppo

MESOPOTAMIA

CYPRUS

Latakia

MEDITERRANEAN SEA

Jebail
(Byblos)

Beirut

DAMASCUS

Tafas

Haifa

Yarmuk

Valley

Deraa

SYRIA

Amman

Azrak

JERUSALEM

Gaza

Dead Sea

Beersheba

Tafileh

Nebk

Wadi Sirhan

PORT SAID

CAIRO

Suez

Maan

EGYPT

Guweira

Tel Shahm

Wadi Rumm

Akaba

Muddowwara

Gulf of Suez

Gulf of Akaba

Sinai

Hejaz Railway

Continuation: not on same scale

HEJAZ

Nakhl Mubara

MEDINA

Yenbo

RED SEA

Wadi Safra

Wejh

Rabegh

Medina to Mecca: 220 Miles

JIDDA

MECCA

Taif

Um Lejj

Wadi Ais

MEDINA

Lawrence in a letter home. There was also 'a very nice fellow en chef' – Herbert's description – in the genial person of Colonel, later Brigadier-General Gilbert Clayton. It has been suggested that Lawrence's role was only that of map officer (indeed he implied that himself in a home letter of January 1916) but in a revealing note held in the Lawrence papers in the Bodleian Library Colonel Newcombe rejects that description, preferring to call him an Intelligence Officer on the General Staff. 'We worked in the same room together,' Newcombe adds: 'T.E., Woolley and myself had breakfast, lunch and dinner together daily at the Continental Hotel for 9 months. So T.E. knew all that any other of us did and of course read all reports which we all discussed together: so "maps" was only a nominal part of his job: and he was in fact as much in the picture as any of us.' Newcombe also makes an interesting observation on Lawrence's well-publicized reputation as an unconventional, scruffily dressed officer in a Cairo filled with impeccably creased uniforms and gleaming Sam Browne belts, stating that 'his senior officer (a Regular of 16 years service) [presumably Clayton] also wore slacks without a belt (and I believe Genl. Maxwell, G.O.C. [General Officer Commanding] did the same.' Yet he undoubtedly gave the impression of being different from the accepted pattern. R. W. Graves, brother of the correspondent of *The Times*, who met Lawrence in early 1916 later wrote that even at that period 'it seemed to be recognized that there was something out of the common about the young man and so far as I know his unconventionalities never brought more than good-humoured expressions of astonishment on the part of the senior staff members of the regular establishment.' (There were exceptions to this rule, as will be seen.)

Lawrence was certainly in the war theatre most suited to his individual style and talents. He was free to put forward his ideas and while he was without military experience he had the authority of one who had for years travelled the future Middle Eastern battleground. He was also able to unleash his talent, already shown at Oxford and Carchemish, for energizing and enthusing people. Ernest Dowson, Director-General of the Survey of Egypt, with whom Lawrence came into contact through his map work, recognized this influence at work among members of his staff who might normally have resented the confidence, which must almost at times have seemed like arrogance, of this knowledgeable and articulate young man. 'His tremendous keenness about anything to do with work was remarkable and infectious,' he wrote in *T. E. Lawrence by His Friends*, 'with the consequence that his frequent walks round the various offices and workshops had a most stimulating effect on the men.' But for the moment his war was an ideas war only, with as yet no prospect of fighting other than with maps and memoranda. There were long hours of work but there was also much frustration – 'Out upon all this show! I am fed up and fed up and fed up' he wrote to Leeds in April 1915 – and when later that year his two brothers lost

'I'm rather low because first one and now another of my brothers has been killed... They were both younger than I am, and it doesn't seem right, somehow, that I should go on living peacefully in Cairo.'

(T.E. Lawrence to E.T. Leeds, 16 November 1915)

Frank Lawrence's name on the Memorial to the Missing, Le Touret Military Cemetery, near La Bassée, France.

Grave of Will Lawrence, St Souplet Military Cemetery, near Le Cateau, France.

their lives, Frank in May and Will in September, his dissatisfaction with a campaign fought from an office became palpable. 'They were both younger than I' – again he was writing to Leeds – 'and it doesn't seem right, somehow, that I should go on living peacefully in Cairo.'[1]

He was still over a year away from finding the moment and the cause which led to his exchanging his Cairo desk for the Arabian desert, but throughout this physically inactive time his mind ranged far beyond the routine tasks of map-work, the interviewing of prisoners and the compilation and evaluation of intelligence. His thorough knowledge of the places and issues involved and his eagerness to strike a blow at the Ottoman Empire were sound platforms for his promotion of, and adding his individual variations to, some of the strategic ideas which were then on the table as options for the further prosecution of the Middle Eastern war. He also did not hesitate to criticize the policies of Britain's allies, Russia and France, particularly the latter, whose Middle Eastern ambitions, especially in relation to Syria, he thought misguided and dangerous. He was not necessarily unique in his ideas; frequently he was arguing the broad consensus; but he quickly established himself as an officer whose trenchant and challenging views could not be disregarded.

In the spring of 1916 Lawrence and Aubrey Herbert found themselves in harness on an extremely difficult and potentially dangerous mission far from Egypt in the hot, fly-infested plain of the Tigris, in what was then known as Mesopotamia. Their first impressions of each other following their original meeting in Cairo seem dismissive. Lawrence called Herbert 'a joke, but a very nice one'; Herbert called Lawrence 'an odd gnome, half cad, with a touch of genius'. In fact they soon came to respect and like each other, though their early friendship was shortly to be interrupted by Herbert's move to the battlefront at Gallipoli, where as a Turkish speaker and a figure of considerable repute in the Middle East from his pre-war days he played an effective and unusual role, even on one occasion securing an armistice so that several thousand bodies could be decently buried. The relationship begun in Cairo was to be cemented at this time and years later Lawrence was to link Herbert with Hogarth as the two men whose death had left 'empty places which no one and nothing can ever fill'.

In Mesopotamia a British military force under Major General Sir Charles V.

1 Frank, a Second Lieutenant of the 1st Gloucesters, was killed by shellfire on the Western Front on 9 May 1915 when leading his men forward preparatory to an infantry assault; Will, having been commissioned as a Second Lieutenant in the Oxford and Bucks Light Infantry, transferred to the Royal Flying Corps as an observer in August 1915. He was shot down on 23 October after less than a week in France. He was originally posted 'Missing', but T.E. took his death for granted. It was officially confirmed in the following May.

Townshend was in trouble. Despatched by the (British) Government of India, it had almost reached the gates of Baghdad, but following a bloody encounter with the Turks as Ctesiphon, just sixteen miles from the city, it had been forced to retreat down-river. It was now besieged by the Turks at Kut-el-Amara between Baghdad and Basra. Exhausted, reduced by sickness and hunger, it had no chance of escape. Herbert, after Gallipoli and a subsequent visit to England, was a naval intelligence officer on the staff of Admiral Wemyss in Mesopotamia. Lawrence was now sent to Basra, commended by the British High Commissioner in Egypt, Sir Henry McMahon, in a letter to the Chief Political Officer in Mesopotamia, Sir Percy Cox, as 'one of the best of our very able intelligence staff here'.

The nature of his mission was a curious one. A War Office telegram addressed to the General Officer Commanding, Indian Expeditionary Force 'D' in Mesopotamia, begins as follows:

> Most secret and for yourself personally. Captain Lawrence is due at BASRA about the 30th March from Egypt to consult with you and if possible purchase one of the Turkish leaders of the Mesopotamian Army, such as Khalil or Negib, so as to facilitate relief TOWNSHEND. You are authorized to expend for this purpose any sum not exceeding one million pounds.

By the time Lawrence joined Herbert and Colonel Beach, the third and senior member of the party who was head of Intelligence Branch of Force 'D', the circumstances were such that there was no longer any possibility of the British buying themselves out of their difficulties. In the event their task became one of attempting to negotiate the best terms of surrender.

Uncertain whether Khalil would see them, they set out towards the Turkish lines bearing a white flag. After some time they were allowed through. As Herbert described it in his diary:

> We were blindfolded and we went in a string of hot hands to the trenches banging against men and corners, and sweating something cruel. Beyond the trenches we went for half an hour, while my handkerchief became a wet string across my eyes.

After a welcome interlude in which they were given coffee and yoghourt they went on again. Herbert's account continues:

> My eyes were bound and I got on a horse that started bucking because of the torture of the flies. Lawrence had hurt his knee and could not ride. He got off and walked, a Turkish officer being left with him. Colonel Beach and I went on.

Eventually, ten miles from the British lines and four miles from Kut, they met Khalil. Lawrence's letter home adds to Herbert's account:

He spoke French to us and was very polite, but of course the cards
were all in his hands, and we could not get much out of him. However
he let about 1000 wounded go without any condition but the release
of as many Turks – which was all we could hope for.

Herbert's diary contains an interesting glimpse of Lawrence that same evening:

I dictated a letter in French to Lawrence, asking [Khalil] for
permission for me to stay and go across to Kut. How Lawrence wrote
the letter I can't think. The whole place was one smother of small
flies, attracted by the candle. They put it out three times. Beach and
I kept them off Lawrence while he wrote. We got an answer at about
two in the morning. Khalil said it was not necessary.

The rest of this melancholy episode is soon told. Townshend surrendered
before the negotiating party had returned to the British lines. He was given
honourable treatment by the Turks, spending the rest of the war comfortably in
Constantinople. His army, particularly the other ranks, were less fortunate, as
Townshend himself had foreseen. Seventy per cent perished, many of them on
a hideous death march to Turkey, others subsequently as prisoners-of-war.
Herbert did not spare the Government of India or the generals on his return to
London that summer, and he raised the subject of the Mesopotamian campaign
in Parliament to such good effect that the Prime Minister, Asquith, agreed to
appoint a Royal Commission into its conduct. Lawrence on the voyage back to
Egypt wrote a comprehensive and outspoken report which had to be suitably
'bowdlerized' before it was shown to the Commander-in-Chief in Cairo, now
Sir Archibald Murray. His report criticized all aspects of the campaign: map
making, transport, health care, tactical dispositions and strategical concepts. His
strictures were later to be vindicated by the findings of the Royal Commission.
He was back in Egypt in June, the month of the beginning of the Arab Revolt.

The majority of the Arab peoples had been under the rule of the Ottoman
Empire since the middle of the sixteenth century. For most of this long period
there had been relatively few signs of Arab political unrest. However, in 1908
a revolution in Constantinople, the Ottoman capital, brought to power the so-
called 'Young Turks', who instead of respecting the susceptibilities of the subject
peoples of the Empire mounted a vigorous campaign of Turkification. This led
to an upsurge of Arab nationalist sentiment and to the formation of a number
of Arab secret societies and political parties, whose ultimate aim was the establishment of an independent and united Arab Empire.

The leader who was to launch the Arab Revolt was Grand Sherif Hussein,
descendant of the Prophet Mohammed, 'Protector of the Two Holy Cities' –
Mecca and Medina – and ruler, 'by Turkish appointment, of the province

bordering the east of the Red Sea known as the Hejaz. Early in 1914 the second of his four sons, Abdulla, visited Cairo. There he met Kitchener, then British Agent and Consul-General in Egypt, and the question whether the British would lend support if there should be an uprising in the Hejaz against the Ottoman government was discussed. Kitchener could give no firm assurance at that time, but when war came later that year he felt able to send from London, where he was now War Minister, encouraging messages first to Abdulla and then to Abdulla's father, the Sherif. The core of his message to the latter, sent in November and cast in mellifluous style, was: 'Till now we have defended and befriended Islam in the person of the Turks. Henceforward it shall be that of the noble Arab. . . . It would be well if your Highness could convey to your followers and devotees who are found throughout the world in every country the good tidings of the freedom of the Arabs and the rising of the sun over Arabia.'

It was a definite invitation to the Arabs to join the Allies; and it clearly implied that Britain viewed with favour Arab aspirations for freedom and independence. Similar indications followed, notably those associated with the British High Commissioner in Egypt Sir Henry McMahon, who wrote to the Sherif of Mecca on 13 December 1915: 'I am . . . directed by the Government of Great Britain to inform you that you may rest assured that Great Britain has no intention of concluding any peace in terms of which the freedom of the Arab people from German and Turkish domination does not form an essential condition.' Yet within months of McMahon's being encouraged to give such assurances, secret negotiations conducted by Britain's Sir Mark Sykes and France's Georges Picot led to a secret understanding between Britain and France and Russia, the Sykes–Picot agreement, whereby the Allied powers agreed to partition large areas of the territories of the Ottoman Empire between them after the war.[1]

Concurrent with the exchanges between the Sherif and the British, the former was in communication with the Turks, who were demanding his support for a Holy War against the Allies. His conditions for agreeing to their request included autonomy for Syria, which the Turks were not disposed to grant. In the spring of 1916 the Turks hanged a number of Arab nationalists in Damascus, the Syrian capital, and threatened to detain his third son, Feisal, who had been sent there by his father to allay Turkish suspicions – and who was given by his

1 The McMahon–Hussein understandings and the Sykes–Picot agreement were not entirely contradictory in that both assumed Arab independence in the Arabian peninsula; the main difference was in terms of the intended fate of Syria (a larger area than the Syria of today) which the treaty divided into British and French 'spheres of influence', apart from the coastal area which was intended to be under direct French control. But the contradictions were enough for one notable Arab historian, Antonius, to call Sykes–Picot 'a shocking document'. Awareness of what he saw as double dealing with the Arabs was to cause Lawrence much heart searching later: see Chapter 8.

Turkish infantry in Damascus

Turkish hosts the dubious pleasure of witnessing some of the hangings. When subsequently the Turks proposed to move substantial reinforcements south to the Hejaz, Hussein became convinced that they were out to curb or even remove him. The Turks did not impede Feisal's return to the Hejaz, and once his son was safely back Hussein moved against them.

He initiated the Revolt with a dramatic gesture. On the 9th of Sha'ban – 10 June 1916 – from his balcony in Mecca the Grand Sherif fired a token rifle shot at a nearby barracks of the Ottoman army. It was the symbolic declaration of what to him and his people was nothing less than an Arab war of independence. As Abdulla was to write in his memoirs: 'Thus the Arabs as a nation began to bear their own responsibilities and to defend their liberty and independence by their own arms and initiative.' He and his three brothers, Ali, Feisal and Zeid, were to play a leading part as field-commanders in the campaign.

In the weeks that followed there was fierce fighting in the course of which

EMIR FEISAL

Is tall, graceful, vigorous, almost regal in appearance. Age 31. Far more imposing personally than any of his brothers... Looks like a European, and very like the monument of Richard I at Fontevrault. He is hot tempered, proud and impatient, sometimes unreasonable and runs off easily at tangents... Obviously very clever, perhaps not over scrupulous... A popular idol, and ambitious; full of dreams, and the capacity to realize them, with keen personal insight, and very efficient.

(From a report by Captain Lawrence, dated Yenbo 27/10/16)

Mecca was cleared of Turkish troops, the Turkish garrison of the Red Sea port of Jidda surrendered after shelling by the British naval cruiser H.M.S. *Fox* and attacks by British aircraft, while two small but important coastal villages, Rabegh and Yenbo, were occupied by Sherifian and allied forces. The inland garrison town of Taif, east of Mecca, surrendered to Abdulla in September.

Lawrence had resumed his intelligence duties in Cairo on his return from Mesopotamia. These included contributions to the political summaries of the Arab Bureau which were the forerunner of the *Arab Bulletin*, first published on 6 June 1916 on the eve of the Revolt, with Lawrence as editor of the opening edition. His initial reaction to the Revolt is made clear in a letter to his mother dated 1 July in which he wrote: 'It is so good to have helped a bit in making a new nation – and I hate the Turks so much that to see their own people turning on them is very grateful [*sic*]. I hope the movement increases, as it promises to do. . . . This revolt, if it succeeds, will be the biggest thing in the Middle East since 1550.' Of his part in events in Cairo he continued: 'The last two weeks we have lived in the middle of a storm of telegrams and conferences, and excursions, and to consider one's private affairs is not possible. . . . Our office is the clearing house through which every report and item affecting the Near East has to pass . . . the mass of Stuff is amazing, and it all fits into itself like a most wonderful puzzle.'

Later in that same month, July, he was engaged in a counter-propaganda exercise to show proof that the Revolt had taken place. 'Arnie will be glad to hear I am printing stamps for the Sherif of Mecca', he wrote to his mother on 22 July, 'I'll send him some when they come out. Of course they are only a provisional issue. It's rather amusing, because one has long had ideas as to what a stamp should look like, and now one can put them roughly into practice. . . . I'm going to have flavoured gum on the back, so that one may lick without unpleasantness.' A month later he sent one or two examples home, adding that he hoped to send his younger brother a few more later. 'They may be valuable some day, for I am not printing many, and have taken steps to prevent any dealers purchasing them in bulk.' His letter continued, however, in less cheerful tone with the brief comment: 'Things in Arabia are not going too well.'

After the initial successes the Hejaz campaign was running into difficulties. Arab forces surrounding Medina, the garrison town at the southern railhead of the Hejaz Railway, were making little impression on its Turkish occupants. Meanwhile instead of the support they expected from the Allies the Arab leadership felt they were getting only lukewarm encouragement from Cairo, while such supplies as they received seemed largely to consist of outdated rifles and guns that were no match for the Turkish artillery. At the same time there were delays while arguments proceeded as to whether Christian troops could suitably be landed in a territory sacred to Islam.

During this period Lawrence felt that Army Command was trying to move him away from Arab affairs. He sought help from Brigadier-General Clayton hoping to transfer to the Arab Bureau. Pending a decision he applied for leave when he heard that Ronald Storrs, the Oriental Secretary at the British Agency in Egypt, was to visit Jidda and asked to accompany him. Storrs was delighted to be asked for he enjoyed Lawrence's company, respected his judgment and was particularly grateful to him for his supervision of the Hejaz stamp issue. He kept a diary of their journey.

> 12.X.16. On the train from Cairo little Lawrence my super-cerebral companion.

> 13.X.16. By 2.0 aboard the *Lama*, a converted B.I. [British Indiaman liner] of 2000 tons. Agreeable neat Commander. I was given the doctor's very adequate cabin; two young vets going to Jeddah to buy, as a first consignment, £10,000 worth of camels. Lawrence shared a cabin with one of the vets.

> 16.X.16. Jeddah harbour 7 a.m. Young came aboard to take us off and we reached Consulate about 9.30.

Thus – much abbreviated – runs Storrs' account. For Lawrence this brief voyage was to mark the transition between the two phases of his war, the move, as it were, from desk to desert. His description of it in his epic work on the Arab war, *Seven Pillars of Wisdom*, is commensurate with the occasion.

> We had the accustomed calm run to Jidda, in the delightful Red Sea climate, never too hot while the ship was moving. By day we lay in shadow; and for great part of the glorious nights we would tramp up and down the wet decks under the stars in the steaming breath of the summer wind. But when at last we anchored in the outer harbour, off the white town hung between the blazing sky and its reflection in the mirage which swept and rolled over the wide lagoon, then the heat of Arabia came out like a drawn sword and struck us speechless. It was mid-day; and the sun in the East, like moonlight, put to sleep the colours. There were only lights and shadows, the white houses and the black gaps of streets: in front the pallid lustre of the haze shimmering upon the inner harbour: behind, the dazzle of league after league of featureless sand, running up to an edge of low hills, faintly suggested in the far away mist of heat.

The purpose of Storrs' visit was to consult with the Emir Abdulla about the progress of the Revolt. Lawrence was inevitably a subordinate figure (one of the 'hangers-on of the staff', he called himself) at the various formal discussions which took place, and also at a notable dinner party at which Storrs and Colonel Wilson, the British Representative in the town, repaid Abdulla's hospitality, while the Turkish band captured by Abdulla when he liberated Taif played execrably in the street outside and the Grand Sherif himself telephoned from Mecca to join in the occasion. But the idea of Lawrence's staying on when Storrs returned to Cairo in order to meet and confer with two of the Sherif's other sons in the field had already been raised, for in his diary Storrs notes that just before dinner, 'I reminded Abdallah [*sic*] of the permission I had that morning extracted, in his hearing, from the Grand Sharif for Lawrence to go up to Bir Abbas and urged him to give L. letters of introduction to Ali and Faisal.'

So it was arranged. When the *Lama* steamed northwards up the Red Sea from Jidda Lawrence sailed with her only as far as Rabegh, where he disembarked. Storrs later wrote evocatively of that moment: 'I can still see Lawrence on the shore at Rabegh waving grateful hands as we left him there to return ourselves to Egypt. Long before we met again he had already begun to write his page, brilliant as a Persian miniature, in the History of England.'

Ali, Hussein's eldest son, was at Rabegh. In his report dated 27 October 1916 Lawrence described him as 'looking a little old already, though only 37. . . . He is obviously a very conscientious, pleasant gentleman, without force of character, nervous and rather tired.' From Rabegh he went to meet Feisal who, with his army of rebel tribesmen and a small contingent of Egyptian regulars, was away inland at a place called Hamra in Wadi Safra. Ali supplied a camel and a two-man escort and with Lawrence wrapped in an Arab cloak and headcloth to conceal his British uniform – they were to pass through a tribal area unsympathetic to the Grand Sherif – the little party set off, beginning its journey by night and with firm instructions 'to avoid all camps and encounters'. At one well they saw but did not speak to another incognito traveller, who was later to ride shoulder to shoulder with Lawrence on some of his most ambitious raids, Sherif Ali ibn el Hussein al Harith. They left Rabegh late on 21 October and rode into Hamra at 3 p.m. on the 23rd. Lawrence described the occasion in his report of 30 October.

> At Hamra the place was swarming with Sidi Feisul's camel convoys and soldiers. I found him in a little mud hut built on a 20 foot knoll of earth, busied with many visitors. Had a short and rather lively talk, and then excused myself and went off to see the Egyptian military; who were very comfortably camped in a palm grove. Zeki Bey received me warmly, and pitched me a tent in a grassy glade, where I had a bath and slept really well, after dining and arguing with Feisul (who was most unreasonable) for hours and hours.

> October 24. Woke late. Sidi Feisul came to see me at 6.30 a.m. and we had another hot discussion, which ended amicably.

This first encounter between Lawrence and Feisal was transmuted into one of the most memorable passages of *Seven Pillars of Wisdom*.

I felt at first glance that this was the man I had come to Arabia to seek – the leader who would bring the Arab Revolt to full glory. Feisal looked very tall and pillar-like, very slender, in his long white silk robes and his brown head-cloth bound with a brilliant scarlet and gold cord. His eyelids were dropped; and his black beard and colourless face were like a mask against the strange, still, watchfulness of his body. His hands were crossed in front of him on his dagger.

I greeted him. He made way for me into the room, and sat down on his carpet near the door. As my eyes grew accustomed to the shade, they saw that the little room held many silent figures, looking at me or at Feisal steadily. . . . At last he inquired softly how I had found the journey. I spoke of the heat and he asked how long from Rabegh, commenting that I had ridden fast for the season.

'And do you like our place here in Wadi Safra?'

'Well; but it is far from Damascus.'

The word had fallen like a sword in their midst. There was a quiver. Then everybody present stiffened where he sat, and held his breath for a silent minute. . . . Feisal at length lifted his eyes, smiling at me, and said, 'Praise be to God, there are Turks nearer to us than that.'

Whether the exchange between Lawrence and Feisal was precisely as written is hardly relevant; Lawrence might well have over-dramatized what was, as he saw it, a most portentous moment for him in the Arabs' war. He had turned what had begun as a break from his duties in Cairo into a mission to find among the four sons of Hussein the leader best able to advance the Revolt. Though his initial reaction to Abdulla had been largely favourable, he did not see in him the qualities he was looking for; in any case Abdulla's role had thus far been as much that of diplomat as of warrior. Ali he had deemed inadequate (though he later gave a more favourable account of him in *Seven Pillars*) and the fourth son Zeid was at twenty plainly too young. Feisal, however, had fulfilled his best expectations. Well over a year before he had dreamed of a revolt which would 'roll up Syria by way of the Hejaz in the name of the Sherif' and 'rush right up to Damascus'.[1] With Feisal this dream was now possible, and indeed in the end it was, in essence, to be realized. In the report in which he wrote coolly about Ali, his comments about Feisal were scarcely less eloquent than the descriptions in his book. He saw him as 'a popular idol, and ambitious; full of dreams and the capacity to realize them, with keen personal insight, and a very efficient man of business.'

1 Letter to D. G. Hogarth, 22 March 1915.

It would not be long before he would write to a fellow officer, Cornwallis, in Cairo: 'The situation is so interesting that I think I will fail to come back. I want to rub off my British habits and go off with Feisal for a bit. Amusing job, and all new country.' And a few weeks later he was writing home: 'It is by far the most wonderful time I have had. I have become a monomaniac about the job in hand, and have no interest or recollections except Arabian politics just now.'

IMAGES OF THE DESERT WAR:
FROM CAPTAIN LAWRENCE TO LAWRENCE OF ARABIA

T. E. Lawrence c.1916. The three shoulder pips indicate a Captain's rank. The head-dress is the standard one worn by British officers attached to the desert campaign.

Lawrence in Wadi Itm, 1917: photographed by George Lloyd.

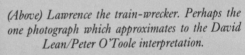

(Above) Lawrence the train-wrecker. Perhaps the one photograph which approximates to the David Lean/Peter O'Toole interpretation.

(Left) One of the numerous carefully posed photographs which were used to publicize him as 'Lawrence of Arabia' after the war.

6

ADVISER TO FEISAL

'I believed in the Arab movement,' Lawrence wrote in *Seven Pillars of Wisdom*, 'and was confident, before ever I came, that in it was the idea to tear Turkey to pieces; but others in Egypt lacked faith, and had been taught nothing intelligent of the Arabs in the field. By noting down something of the spirit of these romantics in the hills about the Holy Cities I might gain the sympathy of Cairo for the further measures necessary to help them.'

He left Feisal having promised to do his best for him and his 'romantics in the hills' and with certain specific recommendations in mind: a base on the Red Sea coast at Yenbo where stores and supplies could be landed; officer-volunteers to be recruited from prisoners-of-war (there were many Arabs in the Turkish armies to whose patriotism appeals could be made); artillery and machine-gun crews to be recruited from internment camps; such mountain guns and light machine-guns as might be available in Egypt to be shipped to the Hejaz; and British officers – 'professionals', Lawrence thought, as opposed to amateurs such as himself – to be sent down to work as advisers and liaison officers in the field. He also had from Feisal an invitation to return 'as soon as might be'. However, such an eventuality seemed unlikely.

> I explained that my duties in Cairo excluded field work, but perhaps my chiefs would let me pay a second visit later on, when his present wants were filled and his movement was going forward prosperously.

In fact he was back within weeks and would be based in Arabia for almost all of the next two years. Yet he plainly left Feisal's camp with no such possibility in mind. A second camel ride brought him to Yenbo, where he spent several days writing reports, until he was able to take ship in H.M.S. *Suva* to Jidda.

I was travel-stained and had no baggage with me. Worst of all I wore
a native head-cloth, put on as a compliment to the Arabs. Boyle
[*Suva's* Captain] disapproved.

From Jidda he sailed in the *Euryalus* to Port Sudan with Admiral Sir Rosslyn
Wemyss, who was on his way to Khartoum to consult with Sir Reginald Wingate,
Sirdar (Commander-in-Chief) of the Egyptian Army and in formal charge of
the British military side of the Arabian campaign. Lawrence accompanied him
to report on his visit to Feisal. At Port Sudan they were met by two British
officers, Joyce and Davenport, both of whom were to be much involved in the
Arab Revolt and one of whom, Joyce, was to become Lawrence's lifelong friend.
Twenty-five years later Joyce recalled his first impressions – not dissimilar to
those Lawrence himself had attributed to Captain Boyle:[1]

> I confess the memory of this meeting merely recalls the intense desire
> on my part to tell him to get his hair cut and that his uniform and
> dirty buttons badly needed the attention of his batman. I should
> certainly have done so had he not been surrounded by such
> distinguished people.

Lawrence felt that his meeting with Wingate was a positive one. 'Khartoum
felt cool after Arabia,' he wrote in *Seven Pillars*, 'and nerved me to show [him]
my long reports written in those days of waiting at Yenbo. I urged that the
situation seemed full of promise. . . . Wingate was glad to hear a hopeful view.
The Arab Revolt had been his dream for years. . . . I went down towards Cairo,
feeling that the responsible person had all my news. The Nile trip became a
holiday.'

The question as to whether Allied forces should be landed in the Hejaz was
still unresolved. Colonel Brémond, Head of the French Military Mission to the
Hejaz, was much in favour; the British Army Command, by contrast, was against,
and Lawrence, on his return to Egypt, proceeded to confirm their doubts. He
wrote a 'violent memorandum' maintaining that if given the necessary materials
there was no reason why the tribes should not continue to operate successfully
for an indefinite time, but that 'the landing of a considerable foreign force . . .
would undoubtedly alarm them and might well result in the return of many
tribesmen to their tents, in which case we shall have contributed to the very
result which we wish to avoid'. His memorandum, written at the request of the
British Commander-in-Chief, Sir Archibald Murray, was described in a covering
note by Clayton as 'observations by Lieutenant Lawrence, an officer of great
experience and knowledge of Arabs'. Clayton took it to Murray, who, admiring its
'acidity and force' (Lawrence's words), promptly wired it to London. Lawrence

---

1 In a BBC radio broadcast, 14 July 1941.

suddenly found himself enjoying a 'novel and rather amusing' popularity at General Headquarters. Meanwhile his recommendation that Feisal should be considered the pre-eminent commander on the Arab side was also gaining acceptance. Lawrence was now confirmed as a member of Clayton's Arab Bureau, and Clayton wanted him to continue in Cairo, but Wingate decided that Lawrence should be sent back at once to the Hejaz, it being considered 'vitally important that an officer with knowledge of Arabs should be there to keep touch with Feisal and arrange for his supplies'. Lawrence urged his unfitness for such work, and reminded Clayton that Wingate had telegraphed to London for competent regular officers to direct the Arab war. To the reply that they might be months arriving he had no argument.

> So I had to go; leaving to others the Arab Bulletin I had founded, the maps I wished to draw, and the file of the war-changes of the Turkish Army, all fascinating activities in which my training helped me; to take up a role for which I felt no inclination.

In view of his earlier statements, such as that following his brothers' deaths claiming that it did not seem right that he should go on living peacefully in Cairo, this reads like protesting too much. Certainly, he soon became entirely absorbed in the Hejaz operation and, indeed, soon began to enjoy it. So much is clear from his letters of the time. 'This show is splendid,' he wrote to Colonel Newcombe in January 1917: 'you cannot imagine greater fun for us, greater fury and vexation for the Turks.' The following month he was equally enthusiastic to his family. 'It is', he wrote, 'by far the most wonderful time I have had.'

But these comments were written after he had settled into his new role and when there were promising developments in the Arab campaign. When he returned to the Hejaz in early December 1916 he found a situation that was little short of disastrous. A sudden move by the Turks had cut Feisal's line of retreat from Wadi Safra, panicked those of his army belonging to a local tribe, the Harb, who had fled fearful of Turkish revenge on their families, and scattered the force camped nearby under the command of Hussein's youngest son, Zeid. Zeid's warriors, in Lawrence's words in *Seven Pillars*, had 'melted into a loose mob of fugitives riding wildly through the night towards Yenbo'.

He reached Feisal's camp at the desert village of Nakhl Mubarak after a hard ride from the coast. 'I had better preface,' he wrote in a report to Clayton, 'by saying that I rode all Saturday night, had alarms and excursions all Sunday night, and rode again all last night, so my total of sleep is only three hours in the last three nights and I feel rather pessimistic. All the same, things are bad.' His faith in Feisal, however, was more confirmed than shaken. Indeed, he saw him as the *beau idéal* of the tribal leader, rallying his men and showing no obvious reaction to adversity. 'I heard him address the head of one battalion last

night before sending them out to an advanced position over the Turkish camp
at Bir Said. He did not say much, no noise about it, but it was all exactly right
and the people rushed over one another with joy to kiss his headrope when he
finished. . . . He is magnificent for to me privately he was most horribly cut up.'

Feisal received Lawrence cordially and throughout this brief stay Lawrence
lived with him in his headquarters tent, seeing and hearing all that was going
on, noting the Sherif's accessibility to any of his men who wished to speak with
him and the extreme patience with which he listened to their petitions – 'a
further lesson to me of what native headship in Arabia meant'.

It was while he was at Mubarak that Feisal asked him to wear Arab clothes.
'I should find it better for my own part, since it was a comfortable dress in
which to live Arab-fashion. . . . Besides, the tribesmen would then understand
how to take me.' He agreed at once, and was kitted out by Feisal's gift in
splendid white-silk and gold-embroidered garments – Meccan clothes which
would mark him out as one of the leaders and allow him to slip in and out of
Feisal's tent without question. 'I took a stroll in the new looseness of them
round the palm-gardens of Mubarak and Bruka, to accustom myself to their
feel.'

Lawrence adopted Arab clothes not merely because he considered them
practical ('army uniform was abominable when camel-riding') but because he
plainly enjoyed wearing them and – perhaps not unimportant to a man of his
stature – they made him a more impressive figure. He was also, unlike most of
his fellow-officers, well used to them from his pre-war experience at Carchemish,
where, as he put it in *Seven Pillars*, he had been 'educated to wear the entire
Arab outfit when necessary without strangeness, or sense of being socially
compromised'. There were times when his new and picturesque appearance
produced incongruous situations; he wrote of a meeting with the French Colonel
Brémond as 'a curious interview, that, between an old soldier and a young man
in fancy dress'. But once he took to Arab clothes he rarely discarded them when
in the desert. That they gave him greater presence is clear from Joyce's
comments. Having felt an acute desire to despatch him for a hair-cut at their
first encounter, Joyce reacted quite differently when he saw him next, at a war
cabinet meeting held by Prince Ali at Rabegh early in 1917.

> On this occasion his appearance was such a contrast to the untidy
> lieutenant I'd met at Port Sudan, that one suddenly became aware of
> contact with a very unusual personality. He was beautifully robed in
> a black *abba* with a deep gold border; a *kaftan* of finest white Damascus
> silk with wide flowing sleeves, bound at the waist with a belt containing
> a large curved gold dagger; a *kofia* or headcloth of rich embroidered
> silk, kept in place by an *agal* [headrope] of whites and gold. Sandals
> on his bare feet. In every detail a truly distinguished picturesque figure

indistinguishable from any of the nobles of the royal house of Hussein seated around us.

Newcombe and certain others also happily adopted Arab clothes in the desert, but some European officers loathed them. One such was Bimbashi Garland of the Egyptian Army (a Bimbashi was the equivalent in rank to a Major), whom Lawrence had just met at Yenbo, a highly competent demolition expert who did much good work mainly in the southern Hejaz throughout the war. 'It is

Colonel Newcombe in Arab clothes.

impossible to conceive of any form of raiment less suitable for the work I had before me,' Garland later wrote of his first railway raid. 'Many a time during that journey I was reduced almost to sobs by the impeding behaviour of my Arab dress.'

On a magnificent bay camel given to him by Feisal Lawrence rode back to Yenbo, but he had barely departed before the Turks launched a further attack, this time scattering the levies of a second tribe, the Juheina. There was nothing for it but retreat. At Yenbo Lawrence saw the dispirited brothers, first Zeid and then Feisal, ride in. As the latter's force, two thousand strong, approached across the level plain, Lawrence climbed to the parapet of one of the town gates and took a series of photographs – a brief aside from more serious concerns, since 'our war', as he wrote in *Seven Pillars*, 'seemed entering its last act'. Subsequently, the leader of the Juheina arrived, explaining that his warriors had fled for reasons of thirst rather than fear, having fought from sunrise to dusk and retired from the field 'only to make ourselves a cup of coffee'. The Juheina were despatched to redeem themselves by keeping pressure on the Turkish lines of communication, while Yenbo prepared to face a likely and possibly crippling Turkish attack. The situation was saved by the British Navy; two ships took station at points from which they could sweep the approach to Yenbo with either searchlights or shells. Meanwhile in the town Garland organized the throwing up of ramparts 'mediaeval fashion', while sailors from the ships 'spotted' from a minaret. Later Lawrence spoke to the man who had guided the Turks in their attempt to take the town. 'Their hearts had failed them at the silence and the blaze of lighted ships from end to end of the harbour, with the eerie beams of the searchlights revealing the bleakness of the glacis they would have to cross. So they turned back.' That night, Lawrence believed, 'the Turks lost their war'.

Over the next days and weeks Lawrence increasingly identified himself with the Arabian campaign. He found he had a natural aptitude for this unusual kind of war, in which the focus was less on the carrying out of precise and detailed orders or on text-book routines than on diplomacy, personality and – perhaps most important of all – awareness of the motivation and psychology of his Arab companions. Here his unconventionality, aided by his Carchemish experience, was a strength. His ability to listen, to gain his points by not pushing too hard for them, and his willingness to tune his behaviour to the practice of his hosts made him acceptable to them and enabled him to assume from the outset a positive and effective role.[1]

---

1 Later in 1917 he set out a code of behaviour for European officers attached as advisers to the Arab armies, which was printed in the *Arab Bulletin* under the title *Twenty Seven Articles*. Lawrence was not alone in such insights, however, rather he was expressing in his particular style a philosophy that was common to the wisest and more experienced officers working in Arabia.

Feisal's depleted force falling back on Yenbo, December 1916.

Three photographs from a sequence of five showing Feisal's approach, taken by Lawrence from Yenbo's Medina Gate.

Bimbashi Garland in British uniform, but with Arab head-dress.

Garland's photograph of stores being unloaded at Yenbo.

As an adviser Lawrence was well equipped, but this was also a fighting war and he needed practice. On the second day of the New Year he took a party of thirty-five tribesmen from Mubarak 'to exercise [his] hand in the raiding genre'. It was only a minor skirmish, a dawn fusillade from high ground with bullets fired through the bell tents of a Turkish encampment, a crowd of Turks leaping 'like stags' into their trenches, and the prompt departure of the outnumbered raiding party with two Turkish soldiers whom they happened to stumble across as they made good their escape. 'We dragged them homeward, where their news proved useful.'

After the bloodless victory at Yenbo the Sherifian forces had steadied and the Revolt was no longer in quite such imminent danger of collapse. But if it was to make progress some new initiative was required. The Arabs were still attacking the railhead garrison city of Medina, but that plus minor skirmishing elsewhere in the southern Hejaz was not enough. Feisal's instinct from the beginning had been to move the Revolt as soon as possible away from the Holy Cities of the Hejaz towards Syria. He had scarcely needed Lawrence to tell him that Wadi Safra was far from Damascus; like Lawrence he saw quite clearly the way the campaign ought to go. As was stated in a British military report of November 1916, 'he [Feisal] is bored with the tactics of the last few months, and wishes to force his brothers to act while he goes northeastwards and cuts the enemy's railway communications between Medina and Syria. . . . His ambitions lie altogether in Syria.'[1] 1917 was to see two substantial moves in the desired direction; one in which Lawrence would play a central role, and one already conceived when he arrived, but to which he would make his own significant contribution.

One hundred and eighty miles north of Yenbo on the Red Sea coast was the port of Wejh. If this were in Arab hands, Feisal would be in a position not only to extend the threat to the Hejaz Railway but also to draw in other tribes. More, a positive movement north would emphasize Arab determination to confront the Turks and boost Arab pride. Lawrence records in *Seven Pillars* a moving moment during the later stages of the march when he was visited in the tent he shared with Newcombe by a young tribal leader who held them for a while in conversation; when at last he rose to go 'chancing to look across the valley, [he] saw the hollows beneath and about us winking with the faint camp-fires of the scattered contingents. He called me out to look, and swept his arm round, saying half-sadly, "We are no longer Arabs but a People." '

Lawrence noted these words in the report he wrote at the time, commenting that the advance on Wejh was 'the biggest moral achievement of the new Hejaz Government, since for the first time the entire manhood of a tribe, complete with its own transport and food for a 200 mile march, had left its own dira, and proceeded (without the hope of plunder or the skirmishes of inter-tribal feud) into the territory of another tribe with a detached military aim.' But he also understood the sadness which mingled with the pride in the young leader's attitude, for a fast camel, superior weapons and a short sharp raid had been among the joys of life for young men like him, joys which 'the gradual realization of Feisal's aims [were] making less and less easy for those in responsible places'.

Lawrence was with Feisal at the first and final stages of Feisal's march but for much of the time his offices were required elsewhere. The advance on Wejh was only possible if it were made to coincide with two other moves on the military chess-board. The first move involved Abdulla, who agreed to transfer his force from a position of minor importance north-east of Medina to Wadi Ais, where he would pose a much greater threat to the Turkish lines of communication and from where he would be able to counter more easily any Turkish

---

1 Unsigned report, headed *Notes on the Military Situation*, apparently by Lieutenant-Colonel Wilson, dated 4 November 1916, based on information supplied by Lawrence.

thrusts towards the vulnerable base-ports of Yenbo and Rabegh. The second move involved the Royal Navy, about whose contribution Lawrence later reported to Cairo: 'The manoeuvre was only made possible at all by the absolute command of the sea and the ungrudging co-operation in transport of ammunition and supplies afforded Feisal by the S.N.O. [Senior Naval Officer] Red Sea Patrol.' Supplies were Lawrence's concern so he was necessarily involved in this part of the operation. The naval officer whose work he praised was Captain Boyle of the *Suva* whom he had met at Yenbo the previous November. Lawrence sailed with Boyle to the coastal village of Um Lejj, half way between Wejh and Yenbo, where in consultation with Feisal a plan was devised to attack Wejh with landing parties from the sea while Feisal's force closed all roads of escape inland: one of the two landing-parties, to be shipped to Wejh in H.M.S. *Hardinge*, was to consist of men of the Harb and Juheina tribes. The prospects seemed good and Lawrence showed his pleasure and excitement, but in doing so provoked a clash with a regular gunnery officer newly arrived in the Hejaz, Major Charles Vickery. Lawrence wrote in *Seven Pillars*:

> Abdulla was almost in Ais: we were half-way to Wejh: the initiative had passed to the Arabs. I was so joyous that for a moment I lost my self-control, and said exultingly that in a year we would be tapping at the gates of Damascus. A chill came over the feeling in the tent and my hopefulness died. Later, I heard that Vickery had gone to Boyle and vehemently condemned me as a braggart and visionary; but though the outburst was foolish, it was not an impossible dream, for five months later I was in Damascus, and a year after that I was its *de facto* Governor.

After Um Lejj he rejoined Feisal's force for the final and more difficult stage of the march to Wejh – difficult because of the virtual absence of water and forage, a serious problem for an army of 4000 camel corps, 4000 infantry and 380 baggage-camels. 'The animals were without food for two and a half days,' he reported, 'and the army marched the last fifty miles on half a gallon of water per man and no food. This did not seem in any way to affect the spirits of the men, who trotted gaily into Wejh singing songs and executing sham charges; nor did it in any way affect their speed or energy. Feisal said, however, that another thirty-six hours of the same conditions would have begun to tell on them.'

They were able to 'trot gaily into Wejh' because the town had already been taken. Feisal was two days behind the agreed schedule and Boyle, fearing the Turkish garrison would run away, had launched his sea-borne attacks without the intended complementary pressure from the Arab force on land. There had been fierce fighting and some casualties. Of the Arab landing force twenty had been killed; in addition a British lieutenant of the Royal Flying Corps had

THE MARCH TO WEJH, JANUARY 1917

Photographs and captions by Lawrence

Emir Feisal and Sherif Sharraf leading the Ageyl Bodyguard northwards on the first stage to Wejh, January 1917.

Arab camp at Wejh.

been mortally wounded during a seaplane reconnaissance. Lawrence was angry because he believed that with better management such losses might have been avoided. 'Vickery,' he wrote in *Seven Pillars*, 'who had directed the battle, was satisfied, but I could not share his satisfaction. To me an unnecessary action, or shot, or casualty, was not only waste but sin. I was unable to take the professional view that all successful actions were gains. Our rebels were not materials, like soldiers, but friends of ours, trusting our leadership. We were not in command nationally, but by invitation; and our men were volunteers, individuals, local men, relatives, so that a death was a personal sorrow to many in the army. Even from the purely military point of view the assault seemed to me a blunder.' As he saw it the tiny Turkish garrison in Wejh, having no transport and no food, must have surrendered if left alone for a few days. Indeed, if they had all escaped, 'it would not have mattered the value of an Arab life. We wanted Wejh as a base against the railway and to extend our front; the smashing and killing in it had been wanton.'

However, by the time he wrote home from Cairo, where he had 'snatched a week's leave', on 31 January, anger had given way to enthusiasm and cheerfulness:

> Things in Arabia are very pleasant, though the job I have is rather a responsible one, and sometimes it is a little heavy to see which way one ought to act. I am getting rather old with it all, I think! However it is very nice to be out of the office, with some field work in hand, and the position I have is such a queer one – I do not suppose that any Englishman before ever had such a place. . . . I act as a sort of adviser to Sherif Feisul, and we are on the best of terms, the job is a wide and pleasant one. I live with him in his tent, so our food and things (if you will continue to be keen on such rubbish!) is as good as the Hejaz can afford. . . .
>
> The war in Arabia is going very well: the Arabs are very keen and patriotic, and the Turks are beginning to get really frightened.

The first important northward move in 1917 was to Wejh; the second was to an even more desirable objective over two hundred miles further on, Akaba – which Lawrence had visited with Dahoum in early 1914 during the Sinai survey. Akaba, at the head of the gulf at the north of the Red Sea, occupied a key position; it was reasonably accessible from Egypt and was an excellent base from which strikes could be made against the Hejaz Railway. Possession of it would bring the Revolt into yet more tribal areas. In Cairo Lawrence found Akaba a subject of much discussion, though the initiative in this case was not from the British side but the French. According to *Seven Pillars*:

Colonel Brémond called to felicitate me on the capture of Wejh, saying that it confirmed his belief in my military talent and encouraged him to expect my help in an extension of our success. He wanted to occupy Akaba with an Anglo-French force and naval help. He pointed out the importance of Akaba . . . [and] began to enlarge on the nature of the ground.

I told him that I knew Akaba from before the war, and felt that his scheme was technically impossible. We could take the beach of the gulf; but our forces there, as unfavourably placed as on a Gallipoli beach, would be under observation and gun-fire from the coastal hills. . . . In my opinion, Akaba, whose importance was all and more than he said, would be best taken by Arab irregulars descending from the interior without naval help.

Brémond did not tell me (but I knew) that he wanted the landing at Akaba to head off the Arab movement, by getting a mixed force in front of them . . . so that they might be confined to Arabia. . . . For my part, I did not tell Brémond (but he knew) that I meant to defeat his efforts and to take the Arabs soon into Damascus.

Lawrence left the same afternoon for Suez and sailed that night for the Hejaz.

Two days later, in Wejh, I explained myself; so that when Brémond came after ten days and opened his heart, or part of it, to Feisal, his tactics were returned to him with improvements.

In fact, Lawrence was determined that the Arabs should take Akaba, and that they should do so not by direct assault from the seaward side but from the rear, with the maximum of surprise and the minimum of bloodshed. More, Akaba for him meant not just the place itself but the whole surrounding hinterland. As he wrote in a letter many years later to Mrs George Bernard Shaw: 'What I wanted was the 50 miles of mountain defiles behind the beach, which could (I still think) only have been taken by us from inland.'

The seizure of Akaba was shortly to take place in line with Lawrence's prescription and was to prove a crucial watershed both in the campaign and in Lawrence's career; indeed in the months that followed the move to Wejh he would not only advance and consolidate an already remarkable reputation but would also experience traumas of self-questioning and of physical suffering which would leave him a changed and disillusioned man. This important period, the subject of the next two chapters, is at the heart of the controversy about Lawrence and his wartime role.

Suppose we were (as we might be) an influence, an idea, a thing intangible, invulnerable, without front or back, drifting about like a gas? Armies were like plants, immobile, firm-rooted, nourished through long stems to the head. We might be a vapour, blowing where we listed. . . .

Most wars were wars of contact. Ours should be a war of detachment. We were to contain the enemy by the silent threat of a vast unknown desert.

(Seven Pillars of Wisdom)

We must not take Medina. The Turk was harmless there. In prison in Egypt he would cost us food and guards. We wanted him to stay at Medina, and every other distant place, in the largest numbers. Our ideal was to keep his railway just working, but only just, with the maximum of loss and discomfort. He was welcome to the Hejaz Railway, and the Trans-Jordan railway, and the Palestine and Syrian railways for the duration of the war, so long as he gave us the other nine hundred and ninety-nine thousandths of the Arab world.

(Seven Pillars of Wisdom)

7

FROM 'WITNESS' TO 'PROTAGONIST'

'After the capture of Akaba,' Lawrence wrote to a friend, H. S. Ede, in 1927, 'things changed so much that I was no longer a witness of the Revolt, but a protagonist in the Revolt.'

At about the same time he wrote to Robert Graves, who was engaged in producing a popular biography of him: 'All the documents of the Arab Revolt are in the archives of the Foreign Office, and will soon be available to students, who will be able to cross-check my yarns. I expect them to find small errors, and to agree generally with the main current of my narrative.'[1]

In fact it was not until fifty years after the war that Foreign Office and War Office papers relating to the Arab Revolt were released to the public domain, by which time Richard Aldington had written his belittling biography and it had become widely assumed that Lawrence had much exaggerated his contribution to the campaign which had made his name. However, as indicated in the Introduction, though the mass of wartime papers now to hand still awaits its proper historian, even a provisional survey of the material tends to support the traditional view that Lawrence was no mere also-ran of the Arab war but an important and much respected participant in it. He was certainly perceived as such at the time. In fact it is arguable that he was being unduly modest in describing himself as only a 'witness', as opposed to a 'protagonist', before the capture of Akaba – though he is surely correct in implying that his role increased significantly in importance after Akaba fell in the summer of 1917.

That his work as adviser to Feisal very quickly made an impact on the Turks is evident from the edition of the *Arab Bulletin* issued on 4 January 1917 (No.

1 *T. E. Lawrence to His Biographers, Robert Graves & Liddell Hart*, p. 117.

37) which included a report based on the evidence of an Arab N.C.O. of the Turkish army who had deserted and made his way to Yenbo. The report concluded:

> Feeling among the Turks runs strongly against the Sherif, and a reward has been offered for the capture of the British officer (Captain Lawrence) who is with Feisal.

That his new role was soon appreciated on the British side is made clear from a report on conditions in the Hejaz sent to the British High Commissioner in Cairo in late February 1917 by a Major Hugh Pearson. The report contained this paragraph:

> Lawrence with Feisal is of inestimable value and an Englishman to take a corresponding place with Ali would immensely increase the probability of co-operation among the armies.

Deputed to reply on the High Commissioner's behalf Brigadier-General Clayton, writing on 2 March, endorsed Pearson's conclusion:

> The value of Lawrence in the position which he has made for himself with Feisul is enormous, and it is fully realized that if we could find suitable men to act in the same way with Ali and Abdulla it would be invaluable. Such men, however, are extremely difficult to get. . . .

On 10 March 1917 Lawrence left Feisal's headquarters at Wejh to visit Sherif Abdulla. A change of policy in Constantinople had led to an order to the Turkish commander in the Hejaz to abandon Medina and retire his troops northwards. They were to put their guns and stores on trains, to enclose these trains in their columns and proceed together up the Hejaz Railway. The last thing the British wanted was the sudden arrival of another 25,000 Ottoman troops opposite their front at Beersheba, so Cairo requested an urgent Arab response. Abdulla's force, positioned inland relatively near to the railway, was the obvious one to counter any such move, so, at the request of Clayton, Lawrence was despatched to Wadi Ais 'to find out why [Abdulla] had done nothing for two months, and to persuade him, if the Turks came out, to go straight at them' (*Seven Pillars* Ch. XXXI). In the event the Turks stayed where they were so that, as far as one of its basic purposes was concerned, his journey proved unnnecessary. Boils and dysentery attacked him on the journey and malaria struck him when he reached Wadi Ais with the result that he was away for a month – a month in which while ill in Abdulla's camp, according to Chapter XXXIII of his book, he rethought the strategy of the whole campaign, and in which he also achieved the second of Clayton's aims by inspiring Abdulla's force to subject the railway to a series of disruptive attacks. His long absence from Wejh produced the following letter to him from Prince Feisal, preserved in the archives together with Lawrence's report to Colonel Wilson on his visit to Wadi Ais. The letter clearly indicates the value which Feisal had come to put on his presence. It also shows that Feisal wanted him for his contribution to more important matters than the relatively straightforward work of attacks on the Hejaz Railway.

> My Dear affectionate friend, May God protect you.
>
> I regret to hear that you were not feeling well. May God show you nothing bad.
>
> I am waiting for your coming because I want to see you very much because I have many things to tell you. The destruction of the railway is easy. Major Garland has arrived and we can send him for this purpose.
>
> You are much needed here more than the destruction of the line because I am in a very great complication which I had never expected.
>
> I beg God, in conclusion to cure you from all diseases.
>
> Accept my sincere salaams for your own self.
>
> Your affectionate friend.   FEISAL

On 28 May 1917 Colonel Wilson wrote a long report for Brigadier-General Clayton, in which he described the advantages which had accrued from the capture of Wejh – now Feisal's headquarters – and the subsequent seizure of two other small ports still further up the coast, Dibaa and Muweilah. His report shows that notwithstanding Feisal's inclination to keep Lawrence for other than railway attacks he had nevertheless made a substantial enough contribution to such activities to deserve honourable mention.

> This northern move not only brought in fresh tribes but enabled raids to be made against the Railway by demolition parties, in which work a fine example of gallantry and energy has been set by Lt. Col. S. F. NEWCOMBE D.S.O. R.E., Captain T. E. LAWRENCE, and Bimbashi H. GARLAND, Egyptian Army. . . .

Describing Lawrence's performance in greater detail, Wilson wrote:

> This officer has made several journeys into the interior which, owing to his knowledge of Arabic and having gained the confidence of the Arab leaders, have had valuable results.
>
> He organized an attack on the Railway with a portion of Emir Abdulla's army by which a train of seven wagons was destroyed and casualties inflicted on the enemy, he also personally carried out demolition on the railway.
>
> His services have been of great value to me and the work he has carried out required both pluck and endurance.

Wilson's tribute is in marked contrast to his first impressions several months before, when, in November 1916, he had written to Clayton that he looked upon Lawrence as 'a bumptious young ass . . . who [had] put every single person's back up . . . from the Admiral down to the most junior fellow on the Red Sea'.

By this time Lawrence was on his way north with Sherif Nasir of Medina and the veteran chief of the Howeitat tribe, Auda abu Tayi, on the journey which was to end triumphantly with the seizure of Akaba. They rode deep into the desert hinterland with a view to raising support among the tribes and subsequently bearing down on Akaba from the north-east, the side from which its Turkish garrison would least expect a hostile approach. The concept of the Akaba expedition has become one of the bones of contention between the pro-Lawrence lobby and some of his critics. For example, interviewed by the authors about Lawrence's assertion, in *Seven Pillars*, that 'Akaba had been taken on my plan by my effort,' Suleiman Mousa has argued:

> I think that he assumed too much in saying that Akaba was captured
> by his plans, and by his own designs. The expedition went to my mind
> its ordinary course of a tribal raid. And this tribal raid reached Akaba.
> I will not deny Lawrence his share, but, to be fair to others, I will not
> give him all the credit.

A claim to sole authorship of the Akaba strategy is difficult to substantiate though Colonel Newcombe many years later insisted to Lawrence's French biographer J. B. Villars[1] that Akaba was 'entirely conceived by Lawrence, who was its real leader and animating spirit'. On the other hand Mousa's assertion in his book that 'the whole expedition was . . . planned with no reference to Lawrence' seems a considerable overstatement on the opposite side. However, reports by Clayton show that, whatever Lawrence's role in planning the Akaba strategy, he was certainly seen at the time as being in the forefront of the operation. Clayton wrote to Sir William Robertson, Chief of the Imperial General Staff, in London:

> Captain Lawrence who was sent Northwards to Maan in company
> with the head Sheikh of the Hueitat [*sic*], has evidently begun to raise
> the Tribes in the Maan neighbourhood, as we have definite informa-
> tion from a reliable source that the tribesmen in that neighbourhood
> are active and are causing considerable anxiety to the enemy.

Clayton's report to the C.I.G.S. is a long one covering four pages of foolscap and discussing numerous aspects of the Hejaz campaign. It ends with the following remarkable postscript.

1 *T. E. Lawrence, or The Search for the Absolute*, 1958.

Since writing the above and just as I send it to the mail, Captain Lawrence has arrived after a journey through enemy country which is little short of marvellous. I attach a rough sketch illustrating his route. He started from WEJH on 9th May with 36 Arabs and marched via JAUF to NEBK (near KAF) about 140 miles N.E. of MAAN, crossing and dynamiting the HEJAZ railway en route. There he met AUDA ABU TAYI of the HUEITAT Tribe, whom he left at NEBK with instructions to raise men for a raid in the MAAN-AKABA neighbourhood. Lawrence himself then rode on with only two men through very dangerous

Key figures of the Arab Revolt

(Above) Auda abu Tayi, veteran chief of the Howeitat tribe.

(Right) Sherif Nasir, leader of the Akaba expedition.

country to a place near TADMUR where he interviewed ANEIZEH
Sheikhs. He then struck due West to the railway at BAALBEK,
destroying a small plate girder bridge in that neighbourhood, and
thence down the railway to within 3 miles of Damascus. From
DAMASCUS he proceeded S.W. and, after visiting the DRUSE Chiefs at
SALKHAD, returned to NEBK where he found ABU TAYI had collected
his force of tribesmen. On 19th June they moved to BAIR (about 60
miles N.E. of MAAN). At BAIR Lawrence left the Arab force and struck
due West across the railway, then turned North and marched West
of AMMAN to UM-KEIS, close to the southern shores of Lake Tiberias,
where he inspected the bridges in the YARMUK Valley. Thence he
returned to BAIR having interviewed various Chiefs on the way,
destroyed the line in several places and derailed a train.

From BAIR the Arab force (some 2000 strong) swept the whole country
down to AKABA, leaving MAAN, but annihilating all the smaller posts
including in one place a whole Turkish battalion of some 500 men.
The ARABS are now in occupation of AKABA where they have 600
prisoners, including 20 officers and a German N.C.O., and Lawrence
estimates the Turkish losses in killed at about 700.

The successful encounter with the Turkish battalion was at Abu el Lissan,
where Lawrence, in the excitement of the attack, shot his own camel through
the head. The victorious Arab force reached its 'goal of months', as Lawrence
called it, on 6 July, racing the last few miles to Akaba through a driving sand-
storm and splashing into the sea. Shortly after this remarkable victory Lawrence
had set off with a party of eight tribesmen on the best camels in the force in an
almost continuous fifty-hour march to reach Suez as quickly as possible and
bring his good news to the British High Command in Egypt. Clayton's enthusiastic postscript concludes:

> I have not yet been able to discuss his journey with Lawrence as he
> has only just arrived and is somewhat exhausted by 1300 miles on a
> camel in the last 30 days. Moreover, E.E.F. Intelligence have first call
> on his information. I think, however, that you would be interested in
> the above brief sketch of a very remarkable performance, calling for
> a display of courage, resource, and endurance which is conspicuous
> even in these days when gallant deeds are of daily occurrence.

On the strength of his reports following this sequence of events Lawrence
was recommended by Wingate, now High Commissioner in Egypt, for the
Victoria Cross, while Wilson cabled the Arab Bureau from Jidda suggesting that
he be granted the D.S.O. immediately for his recent work, making special
mention of his 'personality, gallantry, and grit'. He received instead the C.B.
(Companionship of the Bath), Military Division, and also the personal congratu-
lations of the Chief of the Imperial General Staff, passed on to him by Wingate

Lawrence's own photograph of the dash into Akaba; a remarkable action-
photograph of a remarkable event. '. . . Then we raced through a driving
sand-storm down to Akaba, four miles further, and splashed into the sea. . .'
The capture of Akaba changed the whole complexion of the Arab Revolt, allowing
the desert campaign under Prince Feisal – with T.E. Lawrence as his adviser-
in-chief – to be fought in close relation to the main thrust against the Turk
under the far-sighted command of General Allenby.

'with the liveliest satisfaction'. He was shortly afterwards promoted to the rank of Major.

Some recent critics of Lawrence have cast doubts on one aspect of this performance, namely the journey north through enemy-held territory to Damascus, the Arab historian Suleiman Mousa even going so far as to suggest that it was pure invention. However, it is clear from the contemporary papers that Lawrence was interviewed fully about his recent activities when in Cairo and that much was built on his information and advice. On the strength of his discussions with Clayton, the latter decided to send him to meet Sir Archibald Murray's successor as Commander-in-Chief of the Egyptian Expeditionary Force, General Sir Edmund Allenby. 'After interviewing Captain Lawrence,' Clayton reported to London on 20 July, 'I instructed him to submit his suggestions to the Commander-in-Chief Egyptian Expeditionary Force and give the latter all information obtained.' It is surely basically implausible that Lawrence could have so impressed Clayton and, as he now proceeded to do, gone on to impress Allenby if, as has been claimed, he had stayed immobile in Sherif Nasir's camp at Nebk throughout the time when he was allegedly carrying out his reconnaissance trip in Turkish-held territory.[1]

The meeting with Allenby was a most important one for Lawrence in that, in a matter of minutes, it established his role for the rest of the war. His account of it in *Seven Pillars*, however, has a distinctly light touch:

> It was a comic interview, for Allenby was physically large and confident, and morally so great that the comprehension of our littleness came slow to him. He sat in his chair looking at me – not straight, as his custom was, but sideways, puzzled . . . [H]e was hardly prepared for anything so odd as myself – a little bare-footed silk-skirted man offering to hobble the enemy by his preaching if given stores and arms and a fund of two hundred thousand sovereigns to convince and control his converts.

> Allenby could not make out how much was genuine performance and how much charlatan. The problem was working behind his eyes, and I left him unhelped to solve it. He did not ask many questions, nor talk much, but studied the map and listened to my unfolding of Eastern Syria and its inhabitants. At the end he put up his chin and said quite directly, 'Well, I will do for you what I can', and that ended it. I was not sure how far I had caught him; but we learned gradually that he meant exactly what he said; and that what General Allenby could do was enough for his very greediest servant.

It was a notable encounter between two powerful but entirely different personalities. The future Field-Marshal Lord Wavell, who participated in the Middle Eastern war, compiled its definitive history and subsequently wrote a study of Allenby's life and achievements, while considering Allenby the stronger and greater character, nevertheless described Allenby and Lawrence 'as the two outstanding figures in this campaign'. Allenby's own reference to his relationship with Lawrence, as printed in *T. E. Lawrence by His Friends* is characteristically brief and to the point:

1 For more on this journey and on Lawrence's state of mind during it see following chapter.

Lawrence was under my command, but, after acquainting him with my strategical plan, I gave him a free hand. His co-operation was marked by the utmost loyalty, and I never had anything but praise for his work, which, indeed, was invaluable throughout the campaign.

Allenby's confidence in Lawrence gave him a second identity in Arabia: he was Feisal's accredited adviser, but he was now also, as it were, Allenby's delegate. It was no doubt this change of status which led him to make the distinction, in the letter of 1927 already quoted, between his role as 'witness' before Akaba and as 'protagonist' after it. However, the fact that from now on he was in a situation in which he could make effective decisions and, indeed, devise and carry out much of the strategy of the desert campaign does not mean that he was in actual command or in any clearly defined position of dominance. Much energy has been spent arguing pro and con on this theme, but, as A. W. Lawrence has written, 'the question should be, on which occasion and to what extent did he inspire or control activities by persuasion, whether as a dispenser of British materials and gold to men ill-equipped and unpaid, or through his personal influence.' A. W. Lawrence added, 'Even at the time . . . the question can seldom have admitted of an absolute answer, owing to the informal manner of procedure', quoting as evidence Colonel Joyce's account of the first Arab War Cabinet he attended.

At this, as at dozens of other conferences we attended together, Lawrence rarely spoke. He merely studied the men around him and when the argument ended, as they usually did, in smoke, he then dictated his plan of action which was usually adopted and everyone went away satisfied. It was not, as is often supposed, by his individual leadership of hordes of bedouin that he achieved success in daring ventures, but by the wise selection of tribal leaders and providing the essential grist to the mill in the shape of golden rewards for work well done.[1]

After Akaba he was given the free hand and the backing, which had only been his to a limited extent before, to play a more effective role. He also had the status of being the principal link between Feisal and Allenby at the moment when, with the fulcrum of the Revolt moved north to Akaba (to which Feisal transferred in August) and Damascus no longer a distant dream, the Arab campaign was brought into direct alliance with the main advance of the British eastwards from Egypt and northwards along the Palestinian coast. He would

1 A. W. Lawrence quotation from his 'Comment' in Suleiman Mousa, *An Arab View*; Joyce extract originally from BBC radio broadcast of 14 July 1941, also quoted in Chapter 6.

(Above) General Allenby, affectionately known as 'The Bull'. Lawrence described him as 'the nearest to my longings for a master'.

(Right) Akaba. The ship, moored to the so-called Chatham Pier, is H.M.S. Humber, *a light monitor whose three 6 inch guns constituted Akaba's best defence against Turkish attack.*

henceforward be less concerned with anti-Turkish activities still continuing further south in the Hejaz, though he was sent to Jidda for discussions with the Sherif Hussein (whom he had not previously met) soon after his return from Egypt. His main base would be Akaba and his main work would be, to quote his own phrase, 'up country' from it – with frequent visits to Egypt at first and later to Palestine. He would rarely be anywhere for any length of time.

As in the case of the pre-Akaba period the contemporary files indicate his importance and confirm his reputation.

That he should work directly under Allenby had been proposed by Clayton when he sent him to his crucial meeting with the newly arrived C-in-C.

> If Captain Lawrence's proposals are accepted I suggest he should work under the direction of the Commander-in-Chief, Egyptian Expeditionary Force, as the operations suggested will take place almost entirely in the district north of the Akaba-Maan line and are therefore in the sphere of the Egyptian Expeditionary Force.

They *were* accepted; and indeed other would-be participants who had planned to make attacks on the Turks – for example, the British forces now in Baghdad – were plainly told to desist.

> General Baghdad to Chief London. Repeat Egypt force 27/7/17

> Under altered situation brought about by Lawrence's journey, I agree that any attempt to interfere with railway in Syria would probably prejudice Lawrence's operations.

So he went back to the desert to exercise his new freedom and carry out his promised operations against the enemy. When Clayton compiled a long report on the state of the Arab war some weeks later he wrote: 'I myself visited Akaba on 1st September and had a long talk with Emir Feisal and Major Lawrence' (he had just been promoted); no one else was mentioned, either British or Arab.

At that time the idea of sending British troops from the Imperial Camel Corps to Akaba to assist with operations was still under discussion in Cairo in spite of an agreed policy against their use. Lawrence strongly opposed their being brought into what he knew was a difficult and volatile situation and had written vigorously to that effect to Clayton a few days before the latter's Akaba visit:

> To send the Camel Corps down to Akaba at present, and to attack the railway with it, would, I am convinced, subtract from the Sherif such Beduin as are helping him now, and involve almost a certainty of conflict between the Arabs and our camel corps. One squabble between a trooper and an Arab, or an incident with Beduin women, would bring on general hostilities.

Plainly he did not expect to be overridden without consultation for he concluded:

However I take it that no modification of the policy agreed upon in Cairo will be decided on, without my being given an opportunity of putting forward my views in detail.

Presumably the idea was discussed at the meeting of Clayton, Feisal and Lawrence on 1 September; if so Lawrence's view undoubtedly carried the day for several weeks later, in early November, Joyce, now also based in Akaba, was arguing to Clayton:

> I still hanker for the Camel Corps down here. There are such glorious opportunities for offensive operations if only we could ensure the C.C. being a little tactful with the natives. Lawrence I know is against it and probably has the best of reasons, but we could, I think, down more Turks if we had them, and that is the point I am keen on.

Lawrence's opposition, however, constituted a virtual veto. In the following year the Camel Corps *was* to be used, in a strictly limited operation lasting under a month, but only when Lawrence agreed the time was ripe.

Joyce and he worked well together, however, and Lawrence later wrote generously of him: 'It was Joyce who ran the main lines of the Revolt, while I was off on raids.' Joyce was senior to him in rank, but Lawrence was working directly under Allenby and Joyce respected the situation. He later wrote to Allenby's biographer, Brian Gardner: 'Always a lone bird, [Lawrence] enjoyed much freedom, which I, who had many responsibilities of my own, did not interfere with. When he left Army H.Q. and returned to the desert, he was just Lawrence of Arabia and his movements unpredictable.'

Joyce put the same point perhaps even more pithily at the time, in the letter to Clayton already quoted:

> I would very much like to go out myself [i.e. on raids] for I think I could do a good deal, but it has not been possible to leave this place just lately. There have been practically only Lawrence and myself to run the show for the last two months. Lawrence has had his wonderful stunts to do, and between Feisal, Gaafer [Jaafar Pasha, a former Turkish Army officer in charge of a force of Arab regulars at Akaba] and the cholera my days have been fully employed.

Lawrence was away on one of his 'wonderful stunts' even as Joyce was writing, one which would take him deep into enemy territory. Joyce's letter concludes:

> Lawrence by now must be very near his objective. I hope he is lucky. Fortunately he has got brains as well as dash and the two I trust will pull him through, but one cannot help feeling anxious.

Joyce was writing on 4 November. Clayton wrote back to him on 12 November. The last sentence of his letter reads:

I am very anxious to get news of Lawrence to hear that he is safe.

Lawrence himself, it should be said, did not undertake these 'up-country' journeys with easy confidence; if his superiors were anxious, he shared their anxiety. Captain George Lloyd, whom he had first met in Military Intelligence in Cairo in 1914 and who accompanied him on the first part of the raid he was carrying out at this time, had written to Clayton a few weeks earlier that Lawrence was 'a very remarkable fellow – not the least fearless like some who do brave things, but as he told me last night, each time he starts out on these stunts he simply hates it for two or three days before, until movement, action and the glory of scenery and nature catch hold of him and make him well again.'[1]

The Castle at Azrak: Lawrence's photograph of the castle gatehouse.

1 Quoted in *Lord Lloyd and the Decline of the British Empire*, by John Charmley, 1987. Cf. *The Mint* p. 1: 'One reason that taught me I wasn't a man of action was this routine melting of the bowels before a crisis.'

The raid on which Lawrence was currently engaged had taken him far to the north, with a small force led by Sherif Ali ibn el Hussein of the Harith (whom he had first encountered at the time of his initial visit to Feisal in Wadi Safra). They were using as base, and as shelter against a bout of bitter weather, the old half-ruined fort at the desert oasis of Azrak – 'each stone of it', as he would write later in *Seven Pillars*, 'radiant with half-memory of the luminous silky Eden, which had passed so long ago'. It was an interlude which he would remember vividly, for its own sake but also doubtless for the time of trial which lay only days ahead. It produced one of the most evocative passages in his book:

> In the evening, when we had shut-to the gate, all guests would assemble, either in my room or in Ali's, and coffee and stories would go round until the last meal, and after it, until sleep came. On stormy nights we brought in brushwood and dung and lit a great fire in the middle of the floor. About it would be drawn the carpets and the saddle-sheep-skins, and in its light we would tell over our own battles, or hear the visitors' traditions. The leaping flames chased our smoke-ruffled shadows strangely about the rough stone wall behind us, distorting them over the hollows and projections of its broken face. When these stories came to a period, our tight circle would shift over, uneasily, to the other knee or elbow; while coffee-cups went clinking round, and a servant fanned the blue reek of the fire towards the loophole with his cloak, making the glowing ash swirl and sparkle with his draught. Till the voice of the story-teller took up again, we would hear the rain-spots hissing briefly as they dripped from the stone-beamed roof into the fire's heart. . . . Past and future flowed over us like an uneddying river. We dreamed ourselves into the spirit of the place; sieges and feasting, raids, murders, love-singing in the night.

THE HEJAZ RAILWAY

The Turks' vital Line of Communication, which was subjected to many attacks by Arab forces (usually with a British officer attached) between 1916 and 1918.

A section of the line south of Kalaat el Akhdar, about 760 kilometres from Damascus and 540 kilometres from Medina.

Lawrence became an accomplished destroyer of railways but his methods could at times seem somewhat extravagant to the trained sapper. Lieutenant, later Sir Alec Kirkbride, worked with Lawrence as an intelligence and demolition officer in 1918. Interviewed in 1962 he told the following story:

'I didn't approve of Lawrence's methods of blowing things up. He wasn't trained as a sapper, but he liked to make as big a bang as possible. He wasted a great deal of explosives that had been brought at great trouble on camel back for hundreds of miles. And on this occasion he put everything he could lay his hands on under the bridge. Knowing his habits I said, "Please, sir, give me a bit of warning before you fire your charges and let me get my men away." "Oh yes all right, don't fuss, don't fuss." So we went down, and I was quite happily putting my charges in, and suddenly there was the most terrific bang and the bridge flew into the air and fell all over the station. I was absolutely furious – as furious as a subaltern could be with a colonel, which has its limits. And he sat on a boulder and laughed at me.'

(Above) Locomotive, photographed on the Yarmuk line.

(Left) A relic of the railway war photographed half a century later.

8

RELUCTANT PARTICIPANT

Throughout most of his two years in Arabia Lawrence was plagued by a sense of guilt, because he believed that his Arab friends were fighting on the strength of assurances which the Allies would ultimately disown. He summarized his feelings on this issue in his outspoken introductory chapter to *Seven Pillars of Wisdom* which George Bernard Shaw persuaded him to exclude when he produced his so-called subscribers' edition of the work in 1926 but which is now standard in all modern versions. In it Lawrence made clear the personal conflict he had to endure while serving in Arabia.

> The Cabinet raised the Arabs to fight for us by definite promises of self-government afterwards. Arabs believe in persons, not in institutions. They saw in me a free agent of the British Government, and demanded from me an endorsement of its written promises. So I had to join the conspiracy, and, for what my word was worth, assured the men of their reward. In our two years' partnership under fire they grew accustomed to believing me and to think my Government, like myself, sincere. In this hope they performed some fine things, but, of course, instead of being proud of what we did together, I was continually and bitterly ashamed.

> It was evident from the beginning that if we won the war these promises would be dead paper, and had I been an honest adviser of the Arabs I would have advised them to go home and not risk their lives fighting for such stuff: but I salved myself with the hope that, by leading these Arabs madly in the final victory, I would establish them, with arms in their hands, in a position so assured (if not dominant) that expediency would counsel to the Great Powers a fair settlement of their claims. In other words, I presumed (seeing no other leader

with the will and power) that I would survive the campaigns, and be able to defeat not merely the Turks on the battlefield, but my own country and its allies in the council-chamber. It was an immodest presumption: it is not yet clear if I succeeded: but it is clear that I had no shadow of leave to engage the Arabs, unknowing, in such hazard. I risked the fraud, on my conviction that Arab help was necessary to our cheap and speedy victory in the East, and that better we win and break our word than lose.

He was a British representative with the Arabs, he was trusted by them, yet he had to dissemble; and the more his influence grew the more did his sense of guilt. Plainly for the most part he managed to suppress or live with his mental anguish by concentrating on the many demands of the work in hand. But there were occasions when feelings of guilt and shame became almost overwhelming. One such time was in June 1917, half way through the Akaba expedition – the period of the disputed northern journey into Syria referred to in the previous chapter.

In Chapter XLVIII of *Seven Pillars* he describes how the opportunity for the journey came about. The expedition came to a necessary halt at Nebk in Wadi Sirhan, the 'rallying place', as Auda abu Tayi called it, for the enrolment of the tribal warriors who would march with them to Akaba. It stayed there for over a fortnight. While at Nebk the Syrian political officer on the expedition, Nesib el-Bekri, disagreed with Lawrence about the purpose of their march, with Nesib eager to ignore Akaba and switch targets to his own city of Damascus, while Lawrence argued that with Feisal still in Wejh and the British the other side of Gaza, any such move would leave them unsupported and with no line of communication to their friends. Nesib subsequently rode off to work on what Lawrence dubbed his 'great Damascus scheme'. As soon as Nesib was out of the way Lawrence decided to go off himself, rather as Nesib had done, on what he called 'a long tour of the north country'. His justification was that 'one more sight of Syria would put straight the strategic ideas given me by the Crusaders and the first Arab conquest, and adjust them to the two new factors – the railways, and Murray in Sinai'. He found the prospect an exhilarating one, except that there was a flaw. 'A rash adventure suited my abandoned mood. It should have been happiness, this lying out free as air, with the visible life striving its utmost along my own path; but the knowledge of the axe I was secretly grinding destroyed all my assurance.' That axe was his secret knowledge of Allied duplicity.

When Lawrence was persuaded by George Bernard Shaw to drop his introductory chapter, its main argument and certain key sentences about his feelings of guilt were moved to this point in the book – the point at which he was about to describe his reconnaisance journey. The mutation the statement underwent in being transferred to its new position seems sufficiently interesting for the passage to be quoted at length. Unlike the original version, this second one is specific in its references to the Allies' dealings with – and behind the back of – their Arab co-belligerents.

> The Arab Revolt had begun on false pretences. To gain the Sherif's help our Cabinet had offered, through Sir Henry McMahon, to support the establishment of native governments in parts of Syria, 'saving the interests of our ally, France'. The last modest clause concealed a treaty (kept secret, till too late, from McMahon, and therefore from the Sherif) by which France, England and Russia agreed to annex some of the promised areas, and to establish their respective spheres of influence over all the rest.
>
> Rumours of the fraud reached Arab ears, from Turkey. In the East, persons were more trusted than institutions. So the Arabs, having tested my friendliness and sincerity under fire, asked me, as a free agent, to endorse the promises of the British Government. I had had no previous or inner knowledge of the McMahon pledges and the Sykes-Picot treaty, which were framed by war-time branches of the Foreign Office. But, not being a perfect fool, I could see that if we won the war the promises to the Arabs were dead paper. Had I been an honourable adviser I would have sent my men home, and not let them risk their lives for such stuff. Yet the Arab inspiration was our main tool in winning the Eastern war. So I assured them that England kept her word in letter and spirit. In this comfort they performed their fine things: but, of course, instead of being proud of what we did together, I was continually and bitterly ashamed.

What made him particularly aware of his invidious role at this time was a confrontation with Nuri Shaalan, chief of the Rualla tribe, by whose courtesy they were in Wadi Sirhan.

> Clear sight of my position came to me one night, when Nuri Shaalan in his aisled tent brought out a file of documents and asked which British pledge was to be believed. In his mood, upon my answer, lay the success or failure of Feisal. My advice, uttered with some agony of mind, was to trust the latest in date of the contradictions. This disingenuous answer promoted me, in six months, to be chief confidence man.

'Chief confidence man': in an earlier version of his book, the 'Oxford' text set up for him by the typesetters of the *Oxford Times*, he gave himself an even harsher description. 'A year later', he wrote, 'I was almost the chief crook of our gang.' The evidence is strong that this was one of the major crises of conscience of his war. Nevertheless, though plainly much disturbed and depressed, he decided to go ahead with his plan.

So in resentment at my false place (did ever second lieutenant so lie abroad for his betters?) I undertook this long, dangerous ride.... I had whispered to myself 'Let me chance it, now, before we begin', seeing truly that this was the last chance, and that after a successful capture of Akaba I would never again possess myself freely....

The 'Oxford' text is even more specific on this matter of 'chancing it'.

Accordingly on this march I took risks with the set hope of proving myself unworthy to be the Arab assurance of final victory. A bodily wound would have been a grateful vent for my internal perplexities, a mouth through which my troubles might have found relief.

That he deliberately took risks is confirmed by his brother, A. W. Lawrence, whom he told that on one occasion during this journey he walked up and down a station of the Hejaz line in the vicinity of Damascus wearing British uniform, in the hope of being caught. Perhaps the most revealing evidence of his state of mind at the time, however, was discovered some years ago when his wartime diaries, preserved in the British Museum (now the British Library), were found to contain a message which he drafted for Brigadier-General Clayton but did not send. It is written in faint pencil on a signal pad – which as is clear from other entries was in use during this period – and subsequently heavily crossed out. It is quite readable with a good magnifying glass:

Clayton. I've decided to go off alone to Damascus, hoping to get killed on the way: for all sakes try and clear this show up before it goes further. We are calling them to fight for us on a lie, and I can't stand it.[1]

In so far, therefore, as there is any question over this journey, it is perhaps not so much a matter of whether it actually took place but as to whether it was quite the calm cool reconnaissance which he naturally made it out to be in his official report and his subsequent conversations with Clayton and Allenby. In any case such depression as he suffered was plainly not to prove so disabling as to prevent him from returning with information, intelligence, and numerous ideas for the

1 First published in J. M. Wilson's Introduction to *Minorities*, 1971. The page in the signal pad with the scored out message contains one other interesting fragment of writing, upside down to everything else on the page and written over by part of what is probably a first draft report of his journey: 'I had been 28 years well fed & had no wish to despise these felons for loving their millions. Nesib was of their race, & brothers & sisters may tell the truth, where we cannot. But I wish to God I was quit of it.' The comment shows Lawrence's disillusion with those of the Arabs who saw their Revolt in terms of how much gold they could get out of the Allies; it also confirms that Nesib and Lawrence had little love for each other. It was, incidentally, Nesib who was Suleiman Mousa's principal witness against Lawrence in the matter of the northern journey, stating that he did not believe Lawrence had left Nebk during the fortnight or so of the enrolment. But then Nesib, as indicated in this chapter, had himself left Nebk for Turkish-held territory during this period.

future development of the campaign – ideas which were persuasive enough for his superiors to give them their complete backing. Yet the memory of this unhappy time, and of the reason for it, lingered. In Chapter CXVII of *Seven Pillars*, by which time his story has reached August 1918, he discusses 'life and honour' as seeming to be 'in different categories, not able to be sold one for another'; adding, 'and for honour, had I not lost that a year ago when I assured the Arabs that England kept her plighted word?'

Lawrence made numerous attacks on the Hejaz Railway and in late September 1917 he wrote two contrasting accounts of a recent raid, one to Major Stirling, a regular army officer whom he had met in Egypt and who was about to join the Arab campaign as a General Staff Officer; and the other to his friend at the Ashmolean Museum in Oxford, E. T. Leeds. The letter to Stirling is jaunty in tone and makes light of the event.

> The last stunt was the hold up of a train. It had two locomotives, and we gutted one with an electric mine. This rather jumbled up the trucks, which were full of Turks, shooting at us. We had a Lewis [gun], and flung bullets through the sides. So they hopped out and took cover behind the embankment, and shot at us between the wheels, at 50 yards. Then we tried a Stokes gun, and two beautiful shots dropped right in the middle of them. They couldn't stand that (12 died on the spot) and bolted away to the East across a hundred-yard belt of open sand into some scrub.

> Unfortunately for them, the Lewis covered the open stretch. The whole job took ten minutes, and they lost 70 killed, 30 wounded, 80 prisoners, and about 25 got away. Of my hundred Howeitat and two British NCOs, there was one (Arab) killed, and four (Arab) wounded.

> The Turks then nearly cut us off as we looted the train, and I lost some baggage, and nearly myself. My loot is a superfine red Baluch prayer-rug. I hope this sounds the fun it is. The only pity is the sweat to work them up and wild scramble while it lasts.

The letter to Leeds suggests that he had found the raid seriously disturbing.

> The last stunt has been a few days on the Hejaz Railway, in which I potted a train with two engines (oh, the Gods were kind) and we killed superior numbers, and I got a good Baluch prayer-rug and lost all my kit, and nearly my little self.

> I'm not going to last out this game much longer: nerves going and temper wearing thin, and one wants an unlimited amount of both. . . . I hope when the nightmare ends that I will wake up and become alive again. This killing and killing of Turks is horrible. When you charge

in at the finish and find them all over the place in bits, and still alive, many of them, and know that you have done hundreds in the same way before and must do hundreds more if you can. . . .

Lawrence's 'nerves and temper' were not improved shortly after this by the failure of a mission given specifically to him by Allenby. The latter had asked him to cut the Turks' vital rail link between Deraa, south of Damascus on the Hejaz line, and the Palestine coast. The point selected for attack was the bridge across the Yarmuk river to the west of Deraa. On 8 November Lawrence, Sheikh Ali ibn el Hussein al Harith and a raiding party of sixty or so Arab guerrillas armed with fifteen sacks of dynamite approached the Yarmuk ravine, but unfortunately one of the party dropped his rifle, a Turkish guard heard the sound and the Bedouin had to flee amidst a storm of bullets. Lawrence felt a deep sense of guilt because he had not been able to carry out Allenby's request.

Returning to his base in the old fort at Azrak after this setback Lawrence knew that he could not rest long before his next task. It was on this brief visit that he and his fellow guerrillas enjoyed their evenings of coffee and stories, and dreamed themselves into the spirit of the place with their talk of 'sieges and feasting, raids, murders, love-singing in the night'. However, as his account continues, 'this escape of our wits from the fettered body was an indulgence against whose enervation only a change of scene could avail. Very painfully I drew myself again into the present, and forced my mind to say that it must use this wintry weather to explore the country lying round about Deraa.'

Deraa, the main town of the Hauran district, north of Azrak, was a Turkish stronghold and the vital railway junction on the way to Damascus. Lawrence, with a couple of companions, set off to reconnoitre the town and surrounding country. He was accompanied for part of the way by a local sheikh, Tallal, from Tafas, a village north of Deraa, 'a famous outlaw', as Lawrence described him, 'with a price upon his head; but so great that he rode about as he pleased. In two wild years he had killed, according to report, some twenty-three of the Turks.' Tallal could not enter the town as he was too well known, so Lawrence went in with one of his companions, Faris – 'he was an insignificant peasant, old enough to be my father, and respectable'. Then, according to Seven Pillars, 'Someone called out in Turkish. We walked on deafly; but a sergeant took me roughly by the arm, saying "The Bey wants you." There were too many witnesses for fight or flight, so I went readily. He took no notice of Faris.'

What happened to Lawrence at Deraa has been the subject of speculation by some of his biographers; aspects of his account in Seven Pillars have been questioned and it has even been suggested that he deliberately invented the

1 This is not an incomplete sentence; it ends as printed. The attack in question was the raid at Harret Ammar, Lawrence's official report on which was published in the Arab Bulletin.

story of his being captured, beaten and raped in order to give his book a scene of high drama in which the deception of his Arab friends could have its appropriate punishment. The likelihood is that the episode at Deraa occurred. That it was not devised simply for literary effect is shown by the fact that he referred to it at some length in a report to British Headquarters Cairo written during a visit to Egypt in June 1919. There is even the possibility, not out of the question in the light of his behaviour when last in Turkish-held territory, that he was deliberately taking the chance of being caught. It is certainly improbable that what seems to have been an event of enormous psychological importance in his life was simply imagined. He himself had great difficulty in writing about it. 'About that night,' he wrote in a letter of March 1924 to Mrs George Bernard Shaw, with whom he became a close confidant after the war, 'I shouldn't tell you because decent men don't talk about such things. I wanted to put it plain in the book and wrestled for days with my self-respect. For fear of being hurt, or rather to earn five minutes of respite from a pain which drove me mad, I gave away the only possession we are born into life with – our bodily integrity. It's an unforgivable matter, an irrecoverable position: and it's that which has made me forswear decent living, and the exercise of my not-contemptible wits and talents.'

In *Seven Pillars*, in a chapter much laboured over, Lawrence described how he went into Deraa disguised as a Circassian, how he was captured, and his belt and knife were removed; he was asked to wash himself and spent the day in the guard room:

> Soon after dark three men came for me. It had seemed a chance to get away, but one held me all the time. . . . They took me upstairs to the Bey's room; or to his bedroom rather. . . . He was another bulky man, a Circassian himself, perhaps, and sat on the bed in a night-gown, trembling and sweating as though with fever. . . . At last he looked me over, and told me to stand up: then to turn round. I obeyed: he flung himself back on the bed, and dragged me down with him in his arms. When I saw what he wanted I twisted round and up again, glad to find myself equal to him, at any rate in wrestling.

When Lawrence resisted his advances, the Bey clapped his hands for a sentry who pinioned the prisoner and tore off his clothes:

> Finally he lumbered to his feet, with a glitter in his look, and began to paw me over. I bore it for a little, till he got too beastly; and then jerked my knee into him . . . he leaned forward, fixed his teeth in my neck and bit till the blood came. Then he kissed me. Afterwards he drew one of the men's bayonets. I thought he was going to kill me, and was sorry: but he only pulled up a fold of the flesh over my ribs, worked the point through, after considerable trouble, and gave the

blade a half-turn ... the blood wavered down my side. ... I could not again trust my twitching mouth, which faltered always in emergencies, so at last threw up my chin, which was the sign for 'No' in the East; then he sat down, and half-whispered to the corporal to take me out and teach me everything. ... The corporal came back with a whip of the Circassian sort, a thong of supple black hide, rounded, and tapering from the thickness of the thumb at the grip (which was wrapped in silver) down to a hard point finer than a pencil. ... I locked my teeth to endure this thing which lapped itself like a flaming wire about my body. ... I remembered smiling idly at him, for a delicious warmth, probably sexual, was swelling through me; and then he flung up his arm and hacked with the full length of his whip into my groin. ... I next knew that I was being dragged about by two men, each disputing over a leg as though to split me apart: while a third man rode me astride.

Afterwards the soldiers took Lawrence back to the Bey who rejected him as 'a thing too torn and bloody for his bed'. He was later washed, his wounds bandaged and was allowed to escape. This sexual assault left Lawrence physically and mentally scarred for life. He ended this version of the story with the words 'in Deraa that night the citadel of my integrity had been irrevocably lost'.

In the earlier, unpublished 'Oxford version' of *Seven Pillars* Lawrence ended his account in different, and more revealing words:

I was feeling very ill, as though some part of me had gone dead that night in Deraa, leaving me maimed, imperfect, only half myself. It could not have been the defilement, for no one ever held the body in less honour than I did myself. Probably it had been the breaking of the spirit by that frenzied nerve-shattering pain which had degraded me to beast level when it made me grovel to it, and which had journeyed with me since, a fascination and terror and morbid desire, lascivious and vicious, perhaps, but like the striving of a moth towards its flame.

Although Lawrence had difficulty in writing about his experience at Deraa it is a brave account of his suffering and of his personal degradation and attraction towards flagellation, written at a time when self-analysis was not fashionable. His brother, A. W. Lawrence, has never doubted the truth of the incident, and in the light of information published in 1968 (see Chapter 11) there seems little reason to disagree with him.

The Deraa episode is dated 20–21 November 1917. That same month saw two developments of great historical importance which had major consequences in the Arab world. The first was the Bolshevik Revolution in Russia, which was followed by the disclosure by the new regime of the existence of the Sykes-Picot agreement. There were hurried consultations in London, Cairo and elsewhere and King Hussein of the Hejaz, the former Grand Sherif, was assured that Sykes-Picot was merely a speculative document unratified by the powers whom it concerned. Secondly there was the publication of the Balfour declaration, which stated that the British Government viewed with favour the establishment of a national home for the Jewish people in Palestine – at that time a country largely populated by Arabs. This was not seen at the time as an epoch-making decision (indeed it was not considered worthy of comment by *The Times*), but in the field of Allied-Arab co-operation in the Middle East it was recognized

Lawrence – in conversation, background left – just before the official entry into Jerusalem, 11 December 1917: a still-frame from the newsreel film of the event. 'I only hope he appears in the cinema pictures taken on that occasion, because, otherwise, an unknown aspect of him will be lost.' (D.G. Hogarth to his wife, 23 December 1917) Allenby is in the foreground, centre.

as constituting an extra hazard. To Lawrence's many tasks and burdens was added that of ensuring that the new development did not adversely affect the future of the campaign. He wrote to Clayton, 'For the Jews, when I see Feisal next I'll talk to him and the Arab attitude shall be sympathetic, for the duration of the war at least.' This necessary but unpalatable duty can hardly have produced any easement for his troubled conscience, or increased his enthusiasm for the work in hand.

The following month, December, saw the capture of Jerusalem by Allenby's army, and on 11 December Allenby made his triumphal entry into the holy city. In deference to history he did so on foot. Lawrence was invited by the Commander-in-Chief to take part in the ceremony. Wavell, future Field-Marshal but then a Colonel, was also present and walked beside Lawrence in the official party. 'He was gay that day,' Wavell wrote later of this first meeting, 'with jests at his borrowed uniform and at the official appointment that had been loaned to him for the ceremony – staff officer to Bertie Clayton. He said as usual little of himself, and barely mentioned the great ride to, and unlucky failure at, the Yarmuk Valley bridge, from which he had just returned.'

Lawrence had had no part in the regular campaign to take Jerusalem but was apparently much moved by this historic occasion. 'For me,' he wrote, 'it was the supreme moment of the war.' One cannot help wondering if he so described it because Jerusalem was a place which meant much to him from his Christian upbringing, or because its seizure was the realization of the dream of his much-studied crusaders, or because the event was free of the associations of guilt and bloodshed which would mar the capture of his ultimate goal, Damascus, ten months later.

LAWRENCE AND THE DESERT

We were riding for Rumm.... a place which stirred my thought, as even the unsentimental Howeitat had told me it was lovely....

The crags were capped in nests of domes, less hotly red than the body of the hills; rather grey and shallow. They gave the finishing semblance of Byzantine architecture to this irresistible place: this processional way greater than imagination. The Arab armies would have been lost in the length and breadth of it, and within the walls a squadron of aeroplanes could have wheeled in formation. Our little caravan grew self-conscious and fell dead quiet, afraid and ashamed to flaunt its smallness in the presence of the stupendous hills.

Landscapes, in childhood's dream, were so vast and silent....

(*Seven Pillars of Wisdom*, Chapter LXII)

The abstraction of the desert landscape cleansed me, and rendered my mind vacant with its superfluous greatness; a greatness achieved not by the addition of thought to its emptiness, but by its subtraction. In the weakness of earth's life was mirrored the strength of heaven, so vast, so beautiful, so strong.

(*Seven Pillars of Wisdom*, Chapter XCIII)

9

HERO OF DAMASCUS

Before he left Jerusalem Lawrence agreed with Allenby on a future plan of campaign. Allenby thought he would be immobilized until the middle of February, when he would push down to Jericho. Lawrence's task would be to organize an Arab thrust towards the Dead Sea early in the new year with a view to joining up with Allenby's forces in the Jordan Valley by the end of March. Confident that all the necessary preliminaries were in hand, Lawrence felt able to take a brief leave. 'So I went down to Cairo, and stayed there a week experimenting with insulated cables and explosives.' He was back in Akaba on Christmas Day.

Akaba had been heavily reinforced. Men, munitions and the ever-important gold poured into the small sea port. Armoured cars, Rolls Royce tenders and a squadron of light aircraft had arrived. From now on Lawrence would have other options than a camel if he wished to move swiftly about the battleground. He would also have dealings for the first time in the war with ordinary British servicemen, the other ranks, who immediately realized that he was an officer with a difference. Interviewed about the qualities that set him apart, Laurence Moore, former signaller of the Imperial Camel Corps, stated that he was 'not militaristic in the ordinary sense. I think this is what endeared him to us. No staff college training. He was just a natural guerrilla leader, with a knowledge of the country, its people, its languages, its customs. It impressed us from the start because Lawrence was the first officer we'd ever had who took his troops entirely into his confidence. And remember these were the days of "theirs not to reason why".'

S. C. Rolls, then a Private in a Light Armoured Car Squadron, who became Lawrence's most regular driver, noted the same characteristic. 'In our corps, as in others, orders were snapped out like curses, and salutes to officers were exacted in the fullest measure. . . . Lawrence cared nothing about saluting [and] instead of an order, he usually seemed to raise, first of all, a question for discussion; giving the impression, a true one, that he wanted to have one's opinion of what was best, before he decided on the course to be followed.' As a driver, Rolls found his relationship with Lawrence especially easy and relaxed. 'He talked as we rode side by side in the Rolls Royce tender, he explained the revolt, he discussed the great job that lay ahead, he spoke of his difficulties, of his hopes and fears, of his misgivings and good fortune.'

Rolls had mistaken him for an Arab on first sight. Put on road making outside Akaba he and his comrades were 'fed up and bored stiff', when 'all at once Hassan the Egyptian foreman turned round and pointed with his whip at a group of Arabs coming silently down the pass.' The Egyptians had little love for the Arabs, so Hassan let off a stream of curses and spat on the ground. 'Then I

Armoured cars in the desert, offering the opportunity for what Lawrence called 'fighting de luxe'.

Lawrence (on foot, centre) with his famous bodyguard, his band of 'hired assassins', as he once called them, who much amazed the British who served with him in the desert. 'I chatted with them quite freely and got on well with them. And it was obvious that they were all devoted to the service of Lawrence.' (Laurence 'Rory' Moore, formerly of the Imperial Camel Corps). Lawrence himself wrote of them: 'My bodyguard of fifty Arab tribesmen . . . are more splendid than a tulip garden.'

saw that the leader of the convoy was making his camel kneel. He came shuffling up to me, and I said: "Allah yalla imshi – buzz off", thinking he was after baksheesh, like they normally were. And he parted his kofia and I saw that his face was red, not coffee-coloured, his eyes were blue grey, and there was a smile

on his face. And he said, "Is your captain with you?" I said, "Yes, sir, certainly sir." I didn't know what I was doing. I didn't know where I was. I was flabbergasted. *That* was Colonel Lawrence.'

The convoy of Arabs referred to by Rolls was undoubtedly Lawrence's bodyguard. In this final phase of the war he had his own tiny private army, up to ninety in number, chosen for their bravery and capacity for endurance. They were not always with him; in August 1918, for example, he wrote, 'My bodyguard is as usual spread over a thousand miles of Arabia.' He paid his men six pounds a month, the standard army wage for a man and a camel, but he mounted them on his own camels, so that the money was clear income; the 'eager spirits of the camp' found these terms attractive. They were mostly Ageyli – tribeless men; 'the most reckless daredevils in all Arabia', was Stirling's description of them. 'Fellows were very proud of being in my bodyguard, which developed a professionalism almost flamboyant,' Lawrence wrote in *Seven Pillars*. 'In half an hour they would make ready for a ride of six weeks, that being the limit for which food could be carried at the saddle-bow. . . . In the short winter I outdid them, with my allies of the frost and snow: in the heat they outdid me. . . . In my service nearly sixty of them died.'

The Imperial Camel Corps dubbed the bodyguard 'the forty thieves'. Laurence Moore describes them as being 'all dressed remarkably splendidly. I can remember best of all their fancy waistcoats; they had polka dots, and green and orange stripes. They were all devoted to the service of Lawrence.' Lawrence himself was aware that his bodyguard drew lively comment. He wrote: 'The British at Akaba called them cut-throats; but they cut throats only to my order.'

The presence of the armoured cars, based in permanent camp up country at Guweira, allowed a new and brisker type of warfare. In the last days of the old year, with Joyce in charge and himself as spectator ('the novelty was most enjoyable') Lawrence took part in what he called 'a car-trip down the mud-flats to Mudowwara' – a Turkish-garrisoned railway strong-point the reduction of which was not finally to be achieved until the following August. The mud-flats, bone dry, afforded perfect going, and at times the speedometers touched sixty-five m.p.h. There were two minor brushes with the enemy, but the outing was more of a reconnaissance than a serious raid. Its most important result was to show that thanks to the cars the railway could be under attack from Guweira in a day. This first taste of what he called 'fighting de luxe' was particularly welcome since it gave him relief from his main task, and also a change of company. He relished the rare experience of being encamped with his compatriots, 'happy with bully beef and tea and biscuits, with English talk and laughter round the fire, golden with its shower of sparks from the fierce brushwood. . . . For me it was a holiday, with not an Arab near, before whom I must play my tedious part.'

The 'tedious part' was soon to be resumed, and in earnest. In late January 1918 there occurred the nearest to a conventional battle that Lawrence was ever involved in, at Tafileh, a mountain village some twenty miles south of the Dead Sea. An Arab force commanded by Sherif Nasir, advancing northward in implementation of the plan agreed by Lawrence with Allenby, had encountered little resistance in taking Tafileh on the 15th, the *coup de grâce* having been administered by one of Lawrence's favourite warriors, the 'inimitable Auda', chief of the Howeitat tribe. The latter's booming cry of 'Dogs, do you not know Auda?' caused, according to Lawrence, a failure of heart among the shaky defenders, and 'an hour later Sherif Nasir in the town-house was sipping tea with his guest the Turkish Governor, trying to console him for the sudden change of fortune'. Shortly afterwards Feisal's younger brother Zeid arrived, having been delegated the command of this important push, together with Jaafar Pasha, commander of the Arab regular force which had been training for some months at Akaba. Lawrence came up from Guweira to join them. On 19 January, however, a temporary Turkish regiment, hurriedly collected and short of supplies, began to move by rail and road to retake Tafileh, to Lawrence's considerable astonishment and, indeed, anger.

Their move was, he thought, 'simple greed, a dog-in-the-manger attitude unworthy of a serious enemy, just the sort of hopeless thing a Turk would do'. He saw Tafileh as 'an obscure village of no interest. Nor did we value it as a possession; our desire was to get past it towards the enemy. For men so critically placed as the Turks to waste one single casualty on its recapture appeared the rankest folly.'

Lawrence's account of what followed on 25 January has been disputed, mainly by Suleiman Mousa, the Arab historian, who claims all the credit for Zeid largely on the strength of an account by him in which Lawrence is not mentioned. The essence of the occasion from Lawrence's point of view is that according to all his own precepts and firm beliefs about the nature of the Arab war, he should have advised against a direct confrontation. 'We could have won by refusing battle,' he wrote in *Seven Pillars*, 'foxed them by manoeuvring our centre as on twenty such occasions before or since; yet bad temper and conceit united for this time to make me not content to know my power, but determined to give public advertisement of it to the enemy and to everyone.' In brief, if the Turks wanted a fight, they could have one. 'We would play their kind of game on our pygmy scale; deliver them a pitched battle such as they wanted; kill them all. I would rake up my memory of the half-forgotten army text-book, and parody them in action.' A battle then took place with Lawrence not only approving, but, according to his contemporary reports and to *Seven Pillars*, also devising and directing the strategy. The Turks launched a frontal attack; the Arabs by wise deployment of forces and flexibility of response rebuffed and routed them. The Turks lost an estimated 400 killed while another 250 were taken prisoner; the Arab casualties were twenty-five dead and forty wounded. This was a notable victory and Tafileh was to be saluted in the official history of the war as 'a brilliant feat of arms', while the military historian and biographer of Lawrence, Liddell Hart, called it a 'miniature masterpiece'. But if Lawrence was proud of the battle technically – and it is most unlikely to have been fought without consultation with him as official Allied adviser – he was not proud of it morally. There had been unnecessary bloodshed.

> The day had been too long for me, and I was now only shaking with desire to see the end: but Zeid beside me clapped his hands with joy at the beautiful order of our plan unrolling in the frosty redness of

The aftermath of Tafileh: photograph by Lawrence and captioned by him as
'Tafileh, Turkish prisoners defiling'.

the setting sun.... This evening there was no glory left, but the
terror of the broken flesh, which had been our own men, carried past
us to their homes.

His report on the battle, he commented in *Seven Pillars*, 'was meanly written for
effect, full of quaint similes and mock simplicities; and made them think me a
modest amateur, doing his best after the great models.... Like the battle, it
was nearly-proof parody of regulation use. Headquarters loved it, and innocently,
to crown the jest, offered me a decoration on the strength of it. [The decoration
was a D.S.O. – Companion of the Distinguished Service Order.] We should
have more bright breasts in the Army if each man was able, without witnesses,
to write out his own despatch.'

Snow had fallen on the evening of the battle, and only with difficulty were
the Arab wounded brought in; the Turkish wounded lay ungathered, and were
dead next day. He stayed snowbound in Tafileh until 4 February, he and twenty-
seven of his bodyguard confined in two tiny rooms, 'which reeked with the sour

smell of our crowd. . . . In my saddle-bags was a *Morte d'Arthur*. It relieved my disgust.' Then, in still bitter weather, he set off with four others for Guweira, to collect the gold subsidy essential for the next phase of the campaign. After the winter rigours in the Tafileh hills, he was able to spend three 'lazy nights' in the armoured car tents there, talking to Joyce and to Alan Dawnay, a regular officer of the Coldstream Guards who was to be his strong ally in the desert campaign from now onward. He had Tafileh to boast about, while they by contrast had to report yet another setback at Mudowwara. On 8 February he began the return journey, with the money (thirty thousand pounds in golden sovereigns), three new companions, and his favourite camel, 'Wodheida, the best of my remaining stud.' Conditions were no better in the hills, where 'the wind buffeted us like an enemy'. He arrived on the 11th, having survived various hazards, including a fall into an icy morass.

> Wodheida, sensible beast, had refused to enter the morass: but she stood at a loss on the hard margin, and looked soberly at my mud-larking. However, I managed, with the still-held head-stall, to persuade her a little nearer. Then I flung my body suddenly backward against the squelching quag, and, grabbing wildly behind my head, laid hold of her fetlock. She was frightened, and started back: and her purchase dragged me clear.

Through the same appalling weather another British officer was making his way to Tafileh. This was Lieutenant Alec Kirkbride,[1] Royal Engineers, who had been sent from Beersheba in the west to report on the possibility of making a motor track to supply the Arab army from Palestine instead of via Egypt and Akaba. His party – he was travelling with six Bedouin tribesmen – had lost one of its camels on the journey; 'no brutality on the part of its owner', wrote Kirkbride, 'including a fire lit underneath its belly, would induce it to move, and we had to abandon it to its death.' He had found that the best method of making progress was to walk behind and kick and flog the camel forward: 'this had the advantage of keeping both parties warm'. They staggered into Tafileh late in the afternoon of 11 February 'with both men and animals near to the end of their tethers'. They were billeted on a local shopkeeper, who received them hospitably with scalding hot tea. By 9 p.m. he had settled down in his bedding on the shop floor.

> A couple of hours later someone shook me awake and asked, 'Are you Kirkbride?' Lawrence, whom I had not met before, was kneeling by my bedding dressed in wet and bedraggled Arab clothes and shaking with cold and fatigue. He had just got in through the storm.

1 Later Sir Alec Kirkbride, subsequently British Resident in Transjordan and adviser to King Abdulla of Jordan.

He was in such a poor state that I made him get into my bedding at once, while I went round my men and pulled a blanket off each of them, in spite of their protests, with which to make up another bed for myself in the corner.

Kirkbride was with Lawrence over the next few days, and was finally asked by him if he would like to be attached to the Arab army, an offer which Kirkbride gratefully accepted. Lawrence subsequently made the necessary arrangements with General Headquarters.

Improving weather meant that he could embark on a reconnaisance in the direction of the Jordan Valley. But before he did so he wrote a long, detailed and confidential letter to Clayton on 12 February, covering numerous topics. It was in this letter that he gave the assurance quoted in the previous chapter that the Arab attitude to the Jews would be 'sympathetic, for the duration of the war at least'. He also showed signs of exasperation at what he thought was a dilatory Arab performance: 'If the Arabs had any common spirit, they would have been in Damascus last autumn.' Most interestingly of all, perhaps, he wrote the following:

> I'm in an extraordinary position just now, vis à vis the Sherifs and the tribes and must sooner or later go bust. I do my best to keep in the background, but cannot, and some day everybody will combine and down me. It is impossible for a foreigner to run another people of their own free will, indefinitely, and my innings has been a fairly long one.

Written so soon after the Tafileh battle, this statement might well seem to have a bearing on the question of who was responsible for the strategy of Tafileh. It also has a bearing on the much discussed subject of the importance of his role generally in the shaping of the campaign. There is no doubt, certainly, that his British superiors saw this role as a central one and would appreciate the various difficulties which he had to cope with in the field.

Those difficulties were about to be compounded. He found his reconnaissance to the Jordan Valley 'very assuring for our future. Each step of our road to join the British was possible: most of them easy. The weather was so fine that we might reasonably begin at once: and could hope to finish within a month.' But when he reported this at Tafileh, Zeid heard him coldly. All the money brought up from Guweira had been given away, to people associated with the previous stage of the campaign: there was nothing for the next. 'I was aghast;' he wrote of this setback in *Seven Pillars*, 'for this meant the complete ruin of my plans and hopes, the collapse of our effort to keep faith with Allenby. Zeid stuck to his word that the money was gone. Afterwards I went off to learn the truth from

Nasir, who was in bed with fever. He despondently said that everything was wrong – Zeid too young and shy to counter his dishonest, cowardly counsellors.'

Lawrence decided there was nothing for it but to put his future employment in Allenby's hands. He left Tafileh on the 20th with four companions and rode the eighty miles to Beersheba – five thousand feet down from Tafileh, three thousand up into the hills of Palestine – with only one brief halt for food. At Beersheba he met Hogarth, to whom he poured out his confession. He had 'made a mess of things' and had come to Allenby to beg some smaller part elsewhere. He was tired of free-will, his body so dreaded further pain that he now had to force himself under fire, 'generally he had been hungry, lately always cold'; but worse was the 'rankling fraudulence which had to be my mind's daily habit; that pretence to lead the national uprising of another race, the daily posturing in alien dress, preaching in alien speech'. Also chargeable against him were the 'causeless, ineffectual deaths' of the recent battle. 'My will had gone and I feared to be alone, lest the winds of circumstance, or power, or lust, blow my empty soul away.'

Hogarth said nothing, but took him to have breakfast with Clayton. There he learned of the new plans for the Middle Eastern campaign, which General Smuts had come out from the War Cabinet to Palestine to expound. London was leaning heavily on Allenby to repair the stalemate still existing on the Western Front and Allenby needed help from the Arab forces. In the new conditions as Clayton saw them there was no question of Lawrence being let go. For days they had wanted to bring him to a conference, had even sent out pilots to drop messages for him.

> There was no escape for me. I must take up again my mantle of fraud in the East. With my certain contempt for half measures I took it up completely. It might be fraud or it might be farce: no one should say that I could not play it.

So he went back, but to Feisal not Zeid. He now had different targets, Maan, on the desert plateau up from Akaba, and Amman, north of Maan on the railway, not the area of Tafileh, where it was plainly impossible for him, as a 'flouted adviser', to carry on. The changed emphasis of the campaign left Tafileh highly vulnerable and Feisal feared its loss might do his reputation harm, but Lawrence argued that the place was 'not worth losing a man over – indeed, if the Turks moved there, they would weaken either Maan or Amman, and make our real work easier.' The Turks *did* move there, to Lawrence's complete unconcern. It was no longer relevant. The main thrust of the campaign was elsewhere.

On 8 March he wrote to his mother – his first letter for two months – his account for home reading giving no hint as to the physical and mental difficulties he had recently experienced.

Here I am in Cairo again. At Tafileh I had a difference of opinion
with Sherif Zeid, the 4th son of the old man of Mecca, and left him
for Beersheba. This was about the 22nd. I then went to Jerusalem,
Ramleh, Jerusalem, Beersheba, Ismailia, Cairo, Suez, Akaba,
Guweira, Akaba, Suez, and got back here last night. I hope to be here
four nights. This year promises to be more of a run about than last
year even! ...

They have given me a D.S.O. It's a pity all this good stuff is not sent
to someone who would use it. Don't make any change in my address
of course.

... It will be a comfort when this gypsy mode of life comes to an
end. However, thank goodness the worst of the winter is over. I had
one very bad night in the hills when my camel broke down in the
snow drifts, and I had to dig a path out for it and lead it for miles
down slippery snow-slopes. ...

There, I can't think of anything else cheerful to tell you about –
except perhaps that three of my camels have had babies in the last
few weeks. ...

The letter also helps to pinpoint an important meeting. During one of the
Jerusalem visits referred to, when calling on his old friend, Ronald Storrs, now
Military Governor of the city, he was introduced to the American journalist
Lowell Thomas, whose flare for public relations was to transform Lawrence into
an international celebrity after the war. The letter also contained the information
that he had been promoted; 'apparently ... I'm a colonel of sorts'. He was
officially appointed 'Temporary Lieutenant-Colonel' on 12 March 1918.

From now onward the desert operations were to be less haphazard. As Lawrence put it, 'Allenby's smile had given us Staff. We had supply officers, a
shipping expert, an ordnance expert, and intelligence branch. ... The Arab
Movement had lived as a wild-man show, with its means as small as its duties
and prospects. Henceforward Allenby counted it as a sensible part of his scheme.'
However, the first results of this new phase were mixed. Arab attacks on Maan
in April produced some success in terms of prisoners and machine guns taken,
but appositely, Lawrence headed the passage in *Seven Pillars* dealing with this
period with the terse phrase 'MAAN BEATS US'. A more successful attack
followed, however, on the railway station at Tel Shahm, planned by Dawnay in
the most meticulous detail. Its precison amazed Lawrence who was only disappointed that the Turks surrendered ten minutes ahead of Dawnay's schedule.
Lawrence headed the race for the station. 'Our car won; and I gained the station
bell, a dignified piece of Damascus brass-work.' An attempt on Mudowwara
on the following day, however, found it too heavily defended with accurate
artillery for comfort; 'we made off in undignified haste to some distant hollows.'

Lawrence in Lieutenant-Colonel's uniform, Cairo, 1918.

But a systematic destruction of railway track and bridges between Maan and Mudowwara meant that eighty miles of line and seven stations were now under Arab control.

This was a useful achievement, but a British raid on Amman in late March had been bedevilled by vile weather and difficult terrain. And there was worse news to come, not because of developments in the East but because of the great German attack on the Western Front in France launched on 21 March. This produced a major crisis in what was, after all, the central battleground of the First World War. Allenby was ordered to go on the defensive in Palestine. All troops that could be spared were required for France. He was promised Indian divisions from Mesopotamia, and Indian drafts. 'With these he would rebuild his army on the Indian model; perhaps, after the summer, he might be again in fighting trim: but for the moment', wrote Lawrence, 'we must both just hold on.'

Allenby spelled out the situation to Lawrence when the latter visited G.H.Q. on 5 May. That afternoon at tea-time Allenby mentioned the Imperial Camel Brigade in Sinai, regretting that in the new stringency he must abolish it and use its men as mounted reinforcements.

> I asked: 'What are you going to do with their camels?' he laughed, and said, 'Ask "Q".'

> Obediently, I went across the dusty garden, broke in upon the Quartermaster-General, Sir Walter Campbell – very Scotch – and repeated my question. He explained firmly that they were earmarked for the second of the new Indian divisions. I explained that I wanted two thousand of them. His first reply was irrelevant: his second reply conveyed that I might go on wanting. I argued, but he seemed unable to see my side at all. Of course, it was the nature of 'Q' to be costive.

The matter was resolved that evening, at dinner.

> We sat on the right hand and on the left, and with the soup Allenby began to talk about camels. Sir Walter broke out that the providential dispersing of the camel brigade brought the transport of the —th Division up to strength; a godsend, for the Orient had been ransacked for camels. He over-acted. Allenby, a reader of Milton, had an acute sense of style; and the line was a weak one. He cared nothing for strengths, the fetish of administrative branches.

> He looked at me with a twinkle, 'And what do you want them for?' I replied hotly, 'To put a thousand men into Deraa any day you please.' He smiled and shook his head at Sir Walter Campbell, saying sadly, 'Q, you lose.'

On the following day Lawrence arrived, according to Colonel Joyce, in the middle of lunch at the mess in Guweira.

> He could scarcely eat for eagerness and yet his conversation was about a herd of wild ostriches which had crossed his path on the way over, and describing how his Bedouin escort had fled after them in vain endeavour to make a capture. It was only afterwards, in Feisal's tent, that he announced the glad tidings of the gift of 2,000 camels from G.H.Q. . . . He was like a boy released from school that day and his energy dynamic.

One battalion of the Imperial Camel Corps remained, however, and this too was to be used to Lawrence's purposes in the summer of 1918. Plans were being made for a major raid on Deraa to coincide with Allenby's promised offensive but in the meantime some new factor was required, to maintain pressure on the enemy. It was Dawnay who, writes Lawrence, was 'inspired' to think of this fully trained and equipped force, at that time underemployed in Sinai. He and Lawrence worked out a plan: Mudowwara to be attacked and taken, then a swift northward move across the desert to Azrak, followed by an attack on an important bridge of the Hejaz Railway just outside Amman. The ICC force, under Major Robin Buxton – strength 16 officers, 300 other ranks, 400 camels, 6 Lewis guns – were duly moved to Akaba. Their arrival caused a sensation, as Laurence Moore recalls:

> Lawrence came out to meet us, and rode the last couple of days with us into Akaba, mainly to warn us of the kind of reception we should expect. In spite of this, we were amazed to be greeted by thousands of Arabs milling around shouting, on horse, on foot, on camel, all of them blazing away with their 303's into the air, in what Lawrence called a *feu de joie*. I believe he likened it to a royal salute, but our chaps considered it a shocking waste of small arms ammunition brought across the Mediterranean at great cost and great risk. Some of the bullets whistled uncomfortably close and when we halted some of our fellows found holes clean through their solar topees. Later Lawrence called us together and begged us that no matter what the provocation not to retaliate in any way, because he relied on our western understanding, but mainly because they were so many and we were so few.

With Buxton's permission Lawrence addressed in this way each company in turn. Stirling who was present at one of his briefings said that he gave the men 'the straightest talk I have ever heard'. As well as explaining the general situation to them and warning them to avoid all friction with their Arab allies he also told them that he was going to take them through a part of Arabia where no man had set foot since the time of the Crusades. 'They retired for the night delighted with his talk and fully convinced that they were about to embark on the greatest jaunt in the history of war.' For Lawrence it was second nature to confide in his men, but it was a technique rare for its time.

The ordinary British soldiers liked Lawrence; Laurence Moore claims that those who were with him in the desert 'absolutely worshipped him'. But what of his fellow officers at this time? As the British Mobile Column, the official name for the ICC companies, paused in the magnificent setting of Wadi Rumm to water their camels before moving against Mudowwara, Major Buxton wrote about him in a letter home:

> Lawrence . . . is only a boy to look at, has a very quiet, sedate manner, a fine head but insignificant body. He is known to every Arab in his country for his personal bravery and train-wrecking exploits. I don't know whether it is his intrepidity, disinterestedness and mysteriousness which appeal to the Arab most, or his success in finding them rich trains to blow up and loot. After a train success he tells me the army is like Barnum's show and gradually disintegrates. At any rate it is wonderful what he has accomplished with the poor tools at his disposal. His influence is astounding not only on the misbeguided natives, but also I think on his brother officers and seniors. Out here he lives entirely with the Arabs, wears their clothes, eats only their own food, and bears all the burdens that the lowliest of them does. He always travels in spotless white, and in fact reminds one of a Prince of Mecca more than anything. He will join us again later, I hope, as his presence is very stimulating to us all and one has the feeling that things cannot go wrong while he is there.

But admiration was not universal. For example, Major Hubert Young (an Indian Army officer attached to the Hejaz Operations in 1918) was, by his own account, inclined to be critical of Lawrence's omniscience and of his apparent determination to do everything himself, while Kirkbride wrote of what he described as the femininity of his likes and dislikes: 'If he regarded one favourably, he was charming, but if he disliked you he was spiteful and malicious.' Both these men, however, also found much to admire in Lawrence, Young for example stating that, given certain reservations about his inability to reconcile responsibility with discipline, 'I would rather have served under him than under any regular soldier I have ever met.'

The greatest critic of Lawrence, however, was Lawrence himself. August 1918 was the month of his thirtieth birthday, and, according to Chapter CIII of *Seven Pillars*, 'Myself', he spent his birthday in searching self-analysis.

> It came to me queerly how, four years ago, I had meant to be a general and knighted, when thirty. Such temporal dignities (if I survived the next four weeks) were now in my grasp – only that the sense of the

falsity of the Arab position had cured me of crude ambition: while it
left me my craving for a good repute among men. . . . Here were the
Arabs believing in me, Allenby trusting me, my bodyguard dying for
me: and I began to wonder if all established reputations were founded,
like myself, on fraud.

There is much else in this vein: 'Any protestation of the truth from me was
called modesty, self depreciation; and charming – for men were always fond to
believe a romantic tale. . . . There was my craving to be liked – so strong and
nervous that never could I open myself friendly to another. . . . There was a
craving to be famous; and a horror of being known to like being known. . . .
When a thing was in my reach, I no longer wanted it; my delight lay in the
desire. . . .' It is a remarkable piece of confessional writing, of which perhaps
the keynote is the statement: 'I was a standing court-martial on myself.' The
chapter concludes: 'Indeed the truth was I did not like the "myself" I could see
and hear.'

His birthday fell between the Camel Corps's two missions. The first, the
attack on Mudowwara, was brilliantly successful; at last that most intransigent
of nettles had been grasped. Lawrence was not present but he was with them
for the move against the second target, the railway bridge just outside Amman.
However, he and Buxton decided in the end to abort the attack, since one
condition of the ICC's employment had been a prohibition of all but minimal
casualties; the column had been seen by a Turkish aircraft, so the enemy,
forewarned, might well be better armed. 'The whole cost might be fifty men,
and I put the worth of the bridge at less than five. . . . We decided to cry off,
and move back at once.' The ICC men 'groaned in disappointment', he wrote,
for 'they had set pride on this long raid'; but the purpose of their mission had
been less to fight than to keep the enemy command intent on the east of the
Jordan while Allenby's plans matured on the west. That purpose had been
honourably achieved.

Six weeks later the campaign was over. Lawrence himself told his own, highly
subjective story of this last phase in a final section of eighty or so pages which
is faster and more filled with action and sudden changes of mood than any other
part of the book. It almost has the feeling of a Shakespearean fifth act. Both
Young's and Stirling's accounts confirm the pace of events. In brief, Allenby
broke through in Palestine in mid-September and rolled the Turkish armies
northwards towards Damascus. Meanwhile an Arab mobile column including
Allenby's two thousand camels and consisting of 'aeroplanes, armoured cars,
Arab regulars and Beduin' (Lawrence's description) under the command of
Feisal, having concentrated on Azrak in early September, proceeded to cut the
three railways out of Deraa, isolate and take that vital junction, and, after linking
with advance regular units coming up from Palestine, moved astride the Hejaz

Railway towards Damascus. There are numerous claims as to which of the Allied forces marched into the city first, but the evidence suggests that some elements were in Damascus late on 30 September. Lawrence himself entered on 1 October. On 4 October he left.

Thus the general outline of this last phase, within which certain moments stand out as offering revealing aspects of the character and performance of, if not the central actor, certainly the most self-aware actor taking part.

In a section of his book which he related to 7 September – they were at Azrak, waiting to move towards Deraa – Lawrence stated that 'on this march to Damascus (and such it was already in our imagination) I could feel the taut power of Arab excitement behind me. The climax of the preaching of years had come, and a united country was straining towards its historic capital. In confidence that this weapon, tempered by myself, was enough for the utmost of my purpose, I seemed to forget the English companions who stood outside my idea in the shadow of ordinary war.' Yet in a passage dated five days later he could write that what he called 'the crowd', meaning the massed Arab forces arriving for the coming attack, 'destroyed my pleasure in Azrak and I went off down the valley to our remote Ain el Essad and lay there all day in my old lair among the tamarisk, where the wind in the dusty green branches played with such sounds as it made in English trees. It told me I was tired to death of these Arabs; petty incarnate Semites who attained heights and depths beyond our reach, though not beyond our sight. They realized our absolute in their unrestrained capacity for good and evil; and for two years I had profitably shammed to be their companion!' This was also an occasion for a recurrence of his mood of wanting to be quit of his involvement in the Revolt. 'Today it came to me with finality that my patience as regards the false position I had been led into was finished. A week, two weeks, three weeks, and I would insist upon relief. My nerve had broken; and I would be lucky if the ruin of it could be hidden so long.' However, a fortnight later, after the Arabs had cut the railways and the Turkish Fourth Army was beginning to fall back in disarray, he was totally against the suggestion seriously raised at that point that what had been achieved thus far discharged the Arabs of their duty and that they might without dishonour wait for the British to take Deraa. 'This attitude passed me by. . . . I was very jealous of Arab honour, in whose service I would go forward at all costs. They had joined the war to win freedom, and the recovery of their own capital by force of their own arms was the sign they would best understand. . . . Therefore, for every sensible reason, strategical, tactical, political, even moral, we were going on.'

Two days later there occurred an episode which gave rise to an important and controversial scene in his book. An exhausted Turkish column was allowed to pass northwards in retreat. Their route took them through the small village of Tafas – home of Sheikh Tallal, who had accompanied Lawrence on his attempted reconnaissance of Deraa during the previous November and whom he much admired. Instead of continuing their march the Turks stopped, sacked the village and virtually wiped out its population; the Arab force following on could hear the sound of occasional shooting and see pyres of smoke rising between the houses. As they came near Lawrence saw grey heaps hidden in the grass 'embracing the ground in the close way of corpses'. A child, wounded in the neck, ran towards them, 'then stood and cried to us in a tone of astonishing strength (all else being very silent), "Don't hit me, Baba".... We rode past the other bodies of men and women and four more dead babies, looking very soiled in the daylight, towards the village; whose loneliness we now knew meant death and horror.' If Lawrence saw this with anger, the anger of Tallal was so much the greater.

> Tallal had seen what we had seen. He gave one moan like a hurt animal; then rode to the upper ground and sat there awhile on his mare, shivering and looking fixedly after the Turks. I moved near to speak to him, but Auda caught my rein and stayed me. Very slowly Tallal drew his head-cloth about his face; and then he suddenly seemed to take hold of himself, for he dashed his stirrups into the mare's flanks and galloped headlong, bending low and swaying in the saddle, right at the main body of the enemy.
>
> It was a long ride down a gentle slope and across a hollow. We sat there like stone while he rushed forward, the drumming of his hoofs unnaturally loud in our ears, for we had stopped shooting and the Turks had stopped. Both armies waited for him; and he rocked on in the hushed evening till only a few lengths from the enemy. Then he sat up in his saddle and cried his war-cry, 'Tallal, Tallal', twice in a tremendous shout. Instantly their rifles and machine-guns crashed out, and he and his mare, riddled through and through with bullets, fell dead among the lance points.

Auda said, 'God give him mercy; we will take his price.' 'By my order', wrote Lawrence, 'we took no prisoners, for the only time in our war.' The retreating enemy army was largely slaughtered. It was, as he tells the story, a bloody reprisal for a bloody event. 'In the madness born of the horror of Tafas we killed and killed, even blowing in the heads of the fallen and the animals; as though their death and running blood could slake our agony.'

Criticism of Lawrence's account of this episode stems mainly from his most hostile biographer, Richard Aldington, who considered his conduct at Tafas 'deplorable'. However, first-hand evidence such as that of Major F. G. Peake who was in command of a section of the Egyptian Camel Corps and came on the scene shortly after the Arabs began their killing suggests that he exaggerated his role in supporting savage reprisals against the Turks. 'Immediately Lawrence saw me he ordered me to round up all prisoners as they arrived and to guard them. At nightfall I had 2000 to look after.' Lawrence in his accounts of the episode made no mention of this, his intention being in Peake's view 'to assume the responsibility for an occurrence which neither he nor anyone else could have prevented. He knew that, in future, it would be severely criticized, but as he had originally stirred the Arabs to rebel against the Turks, it was only just that he should be blamed and not the Arabs.' That he had earlier consented to, indeed had given orders for, some killing of prisoners is not in question, but he himself could only have given such orders to his own bodyguard; he had no authority to instruct the whole Arab army. More, many Turks were killed out of hand by enraged villagers of Tafas. He wrote a vigorous defence of the killings in his contemporary report written in Damascus and published on 22 October 1918 in the *Arab Bulletin* under the title *The Destruction of the Fourth Army*. 'The common delusion that the Turk is a clean and merciful fighter led some of the British troops to criticize Arab methods a little later – but they had not entered Turaa [a village where many women had been raped] or Tafas, or watched the Turks swing their wounded by the hands and feet into a burning railway truck, as had been the lot of the Arab army at Jerdun. As for the villagers, they and their ancestors had been for five hundred years ground down by the tyranny of these Turks.' He did not, however, cite this defence in his book. As Peake implies, he wanted to take the responsibility on himself.

But he had always clung to one way of, as it were, expiating his guilt – by success. 'I salved myself with the hope that, by leading these Arabs madly in the final victory I would establish them, with arms in their hands, in a position so assured (if not dominant) that expediency would counsel to the Great Powers a fair settlement of their claims.' This idea seems to have underlain much of his behaviour once the goal, Damascus, was at last in sight.

Kirkbride witnessed two examples in these last days of Lawrence's determination to seize the initiative for the Arabs. The first took place on 28 September, the morning after the Tafas massacres. Lawrence had asked Kirkbride to ride with him to Deraa, which was clear of Turks and ready for occupation. 'Lawrence forced the pace from the start and he made it unnecessary for me to ask why he was doing so by remarking, "We must get there before the cavalry!" I was too tired to feel like hurrying anywhere, especially when the only reason for our haste was to forestall our own side.' They passed close to Tafas, where the bodies of the dead still littered the ground and where a few Turkish stragglers were making their way up the road. 'Lawrence pressed on with a fixed look on his face and it did not seem that he saw the fugitives at all. . . . We reached our destination before the British cavalry came in sight and we hoisted the flag of the Hejaz.' On 1 October (Lawrence had spent the intervening time based in, or rather near, Deraa: 'I had felt man's iniquity here and so hated Deraa that

I lay each night with my men upon the old aerodrome') Kirkbride saw the same phenomenon repeated. That morning all the British formations were by order halted on the outskirts of Damascus. Kirkbride was with a small Arab group under Nuri Said which was about to ride forward towards the city when he was surprised to hear the noise of a car, driving at speed, coming from the rear. 'The source of the noise, a Rolls Royce tender, dashed past us containing only Lawrence and the driver. I waved, but Lawrence did not look round; he was staring ahead in the same fixed way I had noticed a few days before. It was, I told myself, the race to Dera'a all over again with even greater problems at its end.'

Once in the city he set about trying to resolve some of those problems, doing so consciously on behalf of Feisal. As he wrote in the last section of his report *The Destruction of the Fourth Army*:

> I think I should put on record a word of what happened after we got in. I found at the Town Hall Mohammed Said and Abd el-Kadir, the Algerians, who had just assumed possession of the provisional civil government, since there was no one in Damascus who could fight their Moorish bodyguard. They are both insane, and as well pro-Turkish and religious fanatics of the most unpleasant sort. In consequence I sent for them, and . . . announced that as Feisal's representative, I declared Shukri el-Ayubi Arab Military Governor (Ali Reza, the intended Governor was missing), and the provisional civil administration of the Algerians dissolved. They took it rather hard and had to be sent home. That evening Abd el-Kadir called together his friends and some leading Druses, and made them an impassioned speech, denouncing the Sherif as a British puppet, and calling on them to strike a blow for the Faith in Damascus. By this morning this had degenerated into pure looting, and we called out the Arab troops, put Hotchkiss [the Hotchkiss was a machine-gun] round the central square, and imposed peace in three hours, after inflicting about twenty casualties.

It is clear from *Seven Pillars* that his intention was to establish an Arab authority which would prove strong enough to survive the inevitable crises which would follow liberation. 'Another twelve hours, and we should be safe', he writes under the date 1 October, 'with the Arabs in so strong a place that their hand might hold through the long wrangle and appetite of politics about to break out about our luscious spoil.' And again, under the same date: 'Our aim was an Arab Government, with foundations large and native enough to employ the enthusiasm and self-sacrifice of the rebellion, translated into terms of peace.'

In the previous chapter he describes an event of great importance: the welcome of the people of Damascus to their liberators. But this as he tells it was a strictly Arab celebration, in which he took part not as Lieutenant-Colonel Lawrence,

British Army, but as 'Urens', Arab hero among other Arab heroes. More, he and the others, including his new appointee Shukri, went out deliberately to meet the people, to create the necessary occasion. 'We must prove the old days over, a native government in power: for this Shukri would be my best instrument, as acting Governor. So in the Blue Mist [his Rolls Royce tender] we set off to show ourselves, his enlargement in authority itself a banner of revolution for the citizens.' When they first arrived there had been crowds in hundreds; now there were thousands for every hundred then.

> Every man, woman and child in this city of a quarter-million souls seemed in the streets, waiting only the spark of our appearance to ignite their spirits. Damascus went mad with joy. The men tossed up their tarbushes to cheer, the women tore off their veils. Householders threw flowers, hangings, carpets, into the road before us: their wives leaned, screaming with laughter, through the lattices and splashed us with bath-dippers of scent.

Lawrence enters Damascus – driven by S.C. Rolls
– in his Rolls Royce tender.

Damascus, 2 October 1918: crowds in the city streets photographed on the day after its liberation from the Turks.

Poor dervishes made themselves our running footmen in front and behind, howling and cutting themselves with frenzy; and over the local cries and the shrilling of women came the measured roar of men's voices, chanting, 'Feisal, Nasir, Shukri, Urens', in waves which began here, rolled along the squares, through the market down long streets to East gate, round the wall, back up the Meidan; and grew to a wall of shouts around us by the citadel.

In contrast to this triumphal occasion there was much that was squalid and nasty about the first days of liberation: the quarrelling of factions, the settling of scores, looting, revenge killings. He and Kirkbride went out at his request one

*Lawrence by the Official War Artist James
McBey. The portrait was painted in Damascus
on the day before he left to return to England. An
Imperial War Museum memo records that 'while
he was painting him the Arabs were coming in
to him to kiss his hand and say farewell'. By
this stage of the campaign Lawrence had lost
much weight and was physically and mentally
exhausted. He later said of the portrait: 'It is
shockingly strange to me'.*

night to try and stop the slaughter of Turks in the streets. His method was to go up to anybody so engaged and ask them in a quiet voice to stop; Kirkbride's was to shoot first, at which Lawrence got quite angry and said 'For God's sake stop being so bloody-minded.' Lawrence, however, for this and other actions, later recommended Kirkbride for a Military Cross. The appalling conditions at the Turkish military hospital, described by Lawrence in unsparing detail in his book, had to be sorted out, after which there were other problems to be seen to: 'some death sentences, a new justiciary, a famine in barley for the morrow if the train did not work.' There was also a complaint from the commander of the Australian contingent now in the city, Major-General Chauvel, that some of the Arab troops had been slack about saluting his officers. But by the 3rd, as he saw it, Damascus was normal – 'the shops open, street merchants trading, the electric tramcars restored, grain and vegetables and fruit coming in well.'

That day Allenby arrived; a grey Rolls-Royce, 'which I knew for Allenby's', stood outside the Victoria Hotel. 'I ran in and found him there with Clayton and Cornwallis and other noble people. In ten words he gave his approval to my having impertinently imposed Arab Governments, here and at Deraa, upon the chaos of victory.... In ten minutes all the maddening difficulties slipped away. Mistily I realized that the harsh days of my solitary battle had passed. The lone hand had won against the world's odds, and I might let my limbs relax in this dreamlike confidence and decision and kindness which were Allenby.' Some time later Feisal arrived, by special train from Deraa. The two principals were formally introduced – it was their very first meeting – at the Victoria Hotel. Lawrence acted as interpreter. In *Seven Pillars* he touches somewhat lightly on this important occasion.

> Allenby gave me a telegram from the Foreign Office, recognizing to the Arabs the status of belligerents; and told me to translate it to the Emir: but none of us knew what it meant in English, let alone in Arabic: and Feisal, smiling through the tears which the welcome of his people had forced upon him, put it aside to thank the Commander-in-Chief for the trust which had made him and his movement.

An account with a quite different emphasis is that of the Australian Major-General Chauvel. As he remembered it, Allenby seized the occasion to explain the realities of the new political situation to Feisal in line with the Sykes-Picot agreement. He told him that France was to be the protecting power in Syria, that he was to have the administration of Syria (but not of Palestine or the Lebanon) under French guidance and backing, and that he was to have a French liaison officer at once, who would work for the present with Lawrence, who would be expected to give him every assistance. Feisal objected very strongly to all this, saying that he knew nothing of France in this matter; that he was

prepared to have British assistance; that he understood from the Adviser whom
Allenby had sent him – Lawrence – that the Arabs were to have the whole of
Syria including the Lebanon but excluding Palestine; that a country without a
port was no good to him; and that he declined to have a French Liaison Officer
or to recognize French guidance in any way.

> The Chief turned to Lawrence and said: 'But did you not tell him
> that the French were to have the Protectorate over Syria?' Lawrence
> said: 'No Sir, I know nothing about it.' The Chief then said: 'But you
> knew definitely that he, Feisal, was to have nothing to do with the
> Lebanon?' Lawrence said: 'No, sir, I did not.'

Feisal left, after agreeing that he must accept the situation until the matter could
be settled after the end of the war.

> After Feisal had gone, Lawrence told the Chief that he would not
> work with a French Liaison Officer and that he was due for leave
> and thought he had better take it now and go off to England. The
> Chief said, 'Yes! I think you had!', and Lawrence left the room.

Chauvel thought Allenby had been hard on Lawrence and told him so. Allenby
relented to the extent of determining that Lawrence should go back to England
with a letter of introduction to the equerry to the King with a view to arranging
a royal audience, and that he should also be given a letter to the Foreign Office
so that he might be given the opportunity when in London to explain the Arab
point of view.

Lawrence's account in his last chapter of the circumstances which led to the
decision that he should go – in no real way inconsistent with Chauvel's – omits
the harsher aspects of this final exchange with the commander for whom he had
so great a respect. By contrast it emphasizes the factor, crucial for Lawrence,
that he would not be at ease with the 'New Law' – the new dispensation to be
established as the soldiers completed their task and the politicians moved to
take over. His book is the better for avoiding any note of bitterness or distrust.

> When Feisal had gone, I made to Allenby the last (and also I think
> the first) request I ever made for myself – leave to go away. For a
> while he would not have it; but I reasoned, reminding him of his year-
> old promise, and pointing out how much easier the New Law would
> be if my spur were absent from the people. In the end he agreed; and
> then at once I knew how much I was sorry.

So he ends his story, but this is not the end of his book. There is a final page,
the last of almost seven hundred, a kind of soliloquy, in which he states (in what
is usually construed as a reference to his Carchemish friend Dahoum) that his

strongest motivation throughout the war had been 'a personal one, not mentioned here, but present to me, I think, every hour of these two years. . . . It was dead before we reached Damascus.' He also states that as a boy he had longed 'to feel myself the node of a national movement. We took Damascus, and I feared. More than three arbitrary days would have quickened in me a root of authority.' In the last paragraph he writes about 'historical ambition'. 'I had dreamed, at the City of Oxford School, of hustling into form, while I lived, the new Asia which time was inexorably bringing upon us. Mecca was to lead to Damascus, Damascus to Anatolia, and afterwards to Bagdad; and then there was the Yemen. Fantasies, these will seem, to such as are able to call my beginning an ordinary effort.' It is an extraordinary conclusion to the work, disclosing grandiose ideas and concepts which most people would wish to conceal as youthful dreams or aberrations. It makes poignant reading, in the light of the knowledge which we have now and which he must almost certainly have had at the time of writing – several years after the events just described – that he would shortly throw all but his literary ambitions permanently away. Doubtless that was why he felt free to write about them.

[This Document is the Property of His Britannic Majesty's Government.]

153

Printed for the War Cabinet. December 1918. 155

SECRET.

E.C. 38th Minutes.

6

WAR CABINET.

EASTERN COMMITTEE.

Minutes of a Meeting of the Eastern Committee held in Lord Curzon's Room at the Privy Council Office on Thursday, November 21, 1918, at 3·30 P.M.

Present:

The Right Hon. the EARL CURZON OF KEDLESTON, K.G., G.C.S.I., G.C.I.E.
(*in the Chair*).

The Right Hon. E. S. MONTAGU, M.P., Secretary of State for India.

Mr. J. E. SHUCKBURGH, C.B., India Office.

Lieutenant-General SIR H. V. COX, K.C.B., K.C.M.G., C.S.I., Military Secretary, India Office.

Rear-Admiral G. P. W. HOPE, C.B., Deputy First Sea Lord.

Mr. J. M. KEYNES, C.B., Treasury.

Lieutenant-Colonel T. E. LAWRENCE, C.B., D.S.O.

The Right Hon. LORD ROBERT CECIL, K.C., M.P., Assistant Secretary of State for Foreign Affairs.

SIR EYRE CROWE, K.C.B., K.C.M.G., Foreign Office.

Mr. L. OLIPHANT, C.M.G., Foreign Office.

Lieutenant-General SIR G. M. W. MACDONOGH, K.C.M.G., C.B., Adjutant-General to the Forces.

Major-General W. THWAITES, C.B., Director of Military Intelligence.

Lieutenant-Colonel L. STORR, *Secretary.*

Major the Hon. W. ORMSBY-GORE, M.P., *Assistant Secretary.*

(Right) List of people present at one of Lawrence's appearances before the Eastern Committee of the War Cabinet, chaired by the redoubtable Lord Curzon.

(Below) Lawrence and Feisal photographed during a visit to H.M.S. Orion *before the Paris Peace Conference.*

Feisal in Paris, 22 January 1919, with, behind his left shoulder, Lawrence sporting the Arab head-dress which he frequently wore at the Peace Conference; behind his right shoulder, Nuri Said, veteran of the desert war and later to be Prime Minister of Iraq; and, directly behind, the French officer Captain Pisani, who had also participated in the Arabian campaign.

Lawrence, Paris, 1919, by Augustus John. This portrait sketch was done in a two-minute sitting while Lawrence was looking out of the window of Augustus John's Paris flat. (John was an official artist at the Conference.) The first of many drawings and paintings of Lawrence by John – who called it the 'goody-goody' portrait – Lawrence was delighted with it and later selected it for inclusion in Seven Pillars. *It was also used as the frontispiece of* Revolt in the Desert.

10

POLITICAL ACTIVIST

Replying in 1923 to a letter from H. W. Bailey, who had served in the ranks in the Arabian campaign, Lawrence wrote: 'I hear occasionally from most of the officers on our show, but very seldom from any of you: when we got to Damascus I hopped off like a scalded cat and swore that I'd never go back, so couldn't get any addresses.'

'I hopped off like a scalded cat': it is a distinctly less grand way of describing his abrupt departure from Damascus than that given in *Seven Pillars*, but perhaps a not invalid one, for after his exchange with Allenby at the Victoria Hotel the only course of action was to collect his letters of introduction from his chief and return home. His work in the field was now plainly over and what further role there might be for him to play would be a political one and in Europe. Briefly stopping in Cairo on his way back to England he wrote to Major Scott, Commandant at Akaba: 'I'm off, out of Egypt. This old war is closing, and my use is gone. I'm afraid you will be delayed a long time, cleaning up all the messes and oddments we have left behind us. . . . My regards to the Staff – and my very best thanks to you and them. We were an odd little set, and we have, I expect, changed history in the near East. I wonder how the Powers will let the Arabs get on.'

He had begun October in the dust and noise of liberated Damascus; before the month was out he found himself in a milieu which could scarcely have been more contrasting – a meeting of the Eastern Committee of the British War Cabinet in Lord Curzon's room in the Privy Council Office, London. Among those present, as well as Lord Curzon himself, in the Chair, were General Smuts, Lord Robert Cecil (Assistant Foreign Secretary), Edwin Montagu (Secretary of State for India), Sir Mark Sykes (co-creator of the Sykes-Picot Agreement), the

The Colonel who appeared before the Cabinet: Lawrence in the uniform of a
British Army Lieutenant-Colonel.

Adjutant-General for the Forces, the Director of Military Intelligence and two senior officials of the India Office. Lawrence's reputation had gone before him and the men around the table knew the calibre of the young officer they had asked to address them, as the minutes of the meeting of 29 October 1918 amply confirm:

> The Chairman, in welcoming Colonel Lawrence to the Committee, stated that he and every member of His Majesty's Government had for some time past watched with interest and admiration the great work which Colonel Lawrence had been doing in Arabia, and felt proud that an officer had done so much to promote the successful progress of the British and Arab arms. He understood that as Colonel Lawrence had accompanied Emir Feisal on his recent entry into Damascus, he could give information regarding the views that were entertained by the Arab chiefs concerning the settlement of the conquered territories and Franco-Arab relations in particular.
>
> Colonel Lawrence stated that he had left Emir Feisal in possession of Damascus on the 4th October. Feisal was honest and straightforward, and a man of considerable capacity. He was extremely pro-British, and had always worked and would always work in the closest co-operation with General Allenby, for whom he had a genuine admiration. . . .

Lawrence did not merely report to the Committee but got straight to the point and proposed his own political solution, which gave high place to the sons of King Hussein:

> Colonel Lawrence's own idea was the establishment of Abdulla as ruler of Baghdad and Lower Mesopotamia, Zeid in a similar position in Upper Mesopotamia, with Feisal in Syria.

He was fully aware of France's interests – indeed he had met M. Picot, co-deviser of the Sykes-Picot agreement, in Paris on his return journey and had been left in no doubt as to her continuing ambitions – but the scenario he outlined gave her a strictly limited presence. He had plainly decided that there was nothing to be lost, and perhaps much to be gained, in putting forthright views directly and unequivocally to this group of influential men. He appeared before them several times, it being acknowledged by Curzon and his colleagues – an important fact in view of a later tendency to assume that his pro-Arabism was merely a front behind which he was working for British imperial ends – that he was speaking for the Arabs with whom he had fought and with whom he had now come to be identified. He was in fact doing precisely what Allenby had expected and indeed had virtually mandated him to do. 'He is a man with a remarkable career and of great ability', recorded a cabinet minute of 27

November 1918, 'and he represented to us what we may call the extreme Arab point of view, the kind of thing that Faisal would have said if he had been at our table that afternoon.'

That the French would not respond happily to his views could be taken for granted, but he was also to find himself immediately unpopular with the India Office, which still saw Mesopotamia as within its own area of interest and wanted no meddlesome ideas from Lawrence, however great his current reputation. On 20 November 1918 the India Office produced a long, powerfully worded document about the coming peace negotiations in regard to the Middle East which *inter alia* determinedly set out to discredit Lawrence's proposals. The India Office lobby had its own solutions in preparation and already had a nominee for the throne of Iraq in the person of the Naquib of Baghdad, 'but at the eleventh hour Lieutenant-Colonel Lawrence has come home with a proposal to put one of the sons of King Husain in as King of Iraq, and another as King of Northern Mesopotamia . . . [W]ithout in the least wishing to depreciate Colonel Lawrence's achievements and his undoubted genius, it must be said about him that he does not at all represent – and would not, I think, claim to represent – the local views of Northern Mesopotamia and Iraq. . . . It is submitted, therefore, that Colonel Lawrence's scheme has nothing to commend it so far as Mesopotamia and Iraq are concerned, convenient as it may be as a means of providing for the embarrassing ambitions of King Husain's other two sons, when Ali has been installed at Mecca and Feisal at Damascus.'

Meanwhile the question had arisen as to who should speak for King Hussein at the Peace Conference which was shortly to take place in Paris. The inevitable intermediary assigned to resolve this matter was Colonel Lawrence, who as early as 8 November, with Foreign Office approval, had cabled to King Hussein: 'I trust you will send Feisal, as he has gained a personal reputation in Europe through his splendid victories, and this will make his success the easier.'

So it was decided and Lawrence was commissioned to meet Feisal in due course at Marseilles. Before this could happen, however, the matter had to be cleared with the French. There ensued a prolonged argument between the British and French about the precise nature of Feisal's role, with the French claiming that it was inadmissible that Feisal should be accepted as a delegate of King Hussein and some 'hypothetical Arab kingdom', and stating that they would consider him 'only as a distinguished visitor'. Feisal sailed from Beirut, in H.M.S. *Gloucester*, with the matter unresolved, and the Foreign Office gave Lawrence, who flew to Paris for a full briefing at the British Embassy before going down to Marseilles, the discretion to inform Feisal of the situation 'in such a way as he may consider best in the circumstances'. Lawrence's task was made no easier by the fact that it brought him once again in contact with his old rival Colonel Brémond, who met him and Feisal at Lyons. In the event the

French treated Feisal cordially enough and gave him a conducted tour around France which included a visit to the Western Front. Lawrence, however, returned to England; as he wrote some years later to Liddell Hart, 'a foreign hanger-on was out of place', but the suggestion that he should go was not his own but that of his former Allies, 'some coldness' between whom and Lawrence was noted by his colleague of the Arab war, Nuri Said, now accompanying Feisal and beginning the political career which would eventually make him a Prime Minister of Iraq.

At about the same time as these events, on 26, 27 and 28 November, *The Times* published three anonymous articles about the Arab war by 'A Correspondent who was in close touch with the Arabs throughout their campaign against the Turks after the revolt of the Sherif of Mecca'. The correspondent was Lawrence. These first examples of his political journalism – there would be numerous others over the next few years – presented an interpretation of the 'Arab Epic' (head title of two of the three articles) expressly designed to put the Arabs' military achievement, and particularly the contribution of Feisal, in a highly favourable light. In doing so he minimized his own role in a way which he would not repeat in *Seven Pillars*, but then that work was an account for himself and his friends, whereas the articles in *The Times* were political weapons in a public campaign. Almost inevitably, they too, like his presentation to Curzon's committee, drew the wrath of those professionally concerned with the post-war solution of the problems of Mesopotamia. A memorandum of the time from Baghdad to the Secretary of State for India comments on a Reuters report of 27 November referring to the articles and states that this and other similar communiqués will not be republished since 'at this juncture [they] do nothing but harm. Political arguments based on past glories of decayed nations may go down with the British public but they only serve to excite distrust and misapprehension here among sober men: and swell the heads of the fatal theorists of Baghdad.'

Clearly Lawrence was offending powerful opponents: but in the end, if with significant variations and after numerous setbacks, he got his way, with a son of King Hussein of Mecca on a throne in Iraq (i.e. Mesopotamia) and another son firmly rooted in Transjordan – the country now known as the Kingdom of Jordan, where a great-grandson of the old king still reigns. The French, however, as they were always determined to do, acquired Syria.

But that was not until some time later. For the moment there were more immediate tasks to be attended to if he were to make the best possible preparations for the coming peace conference. When Feisal at last arrived in England on 9 December, Lawrence, who had met him in Boulogne and subsequently scarcely left him throughout his stay, set about arranging a number of important meetings; for example, with King George V, and with the Zionist leader, Chaim

Weizmann. Lawrence had met the King some weeks earlier on 30 October, when at a private audience, arranged on the strength of Allenby's introduction, he had refused to accept his wartime decorations – the C.B. and the D.S.O. – on the grounds that he had pledged his word to the Arabs and that the British Government was about to let them down.[1] Now in improved circumstances he met the King again, shoulder to shoulder with Feisal, whom the British were supporting against the French as a legitimate representative of the Arab cause. As if to underline his own unchanged commitment to Arab aspirations he wore an Arab head-dress. Feisal and Weizmann had met before through Lawrence as intermediator in the desert near Amman in 1918; their second discussion in London seemed to confirm the feeling of goodwill and mutual tolerance which had emerged at their previous encounter. Lawrence even got them to sign an agreement, dated 3 January 1919, in which they stated that they would act 'in accord and harmony' at the Peace Conference. But Feisal added his own codicil that he 'would not be bound by a single word of the Agreement' if the British did not live up to their promises to give the Arabs their independence.

Two weeks later, on 18 January 1919, the Peace Conference began.

Writing to the Australian novelist Frederic Manning in 1930, Lawrence began a chronology of his recent life as follows:

> 1914–1918 : the War
> 1919   : Peace Conference: misery

In 1932 he wrote to Harley Granville-Barker, then living in the French capital: 'Paris is pleasant, you say. My largest experience of it was in 1919, during the Peace Conference. So I shall not ever think of it as pleasant.'

Yet though he looked back on his months in the role of diplomat and would-be peacemaker without enjoyment, the fact is that, in a sense, Paris enjoyed him. The distinguished Arabist and traveller Gertrude Bell, a friend from Carchemish days, called him the conference's 'most picturesque figure', while an American history professor on leave in Paris from Columbia University, James T. Shotwell, wrote of him in his diary as 'the twenty-eight year old conqueror of Damascus [he was in fact thirty] with his boyish face and almost constant smile – the most winning figure, so every one says, at the whole Peace Conference'.

---

1 Lawrence's refusal of his decorations earned him some notoriety (particularly since it was widely but incorrectly assumed that he had snubbed the King in public) but it also produced results: e.g. for Churchill it 'opened my eyes to the passions which were seething in Arab bosoms. I called for reports and pondered them.' Churchill was to call on Lawrence when he tackled the Middle Eastern problem in 1921: see later in this chapter.

Feisal's princely presence inevitably drew attention and Lawrence frequently wore an Arab head-dress with his Colonel's khaki, so that the two men together could hardly be ignored. What was also notable was the strength of their relationship; the friendship struck up in the desert had plainly survived the switch from war to peace and from the East to Europe. 'The two men were obviously fond of each other,' Shotwell commented. 'I have seldom seen such mutual affection between grown men as in this instance. Lawrence would catch the drift of Feisal's humor and pass the joke along to us while Feisal was exploding with his idea; but all the same it was funny to see how Feisal spoke with the oratorical feeling of the South and Lawrence translated in the lowest and quietest of English voices, in very simple and direct phrases, with only here and there a touch of Oriental poetry breaking through.'

Something of the flavour of his time in Paris comes across in the one letter he wrote home during 1919. It is dated 30 January and written on Hotel Majestic notepaper.

> I got your letter yesterday, and will answer it this morning, while waiting up here for breakfast. I'm living at the Continental, which is half an hour's walk from the Majestic and Astoria, the British quarters, and this morning I found a taxi, which is a rare thing. In consequence I have ten unexpected minutes.
>
> About work – it is going on well. I have seen 10 American newspaper men, and given them all interviews, which went a long way. Also President Wilson, and the other people who have influence. The affair is nearly over, I suspect. Another fortnight, perhaps.
>
> Everybody seems to be here, and of course it is a busy time. I have had, personally, one meal in my hotel since I got to Paris! That was with Newcombe, who turned up unexpectedly.
>
> Bliss, of the Beyrout College is here, and proving a very valuable assistant of the Arab cause. Tell Arnie I haven't seen a bookshop yet. I cannot come to England to meet Bob, but if he came to Paris could see him. I'm always in my room (98, at the Continental) before 10 a.m. (unless out at breakfast as today) and after 11.30 p.m.

His reference to American newspapermen and to the American President, Woodrow Wilson, is significant (Bliss of the Beyrout College was also an American), for he entertained for a time the hope that the United States, in his view a potentially more benign overlord than the French, might assume responsibility for the administration of Syria. But this prospect faded in the face of the determination of the French to have their way. They wanted Syria as a compensation for their sacrifice in the war and they resented any attempt by Britain or the United States to prevent their attaining this end. Meanwhile Britain's own bargaining position was weakened by the fact that she was practising the kind of direct rule in Mesopotamia which France aspired to establish in Syria. Throughout 1919 Lloyd George retreated steadily before the demands of the French premier Clemenceau. Woodrow Wilson at one point successfully urged the setting up of an international commission to find out the wishes of the inhabitants, but in the event the commission which went out was purely American and its report was ignored.

In such a context Feisal and Lawrence, though they added colour and interest to the Conference scene, got little out of the Conference discussions. Their supreme moment came on 6 February 1919, when they presented the Arabs' case to the leaders of the Allied governments sitting as what was known as the Council of Ten. The two men arrived with their prepared speeches, the text of which was basically Lawrence's; Feisal to speak in Arabic, Lawrence in English. The French provided a Moroccan interpreter to check that the two speeches were identical. What followed was an occasion which, while it did little good for the Arab cause, certainly enhanced the reputation of Feisal's talented British spokesman. A witness of the scene was the future distinguished historian Arnold Toynbee:

> When the moment arrived, Feisal recited Lawrence's speech in Arabic and Lawrence followed him with a recitation of it in English, but then there was a hitch. Clemenceau understood English and also spoke it . . . but the Italians were as ignorant of English as the Ten were of Arabic. The only foreign language that the Italians understood was French. President Wilson then made a suggestion. 'Colonel Lawrence,' he said, 'could you put the Amir Faysal's statement into French now for us?' After a moment Lawrence started off and did it; and when he came to the end of this unprepared piece of translation the Ten clapped. What had happened was amazing. Lawrence's spell had made the Ten forget, for a moment, who they were and what they were supposed to be doing. They had started the session as conscious arbiters of the destinies of mankind; they were ending it as captive audience of a minor suppliant's interpreter.

It is an appealing story, but Toynbee's accurate description of Feisal as a 'minor suppliant' indicates how vulnerable his position was. In April 1919 Feisal left France for Syria – where he still held a precarious rule; he was not ousted by the French until 1920 – with the situation still unresolved but becoming steadily more favourable to the French. Meanwhile earlier that month a sudden illness in the family had brought Lawrence hurrying home to Oxford. His father had fallen victim to the epidemic of influenza then widespread in Europe and Asia. By the time he reached Oxford pneumonia had set in and Sir Thomas Chapman,

Bt, alias Mr T. R. Lawrence of Polstead Road, was dead. It was the end of the
Chapman line, there being no legitimate male heir.

In May 1919 Lawrence decided to return to the Middle East, his intention
being to go to Cairo, visit the Arab Bureau and collect his wartime reports and
other useful material. (Perhaps not surprisingly it was immediately assumed in
some quarters both in Paris and London that his motives were political and that
he was intending some intervention on behalf of the Arab cause.) He chose to
go by air, taking advantage of the fact that a squadron of Handley-Page bombers
was about to undertake an experimental flight to Egypt. The experiment was
not a success. One aircraft crashed in the south of France, with four fatalities,
and Lawrence's own aircraft crashed in Italy, both of its pilots, Lieutenants
Prince and Sprott, being killed. Lieutenant Prince had attempted to land on an
aerodrome unprepared with the necessary guiding flares, had overshot and
crashed in a quarry. Lawrence was himself injured, but not badly, and was able
in due course to resume his journey, which, after further interruptions, finally
ended in June. This experience of the dangers and delays of flight seems not
to have diminished but to have fuelled an enthusiasm for the air which never
left him and was to prove a potent influence on his later career.

He used the long hours of air travel for a purpose which had been in his
mind at least since the second half of 1917. On 2 September of that year he
had written to Colonel Wilson from Akaba:

> The Hejaz show is a quaint one, the like of which has hardly been
> on earth before, and no one not of it can appreciate how difficult it
> is to run. However, it has gone forward, and history will call it a
> success: but I hope that the difficulties it has had to contend with will
> be equally clear. All my memories of it are pleasant . . . and if ever I
> can get my book on it out, I'll try to make other people see it.

He had begun writing his book – his account of the desert war that would
emerge as *Seven Pillars of Wisdom*[1] – in Paris. Now he used the journey to Egypt
to continue, producing, he claimed later, a chapter between Paris and Lyons
the rhythm of which was unlike the rest: 'I liken it to the munch, munch, munch
of the synchronized Rolls-Royce engines!' The labour of drafting and redrafting
Seven Pillars was to become a Herculean one and he would not be rid of it and
its associated problems until 1926. Meanwhile 1919 was to witness another
dramatic twist to his story. Well-known in establishment circles (so that even
his opponents in the India Office could refer while attacking him to his

---

1 Before the war, Lawrence had begun a book about Eastern cities to which he gave this title,
adapted from *Proverbs* 9:1, 'Wisdom hath builded a house; she hath hewn out her seven pillars.'
He named his new book in memory of the earlier one, which he destroyed in 1914.

At Foggia Aerodrome, Italy, during the prolonged flight to Egypt, 1919: the photograph was taken during the resumed flight, subsequent to the accident.

'undoubted genius') he was not known to the public. This was about to be remedied by the remarkable American who had first met Lawrence in Jerusalem in early 1918, and had subsequently been received at Feisal's headquarters in the desert, Lowell Thomas.

In the event, the material Thomas and his cameraman Harry Chase had acquired during their visit to the Middle East was not used (in line with the original intention) to inspire America to support Woodrow Wilson's war, but to glamorize the recent war in time of peace. Thomas devised a popular form of entertainment, which used film, photographs, music and a dramatic style of narration – Thomas himself was the presenter – to tell a number of stories which he had brought back from his visit to Europe and the Middle East. When he first booked the Century Theatre New York in March 1919 he intended to vary his subjects, but, as he later told Professor Mack, the New Yorkers stayed away when the programme was about the Western Front but came in busloads when he featured the more picturesque Arab and Palestinian campaigns. Soon he moved to Madison Square Gardens, where he was seen by a British impresario, Percy Burton, who offered to mount the show in London. Thomas agreed provided Burton could promise either Covent Garden or the Theatre Royal Drury Lane. Burton accepted the terms and on 14 August 1919 Thomas opened at Covent Garden. The original title of his 'illustrated travelogue' was *With Allenby in Palestine*, but the focus of interest soon, though not immediately, shifted from the General in red tabs to the Colonel in Arab clothes. Indeed, some of the earliest reports made no mention of Lawrence at all, but gradually details about him and photographs of him began to appear. *The Sphere*, for example, publishing a little over a week after Thomas's first night, while heading its account *WITH GENERAL ALLENBY at Covent Garden Theatre*, subtitled it *A Remarkable Film Lecture Telling the Story of Colonel Thomas Lawrence, the Leader of the Arab Army*; and the photographs it published were of Lawrence, not Allenby.

Thomas had planned to run for two weeks; instead he stayed for six months. The show moved from Covent Garden to the Royal Albert Hall. In 1920 it was given the accolade of a Royal Command performance during a season at the Queen's Hall. Thomas subsequently took it to Australia, New Zealand and even India; then back home in America he presented it in Washington and Philadelphia.[1]

Allenby apparently went just once to see Lowell Thomas's show, and was given a standing ovation. Thomas claimed that Lawrence went several times, invariably slipping in alone and hurrying away if recognized. Thomas's view was

---

1 Professor Mack believes that it had a powerful impact on the American film industry and on audience taste. 'The wave of popularity in the United States for exotic sun-and-sand commercial films of "Arabia", especially those featuring the Italian-born American actor Rudolph Valentino (*The Sheikh*, 1921; *The Son of the Sheikh*, 1926), may well have been inspired by Lowell Thomas's reportage of the Palestinian campaigns and the deeds of Lawrence, whom he had filmed in flowing Arab costume.'

FROM LOWELL THOMAS'S 'ILLUSTRATED TRAVELOGUE'

(Above) Lowell Thomas and Lawrence, photographed in the Desert, 1918.

(Below) Still frame from the film taken by cameraman Harry Chase when Thomas (centre) was introduced by Lawrence (right) to the Emir Feisal.

that Lawrence 'enjoyed it all, enjoyed the glamour and the honour. But he wanted to remain on the sidelines, he would run miles to avoid the spotlight.' Lawrence now began his love-hate relationship with celebrity which was to be with him for the rest of his life. As he wrote to Sir Evelyn Wrench in his last weeks in 1935: 'to have news value is to have a tin can tied to one's tail'. It was an encumbrance that he generally loathed, but did not entirely want to be rid of. As his friend Sir Ronald Storrs put it: 'He hated public attention . . . but was not disappointed when, as nearly always, his incognito broke down.' Lowell Thomas quoted a description of him that has stuck; in his contribution to *Lawrence by His Friends* he referred to 'an old Turkish saying which admirably illustrates the character of T.E. and which, being interpreted, signifies: "He had a genius for backing into the limelight".'

But Thomas cannot be absolved from shackling on Lawrence some of the more absurd legends that gathered around the man who from now onward would be known as Lawrence of Arabia. In November 1919 the English-Speaking Union gave a complimentary luncheon to Thomas at the Criterion Restaurant, London, 'as a mark of appreciation of his work for the promotion of Anglo-American friendship and his generous appreciation of the British campaign in Palestine in his lecture "With Allenby in Palestine".' Thus *The Times* of 5 November, which reported among other things this jewel from Thomas's speech:

> On one occasion Lawrence blew up a Turkish train. He sat on a rock, and when the engine reached the mine, Lawrence touched an electric button and off went the engine. (Laughter) A number of Turkish soldiers who were about attempted to capture Lawrence, but he sat still until they were a few yards from him, then whipped out his Colt revolver, and shot six of them in turn, after which he jumped on his camel and went off across the country. (Cheers)

To escape from the excesses of rising adulation Lawrence needed a bolt-hole and fortunately his old university of Oxford was able to provide one, thanks to Geoffrey Dawson, who as editor of *The Times* had sponsored his first foray into political journalism in November 1918. Dawson was a Fellow of All Souls College, a foundation which consists of senior members of the university only and lays no requirement on its staff to lecture or conduct students' tutorials. His suggestion that Lawrence should be elected a Fellow was taken up in November 1919, the conditions being that during his tenure of two years' duration he should prosecute 'researches into the antiquities and ethnology, and the history (ancient and modern) of the Near East'. In effect, he was being offered status and support during the writing of his account of the recent Middle Eastern war. On the surface no offer could have been more appropriate or congenial, but he found that he wrote less well and intensively at All Souls than in an upper room of a house in Barton Street, Westminster, which belonged to his friend the architect Herbert Baker. Here he could work entirely to his own time-table, without any impinging collegiate ritual. At All Souls he seems to have spent much of his time in unproductive silence, varying this with bizarre undergraduate-type pranks – such as flying the Hejaz flag from the college flagstaff or ringing the bell which he had acquired during the attack in April 1918 on Tel Shahm station through the window of his room; activities more appropriate to an eighteen-year-old freshman than to an ex-Colonel in his thirties. Meanwhile he had taken steps to realize the dream he had conceived years before of founding a printing press to produce exquisite books, buying (on the day on which he officially became a civilian, 1 September 1919) a piece of land for the purpose at Pole Hill near Chingford, Essex. His friend of Jesus days, Vyvyan Richards, was to collaborate in this enterprise, but in the end it came to nothing and eventually the land was sold.

His chronology for Frederic Manning of his life from 1914 onwards (the beginning of which was quoted earlier in this chapter) continued as follows:

1920–1921 (Aug) : Dog fight in London with the British Government

1922 : Eighteen months work with Winston Churchill settling the Middle East after my lights

His dates are hardly correct in that his 'dog-fight' could be said to have begun in 1919 and his work with Churchill really began in 1921. But this thumbnail description effectively defines the nature of his political activities during his last years in public life. As Britain and France moved towards their inevitable accommodation and the hopes that Lawrence and others had entertained for an equitable settlement in the Middle East duly faded, Lawrence mounted a personal press campaign through letters to *The Times* and articles in other national journals intended to annoy and discomfort the political establishment and remind the general reader of the nation's obligation to its Arab co-belligerents. In April 1920 the San Remo Conference allotted the mandates of Syria and Lebanon to France and of Palestine and Mesopotamia to Britain. These decisions, according to the distinguished Middle East historian Elizabeth Monroe, 'accorded neither with the wishes of the inhabitants nor with the unqualified end-of-war undertakings about freedom of choice. They were pieces of unabashed self interest, suggesting to many onlookers that all talk of liberating small nations from oppression was so much cant.' For the French and British the word 'mandate' eased the conscience; it had almost a worthy, disinterested

LAWRENCE AT ALL SOULS COLLEGE, OXFORD

(Right) Almost certainly written by Charles Graves, editor of Isis *and younger brother of Robert Graves, who was much annoyed at the bantering tone of the profile. Robert Graves wrote to another brother, John, that he now spent 'most of [his] time at Oxford with Col. Lawrence, who smashed the Turks in Arabia & Palestine: he is at All Souls & a great man on poetry, pictures, music & everything else in the world'.*

The front quadrangle at All Souls. In recommending him to the College, Geoffrey Dawson, then Editor of The Times, *had written to the Warden: 'He is so big a man, so modest, and so eminently fitted to adorn our society, that I do hope we shall make an effort to elect him.'*
(Inset) Lawrence's visiting card, representing a conscious shift towards anonymity.

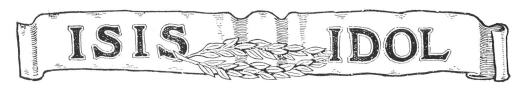

Mr. T. E. LAWRENCE (Arabia and All Souls).

I HAD come to interview the great man fully primed with warnings of what not to say and do—I must not address him as Colonel, I had been told, because that would remind him that he never enjoyed higher pay than that of Captain, though commanding an Eastern Army of some forty thousand effectives for over two years; I must not offer him dates, or ask him what the ruins of Petra look like by moonlight. He is not fond of dates, and never can remember the correct romantic answer to the Petra conundrum. There was a lot more advice of the same nature, but it was all quite useless, because when I arrived I found my Idol sound asleep in bed, at eleven-thirty in the morning. A college scout informed me that this is no sign of sloth; our Idol is not one of the race of man celebrated in the psalm: he does not rise at dawn and go about his long labour until the evening; he is, on the contrary, one with the lions roaring in the night season. When the sun ariseth he getteth him away and layeth him down in his den.

Our Idol, through the propaganda of a certain fancifully-minded popular lecturer, has long ago become a legend throughout the semi-civilized world and in the United States of America; the legend grows every hour, and if he is not pinned down historically pretty soon, he may disappear altogether as a mere Prester John, or a primitive solar myth; a terrible fate for a healthy young man of thirty-one. Hasten, then, masons, brassworkers and engravers, and set up a simple tablet on the wall of No. 2 Polstead Road, North Oxford; what the inscription is to be I cannot tell you. Our Idol wasn't born there, but he lived there for several years, and that is the best you can hope to record. His nationality is problematic, but you may safely put it down as Northern and Western European. What his professional designation should be, I dare not consider. Whether he will go down to posterity as Patron of Contemporary Art, Prince of the Hedjaz, Dynamiter, Historian, Journeyman Printer, Aviator, The Man who Captured Damascus in a Limousine, The World's Authority on Crusaders' Knees, or Fellow of All Souls' College, Oxford, our Idol has not yet decided himself.

But hasten with the tablet, stick up something somewhere before it is too late! Fortunately 'for the world's peace, our Idol is 'standing easy' for the moment, and breaking no new ground, no laws, no heads, and no windows. He has discarded Eastern dress and often wears trousers, he writes chatty letters to the *Times* with the regularity of an old clubman, and has even been known to dine in college, and actually to knock at the gates after dark instead of smashing the lock with his foot.

The price put on his head by the enemy in the 'Late-Great' enlarges with each telling in the popular press: but I understand it was somewhere about twenty million Imperial marks, three hundred million Turkish piastres, forty thousand English pounds, sterling, or forty-three dollars fourteen cents in American currency. Our Idol is hail-fellow-well-met with most of the crowned heads of Europe; to a most important one of these who was complaining, 'Dear me (or *us*), five new Republics to-day!' he replied, 'Never mind, your Majesty, I have just made two new Kings in the East myself.'

I left our Idol sleeping, as I thought, and tiptoed away, but something must have disturbed him, for he yawned, scratched his head, and jumped out of bed; looking round the corner of the door I was relieved to see that, however brazen might be the legs beneath those pyjamas, his feet were at anyrate not of clay.

ring. But, writes Elizabeth Monroe, 'the word struck dismay into all Arab hearts'. 'Mandate' meant that Feisal, having been crowned in Damascus in March 1920, was ejected from his throne in July. 'Mandate' meant the firm suppression of a rebellion in Mesopotamia between the summer of 1920 and the spring of 1921 at the cost of hundreds of British dead and missing and £50 million in money. Lawrence pulled no punches in his scathing attacks. From *The Times*, 23 July 1920:

> The Arabs rebelled against the Turks during the war not because the Turk Government was notably bad, but because they wanted their independence. They did not risk their lives in battle to change masters, to become British subjects or French citizens, but to win a show of their own.

From the *Sunday Times*, 22 August 1920:

> How long will we permit millions of pounds, thousands of imperial troops and tens of thousands of Arabs to be sacrificed on behalf of a colonial form of administration which can benefit nobody but its administrators?

His political agitation had notable supporters. In October 1919 Rudyard Kipling, whom he had met earlier that year, wrote to him that 'we are all sitting in the middle of wrecked hopes and broken dreams', but he nevertheless urged Lawrence to continue his work. 'You will not go out of the game – except for the necessary minute to step aside and vomit. You are young, and the bulk of the men in charge are "old, cold and of intolerable entrails" and a lot of 'em will be dropping out soon.'

Winston Churchill was definitely not one of Kipling's old, cold and intolerable men, and it was he who brought Lawrence back into positive political work, when in 1921, as Colonial Secretary, he made a determined effort to put through a new settlement of the Middle East. Lawrence's press 'bombardment', as Miss Monroe describes it, 'added to the force of circumstances, had shaken the cabinet'. Now the controversial mandates were transferred from the Foreign to the Colonial Office and Churchill was given the opportunity to grasp the Middle Eastern nettle. He got together a small team of experts and resolved to add Lawrence to their number, if he could be persuaded. As Churchill wrote in *Great Contemporaries*.[1]

> They all knew him well, and several had served with or under him in the field. When I broached this project to them, they were frankly aghast – 'What! wilt thou bridle the wild ass of the desert?' Such was

[1] The same essay is printed with minor variations in *T. E. Lawrence by His Friends*.

the attitude, dictated by no small jealousy or undervaluing of Lawrence's qualities, but from a sincere conviction that he could never work at the routine of a public office.

However, I persisted. An important post was offered to Lawrence, and to the surprise of most people, though not altogether to mine, he accepted at once.

Lawrence's own version suggests his persuasion took a little longer. He wrote to Robert Graves that Churchill

in his third attempt to get me to join his new Middle Eastern Department used arguments which I could not resist.

So I'm a Government servant from yesterday. . . .

They let me fix my own terms: so I said a temporary billet and £1000.

So in March 1921 Lawrence returned to the Middle East and at a conference in Cairo – and after – assisted Churchill in establishing a new dispensation which put Feisal on the throne of Iraq (i.e. Mesopotamia), and entrusted the Emir Abdulla with the government of Transjordania. It brought back the British troops from Iraq and gave the responsibility of the defence of that country to the R.A.F. Lawrence proved a valued and effective member of Churchill's team. 'His patience and readiness to work with others,' Churchill later wrote, 'amazed those who knew him best. Tremendous confabulations must have taken place among these experts and tensions at times must have been extreme. But so far as I was concerned, I received almost united advice from two or three of the very best men it has ever been my fortune to work with.'

Thus Churchill's accolade. Elizabeth Monroe, commenting from the standpoint of an impartial historian and after the attacks on Lawrence's reputation by Richard Aldington and others, wrote: 'Photographs of Churchill's Cairo conference of 1921 are good evidence of the galaxy of talent that evolved and supported [its] decisions. Lawrence was not their only begetter, but he used his credit and renown to set the ball rolling in a way that paid dividends both to Britain and the Arabs – perhaps the greatest of the several great services he performed in the Middle East.'

He did, however, have one notable failure. He was sent to Jidda to attempt to persuade King Hussein to accept the settlement arrived at in Cairo. However much Lawrence argued, appealed, threatened, bullied, the old sherif would not do so. Lawrence later described him, when writing to Liddell Hart, as a 'tragic figure, in his way: brave, obstinate, hopelessly out-of-date: exasperating'. His treatment of Hussein at this time is held against him by Arab historians, who see him as high-handedly attempting to force the founding father of the Arab Revolt to put his signature to an agreement which in his, Hussein's, view

Cairo 1921: *Conference outing to the Pyramids. Centre left in front of the Sphinx, Winston Churchill, Gertrude Bell, T.E. Lawrence.*

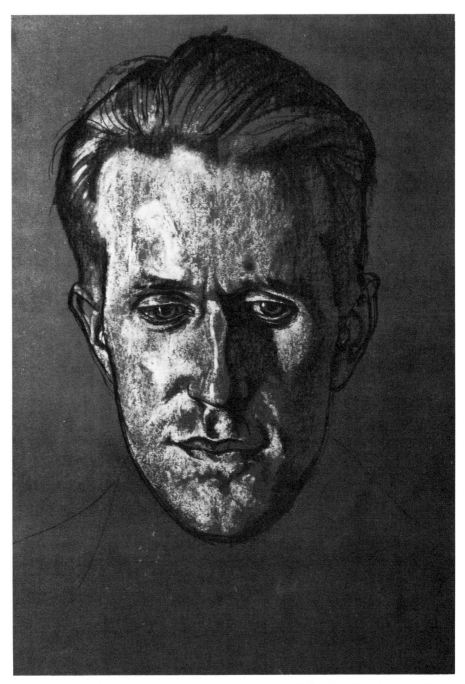

Lawrence, drawn by Kennington, Cairo, 1921. Lawrence called it 'the Cheshire Cat'. 'If one had tickled it, it would have grinned.' But he also said that it was 'too obviously the spider in the web of its own spinning'.

betrayed the strong simple promises of Arab independence which had persuaded him to raise the flag of rebellion in 1916, and which implied acceptance of the basic concept of the Balfour Declaration – the open sesame to the establishment of a Jewish national home in Palestine.

Compared with the immediate post-war situation Churchill's settlement was a considerable improvement; it at least had two of Hussein's sons in notable positions of power – and indeed it was to endure more or less intact until after the Second World War. Lawrence decided that, if not perfect, it was good enough for him. He was later to look back on his work at the Colonial Office as his best achievement. When Lionel Curtis wrote to him in India in 1927 to ask him to provide details for an entry in *Who's Who?*, Lawrence replied:

> I'd be grateful if you'd make it quite clear that in Winston's 1922 settlement of the Middle East the Arabs obtained all that in my opinion they had been promised by Great Britain, in any sphere in which we were free to act: and that my retirement from politics upon that to me happy event was necessarily final and absolute.

What happened to King Hussein and his sons, the bright hopes of the Revolt of 1916? Hussein abdicated in 1924 in favour of Ali, and after some years of exile in Cyprus was allowed to join Abdulla in Amman, where he died in 1931. Feisal reigned in Iraq until his death in 1933, but his dynasty was short-lived, being extinguished in a bloody revolutionary coup in 1958, in the course of which both his grandson Feisal II and Lawrence's old comrade-in-arms Nuri Said were murdered. Ali abdicated in 1925 and died in exile in Baghdad in 1935. Abdulla, having been Emir of Transjordania since 1921, became King of Jordan in 1946 but was assassinated in the Aqsa Mosque, Jerusalem, in 1948 by an Arab fanatic; after a brief tenure his own son Tallal was found unfit to rule and was succeeded in 1952 by King Hussein, who still reigns, the longest serving head of any country in the Middle East. Zeid lived for many years in London where he died in 1961.

Lawrence concluded his chronology in his letter to Manning of May 1930 as follows:

1922 (Aug)–1930 : R.A.F.

He was not strictly correct in that for some two and a half of those eight years he was not a member of the R.A.F.; but it was a forgivable shorthand in that throughout that period and beyond he never wavered from the conviction, amazing and disturbing to his many friends, that only in the ranks of the Royal Air Force could he find home, peace of mind, and personal fulfilment.

Feeling
the Turks

AS I walked northward towards the fighting, Abdulla met me, on his way to Zeid with news. He had finished his ammunition, lost five men from shell-fire, and had one automatic gun destroyed. Two guns, he thought the Turks had. His idea was to get up Zeid with all his men and fight: so nothing remained for me to add to his message; and there was no subtlety in leaving alone my happy masters to cross and dot their own right decision.

He gave me leisure in which to study the coming battlefield. The tiny plain was about two miles across, bounded by low green ridges, and roughly triangular, with my reserve ridge as base. Through it ran the road to Kerak, dipping into the Hesa valley. The Turks were fighting their way up this road. Abdulla's charge had taken the western or left-hand ridge, which was now our firing-line.

Shells were falling in the plain as I walked across it, with harsh stalks of wormwood stabbing into my wounded feet. The enemy fuzing was too long, so that the shells grazed the ridge and burst away behind. One fell near me, and I learned its calibre from the hot cap. As I went they began to shorten range, and by the time I got to the ridge it was being freely sprinkled with shrapnel. Obviously the Turks had got observation somehow, and looking round I saw them climbing along the eastern side beyond the gap of the Kerak road. They would soon outflank us at our end of the western ridge.

460

An example of Lawrence's highly individual concept of book production: each page should if possible have its own illuminated initial letter and end with a completed sentence. He frequently adapted the text to achieve this. The initial letters were specially designed. The drawing is by one of his favourite artists William Roberts. The text is that of Chapter LXXVI in modern popular editions.

CHAPTER LXXXVII

"US" proved to be about sixty men, clustered behind A fine the ridge in two bunches, one near the bottom, one stand by the top. The lower was made up of peasants, on foot, blown, miserable, and yet the only warm things I had seen that day. They said their ammunition was finished, and it was all over. I assured them it was just beginning and pointed to my populous reserve ridge, saying that all arms were there in support. I told them to hurry back, refill their belts and hold on to it for good. Meanwhile we would cover their retreat by sticking here for the few minutes yet possible.

They ran off, cheered, and I walked about among the upper group quoting how one should not quit firing from one position till ready to fire from the next. In command was young Metaab, stripped to his skimp riding-drawers for hard work, with his black love-curls awry, his face stained and haggard. He was beating his hands together and crying hoarsely with baffled vexation, for he had meant to do so well in this, his first fight for us.

My presence at the last moment, when the Turks were breaking through, was bitter; and he got angrier when I said that I only wanted to study the landscape. He thought it flippancy, and screamed something about a Christian going into battle unarmed. I retorted with a quip from Clausewitz, about a rearguard effecting its purpose more by being than by doing: but he was past laughter, and perhaps with justice, for the little flinty bank behind which we sheltered was crackling with fire. The Turks, knowing we were there, had turned twenty machine-guns upon it. It was four feet high and fifty feet long, of bare flinty ribs, off which the bullets slapped deafeningly: while the air above so hummed or whistled with ricochets and chips that it felt like death to look over. Clearly we must leave very soon, and as I had no horse I went off first, with Metaab's promise that he would wait where he was, if he dared, for another ten minutes.

461

11

AIRCRAFTMAN, PRIVATE, AIRCRAFTMAN

To George Bernard Shaw, the fact that Colonel Lawrence – or Lurens Bey as he liked to call him – should suddenly transmute himself into a serviceman in the ranks was as absurd as if Nelson after the Battle of the Nile had insisted on being placed at the tiller of a canal barge. He thought the whole idea 'a maddening masquerade'. But Lawrence joined the R.A.F. because he wanted to do so; when not in the R.A.F. he pined to get back; when allowed to return he remained remarkably and consistently content; and he left the R.A.F. on being retired from it with very great regret. In 1927 when Lawrence was in India a columnist of the Indian *Daily Chronicle* raised the same question of the underuse of outstanding talents that had baffled George Bernard Shaw and was told in the course of an eloquent reply: 'I'm in the R.A.F. because I like it and when people offer me larger boots, and talk of my wasting my "talents" (save the mark) in the ranks, I comfort myself with the sure knowledge that there's nothing else my talented self wants to do.'

His decision to enlist in August 1922 was no sudden whim following the completion of his political work with Churchill; it was the fulfilment of a plan that had been formulating in his mind for some years. As he wrote to his friend Herbert Baker (in whose Westminster house he had compiled much of *Seven Pillars*) in 1928: 'My ambition to serve in the ranks dates – concretely – from 1919: and nebulously from early 1917, before there was an Air Force.'[1]

Present at the Cairo Conference in 1921 had been the Chief of Air Staff Sir Hugh Trenchard. Lawrence had broached the subject of his joining Trenchard's service at that time and in January 1922 he followed this initial approach with

---

1 There was a Royal Flying Corps in 1917; it became the Royal Air Force on 1 April 1918.

a direct request – adding persuasively that he saw the R.A.F. as a fit subject for a book. 'You'll wonder what I'm at. The matter is that since I was sixteen I've been writing: never satisfying myself technically but steadily getting better. My last book on Arabia is nearly good. I see the sort of subject I need in the beginning of your force . . . and the best place to see a thing is from the ground. It wouldn't "write" from the officer level.' He was thirty-three and, as he put it to Trenchard, 'not skilled in the sense you want', so he knew that he was asking a special favour. 'It's an odd request, hardly proper perhaps, but it may be one of the exceptions you make sometimes. It is asking you to use your influence to get me past the Recruiting Officer. Apologies for making it. If you say "no" I'll be more amused than hurt.'

Trenchard was to join the select group of Lawrence's 'admirations' – men of influence to whom he became devoted and who if sometimes mystified by his 'wimbling and wambling' (his own phrase in a letter to Herbert Baker) nevertheless believed in him and supported him with consistent generosity and not a little admiration on their own part. Hogarth had been the forerunner, Allenby had been the dominant figure in time of war, Churchill had assumed the role in the Colonial Office period, and now the mantle passed to Trenchard. Predictably, Lawrence got his way and when he enlisted in the R.A.F. at the Henrietta Street recruiting station, London, on 30 August 1922 he did so with official approval from the highest level and with a carefully prepared litany of answers given to him in advance. He was allowed to declare a correct birthplace, but his birthdate was to be retarded by six years to 1894, he was to describe himself as an architect's clerk (he had after all burned much midnight oil in the house of one of the most distinguished architects of the time) and to the question 'Have you ever belonged to any of the services?' he was to answer 'No'. He was to use the name John Hume Ross. Even with these preparations his enlistment went far from smoothly, partly because of a lack of plausible documentation, partly because the medical examiners, seeing the scars of his Deraa flogging on his back, refused to pass him, and his connections in Whitehall had to be invoked to resolve the matter.

He indeed found the R.A.F. a suitable subject for a book but it was decidedly not the R.A.F. rhapsody that Trenchard might have anticipated from Lawrence's letter of January 1922. Throughout his basic training at Uxbridge Lawrence wrote detailed notes at night of the experiences he had undergone during the day. Nothing was sanitized and conversations were recorded virtually verbatim, so that from the outset he knew that what he was eventually to fashion into a book under the title of *The Mint* was by any contemporary standards unpublishable. Indeed (apart from an American limited edition of 50 copies dating from 1936) it was not published for the general reader until 1955 and even then only in expurgated form, though an unexpurgated text was issued at the same time in a limited edition. The complete version, which included some minor revisions, was not published until 1973, long after his namesake's *Lady Chatterley's Lover* had blazed the trail in the matter of reproducing obscene expressions in public print. By contrast with *Seven Pillars*, the style was plain and austere ('iron' and 'rectangular' was his way of describing it), but then so was the nature of the subject, as different from that of the earlier book as Lawrence's R.A.F. blue was from the Arab robes he had worn in the desert. Writing to Robin Buxton in 1930 Lawrence called his 'bawdy book', as he dubbed it, 'a bit of a come down after the *Seven Pillars*', but some of his friends thought it the more original of his two principal works. E. M. Forster, for example, wrote to him in 1928: 'I inform you that *The Mint* is not as great a write as *The Seven Pillars*, either in colour or form; but it is more new, more startling and more heartening than *The Seven Pillars* or anything else I've read.' Certainly there can be no controversy over the precision and vividness of its documentary observation. Lawrence found the training hard and the treatment meted out to him and his fellow recruits gratuitously vicious and inhuman; his 'Uxbridge notes' faithfully reflected this, so that he could write to Mrs Charlotte Shaw in 1928, 'there never was, I fancy, such stuff put on paper before.'

It is interesting that the kind of literary works with which *The Mint* has been compared are books about people trapped in some kind of real or virtual imprisonment: Dostoevsky's *House of the Dead*, Solzhenitsyn's *One Day in the Life of Ivan Denisovich*, E. E. Cummings' *The Enormous Room*, Frederic Manning's *The Middle Parts of Fortune*.[1] Where Lawrence stands out among these writers is in the fact that his 'imprisonment' was self-imposed, but imprisonment of a kind it was, and Hogarth was not wrong in stating that Lawrence had enlisted 'in order to have the padlocks rivetted on him'. The fact is that though he believed in and admired the Royal Air Force, throughout his ten years in it he was not involved in any serious way in the development of the service or in formulating or advancing its central philosophy. He played no role parallel to that which he had played in the organization of the Middle Eastern war. Significantly, the last entry in his R.A.F. personal service records reads: 'There is little that can be said of a period devoted to self-effacement.' This is arguably unjust to the contribution he made in the 1930s to the development of fast air-sea rescue boats, but basically the R.A.F. provided, to begin with at least, not so much a creative career as an escape hatch and a sanctuary, to which he could withdraw from his public image and from the name and rank which had come increasingly to irk him. 'Please don't call me Colonel. That folly died months ago,' he had written to H. St. J. Philby back in 1919, and his letters had long

1 This point is well made by Jeremy Wilson in his Introduction to the Penguin edition of *The Mint*, first published in 1978. *The Middle Parts of Fortune* has recently been reissued (1986) under its alternative title *Her Privates We*.

contained such disclaimers, while at All Souls his visiting card had simply read 'Mr E. Lawrence', in the hope – a forlorn one – that no one would connect him with the famous Colonel of Arabia. Now he wanted to get rid of 'Lawrence' as well, and this was not only desirable but essential if he joined the ranks. The oblivion he sought would be required of him. When ten years later his old school and Jesus College friend E. F. Hall asked the reason for this 'self-banishment' into the Air Force, he replied, 'to forget and be forgotten'. There were other reasons too. He was physically and mentally exhausted and needed, as he put it to Robert Graves in a letter of November 1922, a 'brain sleep', from which he would come out 'less odd than he went in: or at least less odd in other men's eyes'. As his brother A. W. Lawrence wrote in his introduction to the first published edition of *The Mint*: 'Presumably the years of over-exertion had resulted, when the need for activity ceased, in a condition of mind which allowed only negative decisions to be taken without intolerable effort. Life in the ranks, where a decision would never be required, therefore seemed the right solution.' Lawrence himself made the same point to Herbert Baker: 'If ever there was a man squeezed right out and dry by over-experience, then it's me. I refuse always to say "ever" or "never" of myself, or of anything alive: but I don't think that I'll ever be fit for anything again.'

Different as he was in background, education, interests, experience, age and even voice from his fellow 'prisoners' he did not remain aloof from them. It might fairly be said of him that he had a talent for friendship, and he became firm friends with not a few of the men whom he met in his years in the ranks, such relationships not being discarded when he moved on to a different camp or even to a different service. Nor did their affection for him cease with his death; they remained – in some instances still remain – proud custodians of his memory. One stalwart friend and defender, Jock Chambers, who died in 1986, first met Lawrence when the latter was transferred from Uxbridge to the R.A.F. School of Photography at Farnborough in November 1922. Chambers, as hut orderly, was on duty when Lawrence arrived.

> He was a little bloke, looked rather lonely. I felt a bit sorry for him. He was tied up with all the gadgets we had like a Christmas tree. I helped him off with his equipment and shoved it on the hook; then he poured out his kitbag and I suddenly spotted a lovely book – a beautiful coloured leather book, like a squashed tomato; a beautiful thing. And when I looked at the book it was *Thus Spake Zarathustra*, by Nietzsche. I said, 'Could I have a loan of that?' He said 'Yes, certainly. Have this one as well.' I looked at the other one: Dostoevsky, *The Brothers Karamazov*. So I wrapped them up quick and shoved them in my locker. And just then all the other chaps came in the hut. I felt somehow I ought to be tough with him, I don't know why. I

The Daily Express 27 *December* 1922. *The newspaper reports that ended Aircraftman John Hume Ross's Air Force career.*

said, 'Now don't forget I'm hut orderly here. And when you scrub that bed, Shortarse, you see you do it properly. No tide marks.' He said 'All right', and he scrubbed it twice before I was satisfied. But within half an hour we'd accepted him. He had a cultured voice and he was the ex-officer type which was a bar really, but we accepted him.

Lawrence had contributed to the *Daily Express* and had exchanged letters with its editor R. D. Blumenfeld. Blumenfeld knew of Lawrence's enlistment from a letter he had written from Uxbridge in October 1922; in it he had begged Blumenfeld to 'keep this news to yourself', adding, 'No one in camp knows who I am, and I don't want them to.' In a letter of 24 November written two days after arriving at Farnborough, he again pleaded for silence. 'Please don't publish my eclipse. It will be common news one day, but the later the better for my peace in the ranks. . . . As you say it reads like cheap melodrama.'

Unfortunately Blumenfeld fell ill and in his absence from the editor's chair the *Daily Express* gave a dramatic twist to Lawrence's 'melodrama' by revealing the true identity of Aircraftman Ross in their edition of 27 December. Headlines such as '*UNCROWNED KING AS PRIVATE SOLDIER/Famous War Hero becomes a Private/SEEKING PEACE*' effectively meant that any such peace was instantly destroyed. The press came down to Farnborough to look for him. Jock Chambers was on hand when they arrived.

> I was on guard with him when the *Daily Express* man came along, and *The Times* man. In fact it was *The Times* man who said to Lawrence, who was actually standing on guard, 'Can I go in and see this bloke Lawrence?' So Lawrence said, 'I'm here to stop you.' And he just casually said to him, 'You don't happen to be him, do you?' And Lawrence said, 'Now, do I look like a soldier?' And that was all to it. This bloke just walked away.

However, the resultant furore meant the end, for the time being, of Lawrence's Air Force career. On 23 January 1923 he was discharged and found himself a civilian again. 'The R.A.F. have sacked me,' he told his literary friend Edward Garnett, 'for the crime of possessing too wide a publicity for a ranker.' But he was determined to continue his life in uniform and if the R.A.F. would not have him there was always the army. Two months after his ejection from the one service he joined the other, (thanks to the friendly offices of Sir Philip Chetwode, comrade of the war years and future Field-Marshal), becoming a Private of the Tank Corps under a new alias, T. E. Shaw. He was posted to Bovington Camp in Dorset.

He did not like the army and made no secret of it to his friends. 'Wish I could see you,' he wrote to Jock Chambers in September 1923, 'am home-sick for the R.A.F. The army is more beastly than anything else which the wit of

Lawrence as Private T.E. Shaw of the British Army Tank Corps outside his barrack-hut at Bovington, Dorset.

LETTERS FROM BOVINGTON CAMP

This sort of thing must be madness, and sometimes I wonder how far mad I am, and if a mad-house would not be my next (and merciful) stage. Merciful compared with this place, which hurts me body and soul. It's terrible to hold myself voluntarily here: and yet I want to stay here till it no longer hurts; till the burnt child no longer feels the fire. Do you think there have been many lay monks of my persuasion? One used to think that such frames of mind would have perished with the age of religion; and yet here they rise up, purely secular.

(To Lionel Curtis, 14 May 1923)

I lie in bed night after night with this cat-calling carnality seething up and down the hut, fed by streams of fresh matter from twenty lecherous mouths . . . and my mind aches with the rawness of it. . . We are all guilty alike, you know. You wouldn't exist, I wouldn't exist, without this carnality. Everything with flesh in its mixture is the achievement of a moment when the lusty thought of Hut 12 has passed to action and conceived; and isn't it true that the fault of birth rests somewhat on the child? I believe it's we who led our parents on to bear us, and it's our unborn children who make our flesh itch.

(To Lionel Curtis, 27 March 1923)

The Tanks are interesting, the company hardly tolerable, even to my stomach. There is an animal reek which keeps me awake at night with horror that mankind should be like it; because I feel that we are the unnatural, and that Hut F.12 is the truth about human-kindness. . . .

And why I enlisted? The security of it first; seven years existence guaranteed. I haven't any longer the mind to fight for sustenance. As you realize I've finished with the 'Lawrence' episode. I don't like what rumour makes of him – not the man I'd like to be! and the life of politics wearied me out, by worrying me over-much. I've not got a coarse-fibred enough nature for them; and have too many scruples and an uneasy conscience. . . .

Exit politics. . . Exit Lawrence: and there is most of my earning power gone. I haven't a trade to follow: and won't do the two or three things for which I'm qualified; hence I'm reduced to soldiering.

(To D.G. Hogarth, 13 June 1923)

LAWRENCE'S JOURNAL OF AIR FORCE LIFE

T. E. LAWRENCE

THE MINT

A day-book of the R.A.F. Depot between
August and December 1922
with later notes

by

352087 A/c ROSS

---

1 : RECRUITING OFFICE

GOD, this is awful. Hesitating for two hours up and down a filthy street, lips and hands and knees tremulously out of control, my heart pounding in fear of that little door through which I must go to join up. Try sitting a moment in the churchyard? That's caused it. The nearest lavatory, now. Oh yes, of course, under the church. What was Baker's story about the cornice?

A penny; which leaves me fifteen. Buck up, old seat-wiper: I can't tip you and I'm urgent. Won by a short head. My right shoe is burst along the welt and my trousers are growing fringes. One reason that taught me I wasn't a man of action was this routine melting of the bowels before a crisis. However, now we end it. I'm going straight up and in.

★

All smooth so far. They are gentle-spoken to us, almost sorry. Won't you walk into my parlour? Wait upstairs for medical exam? 'Righto!' This sodden pyramid of clothes upon the floor is sign of a dirtier man than me in front. My go next? Everything off? (Naked we come into the R.A.F.). Ross? 'Yes, that's me.'

Officers, two of them. . . .

'D'you smoke?'

Not much, Sir.

'Well, cut it out. See?'

Six months back, it was, my last cigarette. However, no use giving myself away.

'Nerves like a rabbit.' The scotch-voiced doctor's hard fingers go hammer, hammer, hammer over the loud box of my ribs. I must be pretty hollow.

13

Lawrence's journal of air force life – written under his first service alias, John Hume Ross.

*Lawrence as Aircraftman Shaw, in his second
R.A.F. period.*

man has made. Only of course it wasn't his wit that made it: it came suddenly from him at midnight one moonless time, when he was taken short.'

His first months at Bovington in fact produced some of the most searing letters he ever wrote.[1] The five sent to Lionel Curtis – whom he had met when they were both Fellows of All Souls – between March and June 1923, constitute a *De profundis* statement which suggest a mind almost at the end of its tether. The difference between the men he had been with in the R.A.F. and the majority of those around him in the Tank Corps depressed him deeply. 'There [i.e. in the Air Force] we were excited about our coming service.... There was a sparkle round the squad. Here every man has joined because he was down and out: and no one talks of the army or of promotion, or of trades or accomplishments. We are all here unavoidably, in a last resort, and we assume this world's failure in one-another.... We are social bed-rock, those unfit for life by competition: and each of us values the rest as cheap as he knows himself to be.' The chronicler of the obscenities of Uxbridge found himself mortified by the unbridled language of his new companions when the subject turned, as it did frequently, to sex. 'My mind aches with the rawness of it,' he wrote; and 'a filthy business all of it' was his summing up of the business of procreation, which was not commended to him by the precept and practice of his fellow members of Hut 12. That he could release himself from all this with a word in the right place only added to his mental torment. The surest way he found of temporarily anaesthetizing himself against the reality of his present condition was to escape on his newly acquired motor-cycle, the first of seven Broughs he would have over the next twelve years. 'When my mood gets too hot,' he told Curtis, 'I pull out my motor-bike and hurl it at top speed through these unfit roads for hour after hour. My nerves are jaded and gone near dead so that nothing less than voluntary danger will prick them into life. And the life they reach then is a melancholy joy at risking something worth exactly 2/9d. a day.' Others who received similar confidences were D. G. Hogarth and, from the beginning of 1924, George Bernard Shaw's wife Charlotte. The correspondence with Charlotte Shaw ultimately produced over three hundred letters by him, which have survived, and a presumed equal number by her, which have not; having nowhere to keep them he almost always destroyed them. She was both confidante and safety-valve, and he wrote to her freely and at length about his deepest feelings, about his family, even about Deraa, and also about books and writers and her husband's plays and any other subject in art and life that came to mind. Both Irish, both celibate (by all accounts the Shaws' marriage was unconsummated), both the products of a childhood dominated by a powerful mother, they wrote with an intimacy which belied the gap in age of thirty-one years. It would be

1 See pp. 171–2; Letters from Bovington.

Lawrence in Tank Corps uniform – but the tunic could not have been his: he never rose above the rank of Private.

tempting to assume that he took the name Shaw to align himself with her and G.B.S., who seem to have come to see him to some extent as a surrogate son, except that he chose it before his relationship with them had developed. He himself offered other, and variant, explanations.

Yet the army had its compensations: he found more good friends, for even the 'social bedrock' of the Tank Training School contained kindred spirits – Arthur Russell, for example, from Coventry, still devoted to Lawrence over half a century after his death and with clear memories of him.

> I didn't know who he was, but I was parked almost opposite him in the hut. After a day or two I found out who he was and why he was in the army. He told me he transferred from the Air Force, and he said 'You probably wonder why the name "Shaw" when it was "Ross" in the Air Force. They asked me what name I wanted to go under. I opened a telephone book, jabbed a finger on it, said "that one", and it happened to be Shaw.' There was no connection with G.B.S.[1] It just happened.

> He explained to me that with the Arab Revolt he'd been told to promise certain things to the Arabs, and he felt so let down with making these promises, that he didn't want to make any decisions or promises on behalf of the government or anyone, he didn't want any authority at all. So he came down to the lowest possible rung. That was his explanation. I admired him for that because I realized he could have gone to really great places, but he was so disillusioned.

> I suppose in a way he was a loner and I was a loner; we gravitated. It could be that or that we just got on easily with each other. But we didn't mix with any of the others, there was the odd one occasionally, but we were together most of the time. And then eventually he took on that cottage.

The cottage was Clouds Hill – the other principal compensation of his time in the Tank Corps. Almost derelict, it stood among trees a mile and a half from the camp on the Dorset heathland; it was to become his special refuge from army life and was to be the only real home he would ever have apart from Polstead Road. It was soon in a reasonable enough condition to receive friends; men from the camp, and visitors of a different sort from the literary and artistic world such as E. M. Forster, Siegfried Sassoon, Robert Graves, Edward Garnett, Augustus John. It became a place of books and music, in which ordinary soldiers sat absorbed in poetry and avant-garde contemporary novels, while Bach, Beethoven or Elgar poured from the huge horn of Lawrence's high-quality Columbia gramophone. Food was eaten out of tins and the surrounding rhodo-

---

1 By contrast, Lawrence told Robert Graves: 'I took the name Shaw because it was the first one-syllabled name which turned up in the Army List Index.'

dendron bushes provided the only lavatory – though since to begin with he was 'day-tenant' only (he slept in camp) this was not quite such a disadvantage. He was later to call Clouds Hill, in a letter of 1934, 'my Swiss Family Robinson Cottage', and, in a letter of 1933, 'the real centre of my world'. Though away from it for long periods, it would always be there, and he was still improving and developing it when he died.

His fellow soldiers soon got over any awe they might have felt at having a national war-hero living among them under an assumed name. Indeed, to them he was not 'Lawrence of Arabia', but 'Broughy Shaw', because of his daring and expertise with his motor-cycle. As one of them, 'Posh' Palmer, wrote to Robert Graves in 1927 when the latter was collecting material for a biography of Lawrence (its subject being by then long departed from the army): 'Strangely enough he is remembered, not for anything he did in the war, but for his performance on the "Brough", that wonderful motor-cycle. Hitting the trail they call it in the Tank Corps.'

All in all he found his life at Bovington tolerable despite its drawbacks. As he wrote to Eric Kennington in June 1923: 'The army is loathsome: Dorsetshire beautiful: the work very light. So I can carry on here.'

One other visitor at Clouds Hill, for less cultural purposes, was John Bruce, Scotsman, Tank Corps Private, and accomplice in a punishment ritual to which Lawrence submitted himself on numerous occasions from 1923 onwards. That over a period of ten years or so he had arranged to have himself severely birched by this powerfully built young man, at the alleged insistence of an elderly despotic relation who in fact did not exist, was the shock revelation of articles by Phillip Knightley and Colin Simpson in the *Sunday Times* in 1968, and in their book *The Secret Lives of Lawrence of Arabia* published in 1969. In retrospect it is possible to deduce that something of that nature had taken place from the hint, understandably left vague, dropped by his brother A. W. Lawrence into his Postscript to *Lawrence by His Friends*, first issued in May 1937; A. W. Lawrence wrote that T.E.'s 'subjection of the body was achieved by methods advocated by the saints whose lives he had read'. Interviewed in 1985 A. W. Lawrence described his brother's motivation as follows:

> He hated the thought of sex. He had read any amount of mediaeval literature about characters, some of them saints, some of them not, some ordinary people, who had quelled their sexual longings by beating. And that's what he did.
>
> INTERVIEWER: Did you know about this at the time?
>
> A. W. LAWRENCE: No. I knew about it immediately after his death, but of course said nothing. It's not a thing people can understand easily.

The fact that this happened still amazes friends like Arthur Russell, since the beatings apparently took place on occasions at Clouds Hill. Lawrence, Bruce and Russell were all members of Hut 12 at Bovington but Russell never suspected that Bruce and Lawrence had any kind of close relationship. But then, as Robert Graves has observed, 'Lawrence's friendships were separated by bulkheads'. Indeed it could be said that he had a range of variant personalities so that one man's perception of him might be, and indeed frequently and obviously was, quite different from another's.

Bruce is rarely mentioned in Lawrence's letters, but Russell and Palmer – usually known as 'Posh' – occur frequently, particularly at this time in letters to Mrs Thomas Hardy, for Max Gate, Thomas Hardy's home, was an easy motor-cycle ride across the heath and Lawrence became a regular visitor, often bringing one of his army companions with him. The Hardys developed an extraordinary affection for Lawrence, apparently to the extent of seeing him, as did the Shaws, almost as a surrogate son. When some years later Hardy died Lawrence was away in India and Mrs Hardy wrote to him that she believed that had he been on hand in England her husband might have lived: 'You seem nearer to him, somehow, than anyone else, certainly more akin.' He also gained the reputation of being virtually the only visitor to Max Gate who could cope with the Hardys' fearsome Caesar terrier Wessex. As Robert Gittings wrote in his book *The Older Hardy*, 'The indulged dog was a menace to all guests. . . . According to Cynthia Asquith, it "contested" every forkful on the way to her mouth. . . . The respectable trousers of both John Galsworthy and the surgeon, Sir Frederick Treves, were reduced to tatters. . . . Only T. E. Lawrence of Arabia, perhaps by some esoteric desert magic, managed to remain unscathed.'

Two other things were much on his mind at Bovington. The first was his continuing work on *Seven Pillars of Wisdom*, which after being written several times by hand and subsequently typeset by the *Oxford Times* was now, the advice and comments of his friends having been accepted or rejected as the case might be, in the process of being laboriously printed under his close supervision in its strictly limited 'subscribers' edition'. It was his intention that this full version should never be available for general circulation,[1] though he was not against a popular shortened version being issued to defray the large costs of printing, and lavishly illustrating, the complete work. The reduction, under the popular title *Revolt in the Desert*, was eventually published by Jonathan Cape in 1927. His

---

1 In October 1924 the manager of the book department of the Army & Navy Stores, London, wrote to Hogarth asking for the published price and trade terms of Colonel Lawrence's book. Hogarth sent the request to Lawrence who replied: 'Nothing is being published. Your firm has been misled by inaccurate reports in the press of a private circulation among my friends. There are no copies for disposal.' The title quoted by the book manager was also inaccurate; he referred to it as *The Seven Pillows of Wisdom*.

second obsession was his ceaseless campaign to be allowed to return to the Air Force. In 1925 he even began to hint at suicide after he had been first told he could go back and then had the permission rescinded. On 13 June that year he wrote to Edward Garnett, principal reader at Jonathan Cape and consultant in the matter of the popular reduction:

> Trenchard withdrew his objection to my rejoining the Air Force. I got seventh-heaven for two weeks: but then Sam Hoare [Sir Samuel Hoare, Secretary of State for Air] came back from Mespot and refused to entertain the idea. That, and the closer acquaintance with *The Seven Pillars* (which I now know better than anyone ever will) have together convinced me that I'm no bloody good on earth. So I'm going to quit but in my usual comic fashion I'm going to finish the reprint [i.e. *Revolt*] and square up with Cape before I hop it! There is nothing like deliberation, order and regularity in these things.

Garnett and other friends such as John Buchan became exceedingly concerned; but someone who took such threats less than seriously was Trenchard himself, as Andrew Boyle's biography of him makes clear:

> On the half-dozen occasions he [Lawrence] visited the Trenchards at Dancer's Hill before his wish came true again, the troubled insecurity of the man showed through the habitual charm. Trenchard, who had grown very attached to him, pitied his helplessness. . . . Yet the suicidal frame of mind rarely lasted in Trenchard's presence. It became a sort of private joke between them after the evening Lawrence threatened to take his life and Trenchard said quietly:
>
> 'All right, but please go into the garden. I don't want my carpets ruined.'[1]

In the end it was the Prime Minister Stanley Baldwin who, after appeals by Bernard Shaw and Buchan, intervened to sanction Lawrence's return to the Air Force. Lawrence wrote to an American friend, the publisher F. N. Doubleday, on 17 August 1925: 'I am being transferred to the Air Force from tomorrow. That pleases me. It's like going home.'

Yet there were genuine regrets too. He wrote to Mrs Hardy from his new R.A.F. base three hundred miles away: 'Alas for Clouds Hill, & the Heath, & the people I had learned in the two years of Dorset!'

His new base was the R.A.F. Officer Cadets' College at Cranwell, near Lincoln. 'A very comfortable, peaceful cleanly camp', was his description of it to John

---

1 *Trenchard* (Collins), 1962, pp. 561–2.

Buchan, while to a wartime associate, B. E. Leeson, formerly of the Royal Flying Corps, he explained his new situation thus:

> I'm in Cranwell now. *Name* of Shaw. *No.* 338171. *Rank* A.C.2. *Hut* 105. *Unit.* R.A.F. Cadet College; Cranwell is in Lincolnshire. I'm not a Cadet, but one of their slaves. It is very good to be in the R.A.F. after all the storms and shipwreck.

Returning to the R.A.F. gave him the opportunity and the stimulus to complete *The Mint*, which he did with a series of chapters on Cranwell. In an *Explanation* written to precede this Cranwell section, he stated that the original fifty Uxbridge chapters were meant to be a 'porch, a short porch of selected scenes, to the book I meant to write for the incomparable Hogarth upon Life in a Flying Flight, which is the veritable Air Force: but my sudden dismissal from Farnborough knocked that experience on the head.' Since the Uxbridge Depot was 'a savage place' he had 'for fairness' sake' picked out certain extracts, mainly from letters to his friends, 'in the hope that they may give the idea of how different, how humane, life in Cadet College was'. He concluded:

> There is no continuity in these last pages – and a painful inadequacy: but perhaps some glint of our contentment may shine from between my phrases into your eyes.
>
> How can any man describe his happiness?

Yet his new contentment was far from inviolate. There were times when circumstances conspired to cause him considerable disturbance. One such occasion was a meeting between King Feisal of Iraq, Lord Winterton (who had served with Lawrence in 1918 and was now Under-Secretary of State for India) and Lawrence, now once again Aircraftman Shaw, at Winterton's country home in Surrey in September 1925. Winterton was eager to reminisce about the war and Lawrence felt himself obliged to talk back, as though, as he put it to Mrs Shaw, 'the R.A.F. clothes were a skin that I could slough off at any while for a laugh'. But all the time he knew he could not do so; the Lawrence with whom Winterton and Feisal sought to renew acquaintance was dead, indeed was worse than dead, he was a stranger he once knew. His future lay in the course of deliberate self-effacement which he had pursued since 1922. Yet there was always the haunting thought that he had 'crashed [his] life and self and gone hopelessly wrong. . . . O dear O dear, what a coil!'

By contrast it was at Cranwell that he finished the long labour on *Seven Pillars*. But as that cloud receded another approached, the publication of *Revolt in the Desert*, planned for early the following year. Fearing that this would unleash another rash of tabloid headlines and exaggerated stories he asked to withdraw from the scene. The R.A.F. sent him overseas; late in 1926 he sailed by troopship for India.

He was in India for most of two years. This was certainly, in the words of the R.A.F. report on him already quoted, 'a period of self-effacement'. He deliberately refrained from making any attempt to become acquainted with one of the most remarkable member-nations of Asia and the British Empire, remaining firmly within the confines of the two camps to which he was posted: Drigh Road near Karachi and a remote station at Miranshah on the borders of Afghanistan.[1] In a letter to Trenchard's Secretary T. B. Marson he wrote: 'I am attempting a hard thing: to make the camp suffice for my needs. I haven't been outside its bounds since I arrived: a sort of voluntary C.B.'[2]

One important reason for this new 'imprisonment' was the paramount need to avoid causing the kind of sensation which might lead to his removal a second time from the R.A.F. But there was also the fact that such love as he had once had for the East was now almost entirely gone and while recognizing the wisdom of his absence from England he was heartily homesick for her. He wrote to Dick Knowles, the son of his Clouds Hill neighbour: 'Often in the evening I go out to the music of the camel bells upon Drigh Road, and hang my topee on a cactus branch, and sit under it, and weep, remembering Cranwell and the Great North Road.'

The work and the hours in the Engine Repair Section to which he was attached were undemanding – 'cushy' was his description of depot life in the same letter to Dick Knowles. He wrote to his mother in January 1928, after a full year in India: 'We do not have changes or adventures. We stay still, and are physically taken care of, like stock cattle.'

Mentally, however, he did not lie fallow. He read constantly, and even wrote reviews for *The Spectator*, though not under any recognizable name. As at Bovington he became a one-man library system for his fellow servicemen, and was soon 'astonishing' his room-mates, whose preference was for *Rose Marie*, with gramophone records of Bach and Boccherini. He also at this time typed out a fair copy of *The Mint*, sending it to England to be read by a number of carefully selected friends. There was one other activity to which he devoted, sometimes gladly, sometimes grudgingly, hours of his time. In England he had had many correspondents but he had also had constant opportunity to talk with his friends face to face. Now his only conversation was by post, with the result that he wrote scores, indeed hundreds, of letters during his Indian exile – not only to friends but also to many, though by no means all, of the numerous petitioners, enquirers and other strangers who felt impelled to address him,

1 Both Lawrence's Indian air-stations were in what is now Pakistan.
2 C.B.: Confinement to Barracks – a basic military punishment.

Aircraftman T.E. Shaw at Miranshah, 1928

seeing him sometimes as scholar, sometimes as hero, sometimes as guru, sometimes (though perhaps less now than formerly) as possible husband, sometimes merely as an available celebrity in the public domain to whom they felt free to direct their often vapid, often demented outpourings. His letters frequently contain testy complaints about the pressure the obligation of correspondence put on him. 'Enough of letters,' he wrote to his mother in August 1927: 'They waste my time, & the other people's. Some day I'll be strong-minded enough to stop writing altogether. Till then I'll use half my leisure saying No or Yes to half the world on paper.' He wrote to Dick Knowles in May of the same year: 'Week after week passes, and I sit on my bed in sticky misery staring at the approach of mail-day, and the retreat of mail-day, with on my mind the sense that I must write to some one of the 444 people who have gratified me and honoured me with their best letters in the last eleven years or so, since I landed in India.'

Yet this period produced much that is revealing, eloquent and moving in the correspondence of a man of whom Sir Ronald Storrs wrote in the *Dictionary of National Biography* that 'it has indeed been said that he would have survived (as would Edward Fitzgerald without *Omar Khayyam*) if only as a letter writer.' He wrote to Mrs Charlotte Shaw with extreme frankness and at great length about himself, his family background and his relations with his father and mother. Coupling his stream of letters to her at this period with those to Lionel Curtis during his time of severe depression at Bovington, he told her: 'I've not written any letters of this sort to anyone else, since I was born.' He wrote regular letters to Trenchard, in one of them apologetically about his Air Force book which he knew Trenchard had not liked: 'I wonder if perhaps, had I not been kicked out of the R.A.F., *The Mint* mightn't have gone on to describe squadron life, and flying and airwork. . . . It was a pity the rhythm was broken.' He wrote to his friend Robert Graves, whom he had first met when at All Souls, about novelists and poets and Graves' own poetry; and, when his correspondent took him up on a statement in *The Mint* attributed to an Oxford preacher who had referred to the act of intercourse as lasting less than one and three quarter minutes, defensively about sex. 'As I wrote (with some courage, I think: few people admit the damaging ignorance) I haven't ever: and don't much want to. . . . So I don't feel I miss much: and it must leave a dirty feeling too.' In a letter to his old wartime friend F. G. Peake, now 'Peake Pasha', commandant of the newly formed Arab Legion in Transjordan, he made one of his very few genuinely nostalgic references to the scene of his wartime campaigns: 'I wonder if you still ride up and down that delectable land. I am often hungry for another sight of its hills.' Yet to his American friend Ralph Isham he wrote: 'I hate the East. . . . Did I tell you (I did not go about explaining it) that I consider what I did in Arabia morally indefensible. So I refused pay and decorations while it lasted, and will not take any personal profit out of it: neither from a book about it; nor will I take any position which depends on my war-reputation. "Arabia barred." ' This was in August 1927; it was the same guilt which he had felt so acutely ten years before. At Christmas 1927, however, he could write to his close friend of his R.A.F./Ross period, R. A. M. Guy: 'I have lost everything except publicity value, and am happy . . . or I hope so: but it is very difficult to write that word happy. Always dots run after it on the paper: and I pause to think if I dare say it.'

Two deaths of people close to him also led to a number of notable letters: D. G. Hogarth's in November 1927, Thomas Hardy's in January 1928. Of the former he wrote, for example, to the artist William Rothenstein: 'The death of Hogarth hit me very hard. Oxford was to me a beautiful place, and a home, because he lived there, for me to see for a few minutes whenever I passed. . . . A great loss: the greatest, perhaps, or probably, that I'll ever have to suffer.' Of Thomas Hardy's death he wrote to his widow: 'And now, when I should grieve for him and for you, almost it feels like a triumph. That day we reached Damascus, I cried, against all my control, for the triumphant thing achieved at last, fitly: and so the passing of T.H. touches me. He had finished and was so full a man.'

While in India he decided to make his new identity official. In June 1927 he instructed his solicitors to take the necessary steps to change his name by deed-poll to Thomas Edward Shaw. Meanwhile his former persona 'T. E. Lawrence' was being celebrated in Britain and America following the publication of *Revolt in the Desert*. An instant best seller – in his phrase, it was bought up like 'ripe apples' – it paid off as planned the debts accrued by the printing of the subscribers' edition of *Seven Pillars*. A further boost to his discarded alter ego was given late in 1927 by the publication of a popular biography written, with considerable assistance from Lawrence himself, by Robert Graves, under the title of *Lawrence and the Arabs*.

One other book – his third and last – was in the making during this Indian period. In 1928 the American book designer Bruce Rogers asked him to under-take a new translation of Homer's *Odyssey*, to be produced to a high quality of printing and format. After much hesitation he agreed, and for once he accepted that this would be a commercial venture; if it achieved nothing else such money as he acquired could be used to improve Clouds Hill. The task would occupy him until 1931. One condition he insisted on: anonymity, but this in the event was not achieved. The American edition, published in 1932, would give the translator's name as 'T. E. Shaw'; the British edition, published in 1935 after his death, is credited to 'T. E. Shaw (Colonel T. E. Lawrence)'.

His absence from England had been intended to remove him from the more ludicrous inventions of the popular press, but in late 1928 his presence in India began to cause precisely the kind of sensation which he had tried so hard to avoid. His second posting, Miranshah, was so remote that he could write of it, in a letter to E. M. Forster, 'I like this place: it feels as though I'd dropped over the world's rim out of sight.' However, a revolt against the King of nearby Afghanistan together with the fact that 'the arch-spy of the world' was on hand and masquerading under an incognito was too much for a Fleet Street always hungry for tales of the popular English hero. The *Daily Herald* of 5 January 1929, in a story headed *LAWRENCE OF ARABIA* and sub-headed STARTLING REPORT, made the inevitable Buchanesque connection:

> For some time his movements, as chronicled, have been mysterious, and a few months ago it was stated that he was in Afghanistan on a secret mission, though earlier in the same week it had been reported that he was in Amritsar, posing as a Mohameddan saint.

As Labour Members of Parliament seethed and anti-imperialists burned Lawrence in effigy on Tower Hill, the Foreign Secretary of the Government of India overruled the better judgement of the Air Force and insisted that the subject of all this speculation should be got out of the sub-continent at once, it being considered by him that 'Lawrence's presence anywhere in India under present conditions [was] very inconvenient'. Trenchard proposed Somaliland or Aden as possible sanctuaries, but he also insisted that Lawrence's own views should be sought. Lawrence opted for home. Three days after the report in the *Daily Herald*, he was flown out of Miranshah; by 12 January he was on the liner S.S. *Rajputana*, sailing from Bombay for the port of Tilbury on the Thames. That the man of mystery was returning to England merely multiplied popular interest. It was soon realized that there was little prospect of an incognito arrival in London, so Wing-Commander Sydney Smith, R.A.F., who had met Lawrence in Cairo in 1921, was commissioned to get him off the liner at Plymouth. Fleet Street was not, however, to be so easily outwitted, as Smith later recalled:

> Well, we saw the liner looming through the mist. At the same time I looked round and, my God, I saw all the little boats surging towards the liner, long before the lighter had come to take the passengers off. And I realized to my horror, 'my God, this is the press.' So then I had to get busy and concoct a plan with the lieutenant-commander. He said, 'Right, I'll go along and pay my respects to the Captain as usual, and then I'll get him to open a hatch on the other side of the boat and we'll get Lawrence through the hatch.' Round we went in our pinnace to the other side, and the hatch was opened and the rope ladder let down. But unfortunately it hitched up on the handle of the hatch and of course there was a delay. And there was Lawrence standing at the opening of the hatch. And they photographed him in the hatchway and coming down the ladder and into the pinnace.

However, we shot away as hard as we could in the direction of Plymouth, trying to throw them off.

News film cameras were also present and their less than fully focused images, taken from a boat heaving with the swell of Plymouth Sound, constitute the only shots of Lawrence taken by any of the standard British companies. They would be brought out again a few years later to introduce his newsreel obituary.

LAWRENCE AT CLOUDS HILL

'I liked the place at once. His friends were friendly to me, I felt easy – and to feel easy was, in T.E.'s eyes, a great recommendation. We weren't to care as soon as we were inside the place. We were to feel easy. We weren't to worry about the world and the standards the world imposes. And here we talked, and played Beethoven's symphonies to one another upon the gramophone, and ate and drank. We drank water only or tea. No alcohol ever entered Clouds Hill and we ate – this sounds less romantic – we ate out of tins. T.E. always laid in a stock of tinned dainties for his guests. There were not fixed hours for meals, no tablecloth and no-one sat down. If you felt hungry you opened a tin and drifted about with it.'

(E.M. Forster, from a BBC radio broadcast, 25 August 1938)

My cottage is a gem of gems — in the eyes of its owner. You see, I've almost made it, from the roots up. It is as ugly as my sins, bleak, angular, small, unstable: very like its creator. Yet I love it.

Lawrence to Lady Astor, 15 January 1934.

(Right) The doorway at Clouds Hill, with its Greek inscription 'ου φροντις'.

'In Athens was a gentleman called Hippo-clides who became engaged to a rich man's daughter: and they arranged him a slap-up and splendid marriage. The feast preceding it was too much for his poor head, though. He stood on his head on the table and did a leg-dance, which was objectionable in Greek dress. "Hippoclides, Hippocleides" [*sic*] pro-tested the shocked merchant. "You dance your marriage off." "Wyworri?" said Hippo-leides: and Herodotus tells the tale so beauti-fully that I put the jape on the architrave. It means that nothing in Clouds Hill is to be a care upon its habitant. While I have it there shall be nothing exquisite or unique in it. Nothing to anchor me.'

(*Lawrence to Mrs Eric Kennington,* 18 October 1932)

12

CONTENTED MECHANIC

Lawrence was angered, disturbed and disorientated by being made the subject of a pointless fracas in the press. 'I am in London,' he wrote to his wartime comrade Colonel Newcombe on 22 February 1929, 'rather distractedly and jerkily, with one suit of plain clothes, & two suits of uniform, & a motor-bike: I see hardly anyone, & don't know what to say to them, when I do see them.'

One person to whom he did know what to say was the Labour M.P. Ernest Thurtle who had been asking questions in the House of Commons about his alleged espionage activities. In early February he telephoned Thurtle, then next day marched into the Houses of Parliament and confronted him and his colleague the Independent Labour Party leader James Maxton. The meeting was a success in that the two members totally accepted his explanations and subsequently he and Thurtle became close friends and correspondents. His forthright action, however, produced a stern reprimand from the R.A.F. He typed a vigorous defence to Trenchard – singularly unabashed by the fact that he was an ordinary Aircraftman addressing his ultimate chief.

> As for the House of Commons raid, I think I was right. Mr. Thurtle was enquiring into what was very much my private business. In explaining this I explained practically the whole affair, and probably the Labour Group will ask you no more questions on my account. In that case, I expect you to feel sorry that I did not go sooner to the House!

Evidently a re-reading of this letter after signing it persuaded him that he had argued his case somewhat too vehemently. He added by way of postscript:

> I'm afraid the above reads too stiffly. That is the worst of type. I am

'Tes' and his C.O.: Aircraftman T. E. Shaw and Wing Commander Sydney Smith.

'I'm web-footed now and quack before meals': Aircraftman Shaw standing on the float of a de Havilland 60x Moth seaplane.

very sorry to have annoyed you by my slight activity, and will be very patient henceforward. . . .

As it happened, this turmoil preceded one of his happiest postings. He was sent in March to the R.A.F. Flying Boat station at Cattewater, on Plymouth Sound, commanded by the officer who had attempted to smuggle him off the *Rajputana*, Wing-Commander Sydney Smith. Smith, his wife Clare and Lawrence became friends, their relationship untroubled by the lowly rank of the new arrival, who was soon known to them, from his now legal initials, as 'Tes'. The friendship extended to the Smiths' young daughter, Maureen, known as 'Squeak', and to the family's lively complement of dogs. A product of this easy openness between commanding officer and Aircraftman was the choice of a better name for the base, as Clare Sydney Smith wrote in her account of the Smith-Tes friendship *The Golden Reign*:

One of the things they agreed upon unanimously was their mutual dislike of the name 'Cattewater' R.A.F. Station. One evening Tes joked about it and said: 'Why, if you instructed the laundry to deliver your clean clothes at Cattewater the vanman would be justified in throwing them into the sea!' This was such a ridiculous thought that he and Sydney promptly concocted a letter to the Air Ministry asking that it should be named Mount Batten after the pier on the other side of the peninsula. This was done officially soon afterwards.

The cold of Britain's weather had worried him to begin with as did talk of a possible film based on his book and a sudden upsurge of interest in his Dorset retreat. But by July 1929 he was writing with unwonted contentment to Dick Knowles:

> The wish of people to see Clouds Hill will soon fade: if only the press will leave me alone now, then all the troubles will be forgotten. The papers feel sore at having made fools of themselves over me and Afghanistan: and will not readily invent another yarn. That film project is dead, too, I think. In fact, all's looking well for my peaceful old age.

The motor cycle referred to in his letter to Newcombe was a new Brough Superior given to him by Mr and Mrs Bernard Shaw. 'It's a heavenly bike,' he wrote to his wartime comrade and now financial adviser, Robin Buxton. 'Goes like smoke & is smooth as milk to ride.' On it he had ridden down to Cattewater and because of it he was able, when opportunity offered, to pick up the threads of his social life, renew old friendships and make new ones. One notable new friend, who even occasionally rode pillion with him, was Lady Astor, whose principal addresses were 4 St James's Square London and Cliveden House Buckinghamshire, but who as M.P. for the Sutton Division of Plymouth also had a home in Lawrence's vicinity – indeed, on Plymouth's famous Hoe. He described in a letter of April 1929 to Mrs Shaw how on paying a reluctant visit to the town (which he tended to avoid almost as much as he had avoided Karachi) 'a pea-hen voice screamed "Aircraftman" from a car: and it was her'. The following day Lady Astor visited the air station, was 'allowed all over it' and subsequently Lawrence drove her back into Plymouth. The episode was noted in the press. 'Serves me right', he commented to Charlotte Shaw, 'for walking around with a talkie sky-sign.' But the Aircraftman and the Peeress (as he delighted to address her) began a firm friendship, enlivened by often breezy and witty correspondence – and, from time to time, by lively and, to anyone who might overhear them, entertaining telephone calls. In one of his letters, dated 6 June 1929, after refusing an invitation to Cliveden, he ended with the suggestion: 'Some day, if you revisit Plymouth quietly, ring up 1634, and we'll brighten the life of the Exchange girls, again.' A typical example of his breezier

Lawrence on Boanerges *(the sons of thunder) – the Biblical name he transferred from motor-bike to motor-bike. Ironically he once described his current machine to Robin Buxton as his 'safety-valve'.*

style is the following, from a letter written on New Year's Eve 1930; the extract also shows his continuing taste for speed.

> I feel inclined to send a postcard to Sandwich [another Astor address], explaining how much I enjoyed Cliveden and what an excellent ride back I had (including a race across the Plain with a sports Bentley: well, not so much a race as a procession for the Bent, which did only 88. I wished I had a peeress or two on my flapper bracket!)

Their correspondence continued, with occasional long gaps, until the month of his death. The gaps annoyed her. A characteristic note from her to him (in May 1934) ran as follows:

> Do you never want to see me again.
> If so write & say so to
>   4 St James' Square
>   Greetings   Respfy
>   N. Astor

Nevertheless the friendship remained strong and he had no compunction in his self-imposed poverty at becoming the associate of one of the richest society hostesses in the land. Of her and her husband he commented, in a letter of January 1934, 'You and Waldorf are two of the rich who would very easily pass through the eye of the needle, I reckon. If only the rest of us were as unselfish with our money.' His best letters to her catch almost the same intimate tone as his letters to Charlotte Shaw, particularly when writing, for example, about his mother, who for most of his last years was away in China with his eldest brother Bob, now a medical missionary of the China Inland Mission. He disapproved of the nature of the 'call' that had taken them there feeling that, as he told Lady Astor, 'the spirit of the day is against the missionary profession. We do not feel confident in ourselves to preach or inculcate.' Yet he cared deeply for their welfare, and he was moved by their reaction when Lady Astor made them a present of rugs to take with them when, after a furlough in England during which they had lodged at Clouds Hill, they returned to China in late 1932. 'The rugs were well taken, indeed,' he wrote. 'You would have been touched at their reception. I wish these poor things hadn't this cast-iron sense of duty. They are not fit for life in rough places, and they were so quaint and happy in my Dorset cottage, improbable home as it is.'

Eighteen months later in a revealing passage in a letter to Lady Astor dated 27 July 1934 he referred to the rugs again:

> In a recent letter she told me how useful your parting gift to her of rugs had been. They have great cold winter journeys. I am sure she would be hurt if I did not take a chance that offers and repeat my gratitude to you. My mother does not encourage kindness, in her brisk utility: but when she receives it, she is touched.

He had already elsewhere in the letter made further frank comments on his surviving parent's character ('my mother has never learned our lesson, of giving in, and of doubting our own competence universally. She is fitted only to dictate in a *small* world,' etc) and he concluded the passage with the following comment on himself and his whole family:

> With such a father (you did not know him, I expect ... before your time) and such a mother, we have no chance of being useful citizens of this great country. If only they sold single tickets to the Moon, now! I think they would elect me President, there.

Another new friend of this period was the novelist Henry Williamson, about whose *Tarka the Otter* he had written, in a letter from India to Edward Garnett, a long and detailed critique which Williamson, far from resenting, had much appreciated. The two men opened correspondence and arranged to meet. Williamson was to be one of many who felt the curiously powerful impact of

Lawrence's personality. He arrived at Williamson's home on a day of pouring rain:

> Finally he turned up one Sunday, coming right across Dartmoor from Plymouth to North Devon, where I lived, on his ten horse power 100 mile an hour Brough Superior nickel-plated motor cycle. I remember I waited for him and I looked below and suddenly this man appeared from nowhere, his bike shining from the rain was put in the stand, and a little man came up the stairs, with a minesweeper's suit on from head to foot. And he came in and he smiled, and he nodded to our maid and spoke to the boy and patted his head. I just looked at him, he never looked at me, and I thought, what a marvellous person. And I began to feel very big and strong and happy and confident. And when he'd gone we all felt rather sad and empty, this wonderful party was over, and I said to my wife, how does he do it? She said, I don't know. I said, do you like him? She said, he's a marvellous person. I said, in what way, did he pay you compliments? She said, no, he was simply like a spirit that came in, we all felt fine, and he just vanished. And I think that's the effect he had on the Arabs.[1]

Not only was he contented with the friendly social atmosphere of Cattewater/ Mount Batten, he also found a fulfilment in the work into which he was now drawn and which was to absorb him increasingly throughout the rest of his R.A.F. career. In 1929 he worked closely with Sydney Smith as a member of the R.A.F. team which managed the seaplane races for the Schneider Cup. But more significantly he became involved with the marine side of the base, bringing his untrained yet effective mechanical expertise and his resourceful intelligence to bear on the problems which afflicted the boats which were used as tenders and rescue vessels for the seaplanes which were Mount Batten's *raison d'être*. His awareness of their inadequacy – they were cumbersome craft of naval design and constantly prone to breakdown – was heightened when he was given by a wealthy friend the use of a Biscayne Baby speedboat produced by the American Purdy company. The *Biscuit*, as she was called, was not in good working order when she arrived at Mount Batten so Lawrence set to, undeterred, to get her

---

1 From Williamson's interview of 1962, included in the BBC Television Documentary *T. E. Lawrence* 1888–1935. Siegfried Sassoon, in an interview recorded that year but only briefly used, made a somewhat similar statement about Lawrence's personality: 'He had a terrific power that could be frightening, but it was his gentleness which left a particular impact on my mind. . . . He had some indescribable magnetism, which he could exert when he liked but in later years he used very little. It seemed to me that he had what I can only describe as "power over life", by which I mean that he could make things happen by his influence on other people. He was almost like a too high powered motor bicycle, almost *over*-powered. . . . To call him a charlatan as some people have done is a wicked representation of the worst possible kind. Everything I know of his character belies it. He was absolutely true mettle all through.'

into prime condition. Clare Sydney Smith witnessed her not undramatic first outing:

> Would she go? The Commanding Officer, officers, sergeants, corporal, aircraft men – all stood by in eager groups watching the long-awaited launching. . . . Beaming, Tes settled himself at the wheel with Corporal Evans beside him; pressed the button, accelerated, and with a roar she was off. Turning and twisting, she was a flash of silver in the blue water. Never have I seen such antics from a speed-boat. Tes turned her round in her own length and showed her off like a small boy with an exciting toy.

The *Biscuit* was to be much used for trips round the bay or picnics up the River Tamar, Clare Sydney Smith being perhaps the most frequent of his numerous passengers – though Lady Astor enjoyed her outings too.[1] But the speed which he could command in the *Biscuit* was not available to the R.A.F. when confronted by the necessity of air-sea rescue and he now began to lobby for the devising and introduction by the Air Ministry of a new generation of boats more suitable for this important purpose.

He soon made a second firm friend among the officers of his service when he met Flight-Lieutenant Beauforte-Greenwood, Head of the Air Ministry's Marine Equipment branch, for whom he began work in the autumn of 1930 on the testing and tuning of various experimental craft. This work took him for much of his time to Hythe near Southampton but he was at Mount Batten on 4 February 1931 when in perfect weather conditions he and Clare Sydney Smith witnessed a fatal air accident in Plymouth Sound:

> Two or three flying-boats were up as usual, practising firing at targets at sea. Presently one of them began to circle downwards as they always do before landing. As the boat circled over the breakwater Tes said 'that boat looks queer'.

> . . . Suddenly before our horrified eyes she nose-dived straight into the sea with hardly a splash. As she slowly rose to the surface we could make out no movement or sign of human life in her.[2]

Lawrence and Sydney Smith hurried to the rescue but as the latter subsequently told his wife it was the Aircraftman who mastered the situation. 'His gift of quick, crystal-clear thinking and natural leadership made his authority instantly acceptable to everyone there – including his own Commanding Officer.' Lawrence dived with the other rescuers and released the body of the Wing-

---

1 Lady Astor to Aircraftman Shaw, 18 March 1931: 'I am arriving at Plymouth tomorrow at about three or four o'clock. This is to warn you that I shall call you up, and hope that if the weather is fine you will take me out in your boat. If it isn't fine, I should prefer pillion riding!!!'
2 From *The Golden Reign*, p. 102.

Commander who had been at the controls, but he had been caught between the control column and the pilot's seat and had drowned. However, six of the twelve on board were saved. The inevitable inquest brought Lawrence more unwelcome publicity; but the accident underlined the urgency of the work to which he was now fully dedicated, and which gave him a special satisfaction, as he stated with much conviction on one occasion to Henry Williamson:

> He said to me, the only thing to do on this earth is to use the mind and the body together; we must use hands, we must think with our hands. He inferred that people who were all headwork only were going wrong. He tried to live this belief, and he was very happy towards the end of his R.A.F. life, testing speed-boats in the Solent and even taking them up to Yorkshire. He wrote to me: I'm web-footed now and quack before meals.

This pride in the joint use of mind and hand was not a new phenomenon. Before the war in Carchemish days he had written proudly to his family about what he called 'my faculty of making and repairing things' – which, he told them in a letter of 31 March 1911, 'has recently demonstrated how to make paint (black and red) for marking antiques, how to render light-tight a dark slide, how to make a camera-obscura, how to reworm a screw, (difficult this without a die), how to refit a plane-table, and replace winding mechanism on a paraffin lamp. Also I have devised a derrick, and a complicated system of human-power jacks (out of poplar poles, and rope, and Arabs). . . .' David Garnett, who came to know him after India when he was absorbed in his mechanic's role, concluded that he was happy in the R.A.F. not because it provided a monastic way of life or a retreat from the world, 'but because he valued more than anything the intimacy which comes from doing a bit of work with other men. The Air Force gave him that. He was very proud of his boats, explained in detail all the improvements he had made in them and spoke with enthusiasm of their designer, Scott Paine.' In September 1934, when only months away from leaving the R.A.F., he declared his pleasure at his recent achievements in a letter to his old friend of wartime days, George Lloyd (now Lord Lloyd and ex-High Commissioner in Egypt). 'After having dabbled in revolt and politics,' he wrote, 'it is rather nice to have been mechanically useful.'

But that was written when in sight of the end of his work and his service career. 'At Hythe listing a new English motor-boat engine for R.A.F. acceptance,' he wrote to S. F. Newcombe in April 1931. 'Hard work, cold work, wet work. Such aquatic sports would be better in the Mediterranean!' Yet in the same month he could write to Liddell Hart that 'my two-year war with the Air Ministry over the type of motor boats suited to attend seaplanes is bearing results now'. By March 1932 following a further year of intensive experimentation he felt confident enough on the eve of some important trials in Southampton Water to write privately to the Editor of *The Times*, inviting him to cover the story in his newspaper. The only necessary condition was that his name should not be mentioned. The Editor was Geoffrey Dawson, through whose offices he had become a Fellow of All Souls and who had published his first essays in political journalism in 1918. Dawson sent down his aeronautical correspondent and subsequently printed two articles, applauded by Lawrence himself as 'admirably expressed and arranged'. It all advanced the cause.

The year 1932 saw his final release from a more private labour which had burdened him for several years, with the publication – in the U.S.A., with a limited edition in Britain – of his translation of the *Odyssey*. As ever, he was dismissive of the quality of any written work he produced; however in this case he had raised no moral objection against payment. As he put it to Harley Granville-Barker, the *Odyssey* meant 'a bath, a hot-water plant and bookshelves for my cottage. So I have no regrets: but it is not one of my collected works.'

In the same year he was portrayed on the stage, not as himself but as the caricature figure of Private Napoleon Alexander Trotsky Meek in George Bernard Shaw's bizarre political extravaganza *Too True to be Good*. Meek arrives, off-stage, on a motor-cycle with, according to Shaw's stage directions, 'a sound like a machine-gun in action' and subsequently displays remarkable leadership and powers of command in a sudden military crisis. A rehearsal copy was sent to Lawrence for his comments. 'What excellent reading "Too True" is,' he wrote, not to the playwright, but to his most faithful of correspondents, the playwright's wife. 'I have read it again and again for pure enjoyment.' Through Charlotte he offered corrections to Shaw's text: 'I regret to see that . . . on page 51 the rifles have "cut-outs". These should be "cut-offs" of course. I am also not sure if Pte. Meek should twice "double" or "trot" out (pp. 32 and 53). In the R.A.F. and Navy other ranks double *to* an order. In the army progress is always at the march. Perhaps I pettifog? I suppose, too, that Articles of War is correct for the Army Act? We always called it the Army Act, officially.' His enjoyment of the play was not merely because of the personal connection – G.B.S. almost always drew his plaudits. ' "Too true" is the only bright spot in my existence at Hythe this winter. I went about for days with a feeling, that some great unknown benefit to me had happened. And that does *not* mean Pte. Meek.' The play was first performed in New York and subsequently at the Malvern Festival, where Walter Hudd took the role of the eccentric Private. After Malvern it ran for three weeks in Birmingham and it was there, at a matinée, that Lawrence managed to see it, in the company of G.B.S. He shrank from meeting Hudd backstage but wrote to him warmly from London on his way back to Hythe, admitting that since the part of Meek was 'obviously a hit at me' he had felt rather nervous, until all was over, 'lest something in it should hurt. Actually,' his letter continued, 'I thoroughly enjoyed it – or rather I should say that I hope to come one night in London and see it again, for enjoyment's sake. The first time my stomach felt a bit hollow all through.' He complimented Hudd on his performance, adding that 'you looked decent . . . and I only wish nature had let me look half as smart and efficient as you.' He wrote to Charlotte immediately afterwards: 'I have sent poor little Meek a line, saying that he does me proud and I wish I was half as good looking.'

Overall he was much changed from the disenchanted near-recluse who had sought humiliation – degradation even – in society's lower depths. In this final post-Indian phase of his R.A.F. career he plainly felt able to take up causes other than the one to which he was now devoted by profession. He lobbied his M.P. friend Ernest Thurtle on such subjects as the admission of Trotsky into England or the abolition of the death penalty for cowardice in war ('I have run too far and too fast . . . under fire, to throw a stone at the fearfullest creature'). He itemized in detail and at length to Liddell Hart those aspects of R.A.F. discipline which the ranks found irksome and absurd, with a view to giving his influential correspondent ammunition for use in the appropriate high places. He attempted to persuade Trenchard to use the first flight of the airship R101 to explore from the air the Empty Quarter of Arabia: his argument failed, but even if it had been accepted the fate of the R101 on its disastrous maiden voyage of October 1930 would have prevented its implementation. All such initiatives were of course confidential; he baulked at any move which might lead to his being exposed to public interest or concern. When in 1930 St Andrew's University offered him the honorary degree of Doctor of Laws he instantly refused, and he joked later to his friend Reginald Sims (another Air Force officer) about the problem he would have faced had he agreed:

> Should I be A/C1 Doctor Shaw???
> Doctor A/C1 Shaw???
> A/C1 Doc Shaw???
> and if I were made Leading Aircraftman, how would
> LAC DOC SHAW or DOC LAC SHAW sound?

Similarly when in June 1933 the B.B.C. approached him with a view to his broadcasting a talk about King Feisal, then on a state visit to the country, his answer was firmly if jauntily negative. The proposal was put to him by his old wartime friend Colonel Alan Dawnay, at this time occupying a senior post at Broadcasting House. 'Only one thing tempted me,' Lawrence replied: ' "They will require the manuscript. . . ." I saw myself approach the mike and mellifluously say "The B.B.C. caused me to deposit with them the text of my possible delivery upon Feisal tonight. I have forgotten that stupidity. Here goes for what

I really think . . ." and then the red light would pop out and the announcer would say "Now we will have a short programme of gramophone records. . . ."' However, he concluded his letter: 'I hope you do the Feisal touch. If you see the dear man remember me very kindly to him. Say I am very proud of having helped his beginning.' The BBC has no reference in their records to any broadcast of note about Feisal at that time; however in September that year Allenby was on the nine o'clock news to broadcast a brief obituary. Feisal had died of a heart condition in Switzerland.

His statement that he was 'proud of having helped [Feisal's] beginning' was an unusually benign reference to his war years. Often people who tried to get him to write or reminisce about that period were given brusque replies. A former member of the Royal Naval Volunteer Reserve living in Canada in 1931, who claimed to have met him in the Arabian campaign when they were together on board the troop and stores carrier H.M.S. *Hardinge*, was told, 'It wasn't a good time and I like to forget it.' 'As for the Arab business,' he wrote to the United Press correspondent Henry T. Russell, who asked him for an interview, also in 1931, 'I had a hateful war: and after it $2\frac{1}{2}$ years of a dog-fight with the British Cabinet to secure the fulfilment of the promises to which they had made me an unwilling and post-facto accessory. When Winston Churchill fulfilled all that was humanly attainable of those promises I was free to quit events and return to the class & mode of life that I belong to and feel happy in. . . . So while, as I said, I haven't the smallest objection to seeing you, the result, on your side, will be nil. There are no wrongs to put right, no remorse or agony. Only a very ordinary and pleased creature whose position in the R.A.F. forbids him to give interviews for publication.'

He had not forgotten how Fleet Street's exposure of Aircraftman Ross at Farnborough had resulted in his peremptory expulsion from the Air Force in 1923 and there were one or two occasions in his last service years when the alarming possibility of a similar disaster confronted him. One such time had been at the Schneider Cup races in 1929 when the Air Minister Lord Thomson had been infuriated by a report that Aircraftman Shaw had been seen in apparently equal conversation with the Italian Air Marshal, General Balbo; only after some hard negotiation by his friends in London was the threat of a second expulsion withdrawn. Some years later Henry Williamson witnessed a smaller, but nevertheless upsetting occasion when Lawrence found himself unexpectedly snared and dismayed by the ever-lurking publicity machine.

> I was going to America, I'd been ill, and he came on board [the liner] – it was at Southampton – and a friend of mine, John Heygate, came too, and we were all talking quite happily, enjoying it, and suddenly a man came up, recognized him, and said, 'May I take your photograph

for publicity, sir?' Well, I've never seen a man wilt like that, he seemed
to shrink and leave his uniform with nothing in it, and he mumbled
something and shuffled away, obviously very worried in case it was
reported that he was doing it again and would have to leave the Air
Force. That was in March 1934.

Try as he might to distance himself from it, his legend would not quite leave
him alone. Also in March 1934, during a brief retreat to Clouds Hill, he tried
to disabuse an American admirer, Lincoln Kirstein, the young dancer and writer
– who had just reviewed the new biography of him written by Liddell Hart – of
what he saw as overblown assumptions:

> 'Man of action' you call me, in the last words of your letter 'who has
> done what he chose to his full extent.' Do, for heaven's sake, travel
> down to where I am next time you reach England, and put these ideas
> straight. We are all poor silly things trying to keep our feet in the
> swirl. Even if we succeed, it is not more than a static performance,
> nor deserving of applause. So I beg you to see me, and disabuse
> yourself of an illusion.

In a second letter to the same correspondent on 11 May he put the point even
more precisely:

> If we ever come together you will see that I am human. There ain't
> any such super-creatures as you would fain see: or if there are, I
> haven't been lucky enough to meet one.

With the light of hindsight we can look at these dates and note that Lawrence
had only one year to live. Coincidentally just a few days before this second letter
to Kirstein, on 3 May 1934, he wrote a letter to the motor-cycle manufacturer
George Brough which contained the sentence: 'It looks as though I might yet
break my neck on a BS [i.e. Brough Superior].'
Just one month later notes made by Liddell Hart, following what he called
Talk with T.E. at Hythe and in Evening at Otterbourne/2 June 1934, included this
paragraph:

> On care in driving – T.E. talked of way he will try to avoid running
> over even a hen, although to swerve is a risk. Said that only on a
> motorcycle was the driver compelled to take fair proportion of risk.
> In a big car can hit anything with impunity. On a motorcycle almost
> certain to be killed – quite right if careless. He would like to see cars
> fitted with a backward projection from bumper ending in a spearhead
> just in front of driver's chest, so that if he hit anything, point would
> pierce him.

A rare glimpse of Lawrence in civilian clothes.

'Tes' and Mrs Clare Sydney Smith in Biscuit.

Lawrence and an unidentified lady.

It is not suggested, however, that there was any sense of premonition in this. If there was one thought that was weighing on him in 1934 it was not that of imminent death but of his imminent departure from the institution which had been his home and life-support system for so long, for in early 1935 his period of service was due to come to an end. He had almost been discharged from the service in early 1933 but there had been an eleventh hour reprieve. Now, however, he could not see, and the R.A.F. did not in the event see, any reason why he should not go. As his personal file states in a note dated 20 December 1934: 'It has been decided unless anything to the contrary is heard from Shaw normal discharge action should proceed.'

The R.A.F. had moved him briskly about England in his last Air Force years. Typical is a time table included in a letter of August 1933 to the Sydney Smiths, like himself by then long departed from Mount Batten:

        Movements:
            Aug. 13–17 – Bridlington
            Aug. 18   – road to Southampton
            Aug. 19   – Hythe
            Aug. 20   – Fareham
            Aug. 21   – Cowes – preliminary trial of pinnace
            Aug. 22   – Air Ministry
            Aug. 23   – Cowes (acceptance trials)

One other R.A.F. station not mentioned above was Felixstowe, where he had been posted immediately following his reprieve of April 1933, and it was to Felixstowe that he consigned his much loved speed-boat *Biscuit* in the last month of his service, January 1935. 'A sad week, this,' he wrote to the Smiths, by this time based in Singapore: 'the *Biscuit*, of tender memory, has journeyed to Felixstowe. Her new owner is F/Lt. Barlow. I hope he will be kind to her. She ran like a race-horse last time I drove her, in November. Leaving her is training for the wrench next month when I lose the service too. A bad year, 1935, for me. I hope it will go on being fine for you, at any rate.'

He had been preparing for the 'wrench', as he put it, for some time. Just before Christmas 1934, writing from his last R.A.F. address in Bridlington, Yorkshire, he summed up his service career in an important and moving letter – in effect an 'Apologia pro Vita Sua' – to John Buchan:

> If you meet Mr Baldwin in the near future, will you please tell him
> that the return to the Air Force secured me by him (on your initiation)
> has given me the only really contented years of my life? Please say
> that I've worked (and played) all the time like a trooper: that my spell
> of service has been spent in doing my best to raise the pride and
> respect of the ranks, and to make them pleased with their duties: that

amongst my jobs have been a re-organization of aero-engine overhauls in India, the ground-work for the 1929 Schneider Cup, and lately the development of the marine-craft side of the R.A.F. In four or five years we have trebled the speed and yet reduced the prime cost and running cost of *all* the R.A.F. boats: and now the War Office and the Admiralty are borrowing our boats and copying or adapting our designs for their purposes.

I tell you this not to boast of it, but to show that you and Baldwin, in gratifying what may have seemed to you my indulgence, have not harmed the public service. I have done all I could, always: and could have done far more, if they had given me more rope: the Air Force is pretty good, down below. I think it deserves more imaginative handling than it gets.

However this note (meant to be a paean of gratitude to two admirable men) mustn't descend into politics. I owe the two of you more than my twelve years work (and another twelve on top of it, were I young enough) in the sheer satisfaction it has been. You have me very hopelessly in your debt: and thank you both very much for it.

His attitude to the termination of his R.A.F. career had two aspects, apparently conflicting. He expressed one of them in a letter to Liddell Hart at Christmas 1934: 'For myself I am going to taste the flavour of true leisure. For 46 years I have worked and been worked. Remaineth 23 years (of expectancy). May they be like Flecker's "a great Sunday that goes on and on".'

There are more examples of his other, more pessimistic mood. He wrote to his old friend of Carchemish days, Mrs Fontana, in November 1934: 'Bridlington in winter is a silent place, where cats and landladies' husbands walk gently down the middle of the streets. I prefer it to the bustle of summer, because my February-looming discharge from the Air Force makes me low-toned. It's like the hermit-crab losing his twelve-year-old shell and I hate the pleasure that my service has been, coming thus to an arbitrary end.' In January 1935 he wrote to Sir Ronald Storrs, with whom he had sailed on his first visit to Arabia in 1916: 'After my discharge I have somehow to pick up a new life and occupy myself – but beforehand it looks and feels like an utterly blank wall. Old age coming, I suppose; at any rate I can admit to being quite a bit afraid for myself, which is quite a new feeling. Up till now I've never come to the end of anything.'

A friend who had no doubt that he was genuinely apprehensive about his future was Henry Williamson:

The R.A.F. was his family and he was happy in it; he said to me, I'm happy here, these plain men here are my equals and it gives me a root in the ground. When he had to retire from the Air Force he went into nothing; he went into a cottage by himself, he missed his friends and he was quite frightened. Anybody would be, especially after, in his words, a 'mort' of experience, a 'death' of experience – we all did in my generation, we found it very hard to get back. . . .

So the time of his departure came. There was a farewell party or two and then on 26 February 1935 he mounted his push-bike (his motor-cycle was not licensed at the time) and rode south from Bridlington.

At Birmingham, December 1934: photographed during a visit to his former R.A.F. friend Arthur Hall, known as 'Brum'.

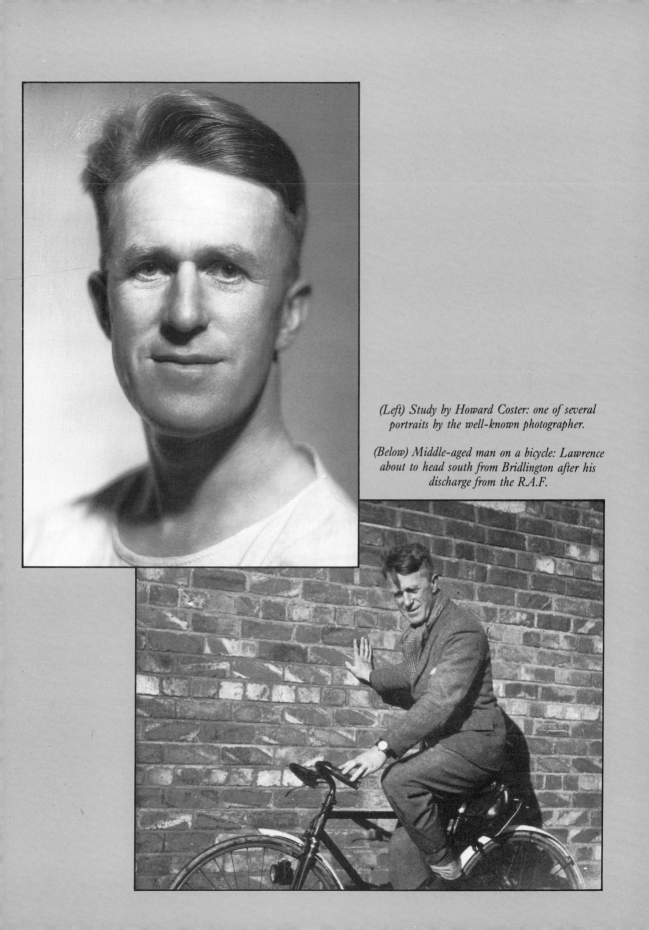

(Left) Study by Howard Coster: one of several portraits by the well-known photographer.

(Below) Middle-aged man on a bicycle: Lawrence about to head south from Bridlington after his discharge from the R.A.F.

13

CASUALTY AT
CLOUDS HILL

His ultimate destination was Clouds Hill but he intended to make various visits on the way. One person high on his list of favourite writers was the Australian Frederic Manning, author of the war novel *Her Privates We* – based on Manning's own experiences as a soldier in the ranks on the Western Front – with whom he had been corresponding occasionally since 1930. Manning's home was at Bourne in Lincolnshire, comfortably on his route home. But, as he wrote to Manning's publisher Peter Davies on 28 February, 'On Tuesday I took my discharge from the R.A.F. and started southward by road, meaning to call at Bourne and see Manning: but to-day I turned eastward, instead, hearing that he was dead.'

Continuing his journey he visited his brother Arnold in Cambridge. In his letter to Peter Davies he had written: 'My losing the R.A.F. numbs me, so that I haven't much feeling to spare for the while. In fact I find myself wishing all the time that my curtain would fall.' Yet his brother found him relaxed and content, and ready to discuss such ideas as the possibility of resuming his printing interests or of spending time exploring the countryside. Another call he made before he returned to Clouds Hill was on John Buchan at Elsfield Manor, near Oxford, impressing Buchan, according to the latter's biographer, Janet Adam Smith, 'with his splendid health and calm nerves'.[1] This is a significant description, because over the next weeks his letters were at times to suggest a man of undiminished sharpness and vigour, at times a man who was almost broken by the unease and uncertainty of his new situation.

Early March found him in London having heard to his anger that the press

---

1 *John Buchan*, pp. 243–4.

were waiting for him at Clouds Hill. He took lodgings under an alias he had used before, Mr E. Smith, sending off a number of letters to explain his predicament. 'My Dorset fastness is beset, they tell me, by pressmen,' he wrote to Ernest Thurtle M.P., 'so I wander about London in a queer unrest, wondering if my mainspring will ever have a tension in it again.' To his former Tank Corps friend, Alec Dixon, he wrote in similar terms – 'It is a feeling of aimless unrest: and of course I am sorry, while knowing it had to be' – and added that he might wander in the Midlands for a while, until the pressmen went away. 'After they tire, the cottage should be a peaceful place.'

With almost every letter at this time he sent out a specially printed card, bearing the message:

> To tell you that in future I shall
> write very few letters   T.E.S.

He included one with the letter to Alec Dixon, stating: 'I'm sending out dozens of the enclosed. Good idea?' It was a ruse he had thought of long before, in India, and now at last he had taken action. Some of his last messages were written on the reverse side of these elegantly printed cards.

Sergeant W.A. Knowles, once of the Royal Tank Corps, who had been his near neighbour across the road at Clouds Hill, had died, as had his widow, and the Knowles homestead was now manned by their son Pat, who was both friend and aide to Lawrence at this time. He wrote to Pat from London on 19 March that he had been making ground with the Press Association bosses and Press Photographing Agencies, that there were good hopes that he would be left alone, and that he hoped to return early the following week. Back at Clouds Hill he decided in spite of his frugal resources to re-license his motor-cycle. 'It goes like stink', he wrote to H.S. Ede, 'and is altogether a marvellous machine.' But one Sunday morning some time after his return two more gentlemen of the press arrived at the cottage and the result was an ugly fracas in which Pat Knowles was involved. Interviewed in 1962 he described the occasion.

> On that morning I came across to tell him that breakfast was ready and saw two men alongside a motor-cycle up the road, and as I got near them I saw they had got cameras under their coats. I asked them what they wanted, and they said they wanted a photograph of Shaw, so I told them that he was averse to having his photograph taken and I didn't think they'd have much chance. I went in and told Shaw that these men were here. He didn't seem unduly worried. He said, 'Well, I'll just stay here. Bring me some food over and we'll just wait.' I brought him some food over and kept an eye on these chaps, and went about something else. Well, later on in the morning I came in, and his mood had changed completely. His face was red and he wouldn't look at me, and his eyes were blazing. He couldn't sit still.

Lawrence in mechanic's overalls:

*'After having dabbled in revolt and politics it is
rather nice to have been mechanically useful.'*
(Lawrence to Lord Lloyd, 26 September 1934)

First of all he sat on the fender, and he got on to the settee, then he went to the chair, then he came back again. I've never been in the presence of anyone before or since in whom I felt such distress and anger and frustration. If it were possible for a human being to evanesce, to just disappear like smoke, he would have done it that morning. It was almost like an aura about him, almost something solid, and I just couldn't stay there in the same room. I came down to the lower room and I tried to read a book, but I couldn't even stay inside the cottage, so I went out. He called me and said, 'Don't go very far', so I stayed around and sawed some wood or did something. Then he called me back and said, 'I'm not going to have any more of this. Go and get one of them, and we'll see if we can talk them out of it.' I got the two chaps and I took their camera away from them, and followed them inside. One of them got into the top room and I heard him talking, and then suddenly there was a scuffle. There was a shout from Shaw, 'Come on, Pat, let's chuck these chaps out!' And a free-for-all developed and we pushed them out on to the brick-path and slammed the door. They hammered on the door and shouted a lot of abuse, and Shaw went upstairs. When they went away from the door, I went upstairs and Shaw was sitting on the fender, and he was shaking, and he was chewing his knuckles. And he turned to me and said, 'It's years since I struck a man.'

He exiled himself from his home more than once at this time. E. T. Leeds, his colleague and correspondent of the Carchemish and Arabian years, concludes his contribution to *Lawrence by His Friends* as follows:

So comes the last memory of him three weeks before his death, when driven from Clouds Hill a third time by the gadfly torment of an insatiable and inconsiderate Press, he escaped to Oxford. There he made one of his never omitted, however short, calls, loyal to a favourite haunt of other days, to learn how the Ashmolean still fared. A restatement of certain facts surrounding an archaeological conundrum for which he himself had been largely responsible over twenty years before, a brief discussion of the ways and means to solve it, the smile and jest of farewell, and quietly he was gone for ever.

His friends had always hoped that leaving the R.A.F. service might release him to take up work of importance appropriate to his energies and intelligence. He had been approached by the Hon. Francis Rodd on behalf of Sir Montague Norman with the offer of the Secretaryship of the Bank of England, which, while admitting that the approach had given him 'a moment of very rare pleasure which I shall not tell to anyone, or forget', he had firmly declined.[1] Now Lady

1 This offer is fact and not fiction, as surmised in a recent best-selling biography, *The Secret Lives of Lawrence of Arabia*. Further discussion on this point is to be found in *The Letters of T. E. Lawrence* edited by Malcolm Brown, 1988.

To tell you that in future I shall

write very few letters.

T. E. S.

The card which Lawrence included with almost all the letters he wrote in the last months of his life.

8. V.35

No: wild mares would not at present take me away from Clouds Hill. It is an earthly paradise and I am staying here till I feel qualified for it. Also there is something broken in the works, as I told you: my will, I think. In this mood I would not take on any job at all. So do not commit yourself to advocating me, lest I prove a non-starter. Am well, well-fed, full of company, Calorious and innocent - customed. News from China — NIL. Their area now a centre of disturbance.   TES

His last message to Lady Astor, written on the back of one.

Astor and others conspired to draw him into discussions about a subject much closer to his known capabilities and achievements. 'I believe when the Government reorganizes,' she wrote to him on 7 May, 'you will be asked to reorganize the Defence Forces. . . . If you will come to Cliveden Saturday, the last Saturday in May, you will never regret it.' She then listed a number of leading people who would be there, including Stanley Baldwin (who was to resume the Premiership, succeeding Ramsay MacDonald, precisely one month later), Lionel Curtis and Lord Lothian. With a nice wit in spite of his somewhat sombre mood, Lawrence replied:

> No: wild mares would not at present take me away from Clouds Hill. It is an earthly paradise and I am staying here till I feel qualified for it. Also there is something broken in the works, as I told you: my will, I think. In this mood I would not take on any job at all. So do not commit yourself to advocating me, lest I prove a non-starter.

Someone with a different political initiative in mind for Lawrence was Henry Williamson, who at this time was emerging as supporter of the British Fascist Movement and showing a distinct sympathy for the eccentric leader of Germany, Herr Hitler. He had been a soldier on the Western Front from the early months of the Great War and been a participant in one of the most remarkable episodes of that first phase, the Christmas Truce of 1914. Meeting ordinary German soldiers in a No Man's Land untouched for once by shot or shell, and talking with them as man to man, had convinced him of the essential benevolence of the nation against whom Britain had fought with such ferocity and anger – and also made him deeply anxious to avoid such a confrontation happening again. On or just before 12 May he wrote to Lawrence at Clouds Hill, asking if he might come to see him. Henry Williamson, again from his interview in 1962:

> I thought the world was dropping down into war and I felt that if the two white giants of Europe grappled again it would be the end of our civilization and Bolshevism would come over. So I wrote to Lawrence in desperation and said, if I can arrange a meeting with Hitler, will you come and see him? I thought Hitler would be influenced by that man, because Hitler was balanced between a psychotic nature and a nature of tremendous common sense and sensitivity. And the answer to my letter was a telegram from Lawrence 'Come tomorrow lunch cottage Bovington Camp wet fine'.[1]
>
> INTERVIEWER: What do you think his reaction would have been if you had been able to discuss this?
>
> I think he'd have said, You must be a writer, Williamson, and not a

---

1 The precise text of the telegram was: 'Lunch Tuesday wet fine cottage one mile north Bovington Camp Shaw'.

politician, and don't get involved in things as I did in the past. Just live as happily as you can and do your own work.' And I of course would have done exactly what he would have told me to, because I looked upon him as a man of great wisdom and kindliness.

Pat Knowles later recounted what happened on the morning of Tuesday 13 May:

> There was a letter from Henry Williamson, saying that he was proposing to visit Clouds Hill the following day, and Shaw said that he was going to go down [to the camp] and send a telegram. He came across to me shortly before he went and asked me if there was anything I wanted, and shortly afterwards I heard him move off. Well, it was one of those bright clear days in May when the wind was southerly and it was very pleasant, and I could hear the drill sergeants on the squares. And later I heard the motor-cycle coming back. I heard the engine suddenly race – and then stop.

Attempting to avoid two errand boys bicycling up the road from Bovington Camp towards Clouds Hill Lawrence had apparently swerved but had clipped the wheel of one of the bicycles and the Brough had gone out of control. Flying over the handlebars he had hit the ground hard and instantly, or almost instantly, lost consciousness. He was taken to Bovington Camp Hospital where he lay in a coma and died six days later. He was aged 46.

That a man about whom there were many bizarre stories in life should be made the subject of much speculation in death was almost inevitable. There were – indeed still are – theories of conspiracy and murder. It is, however, surely much more plausible that the man who told Liddell Hart that when driving he would try to avoid even a hen in the road would attempt to spare two errand boys on bicycles. It is also possible that the mood of 'something broken in the works' of which he wrote to Lady Astor was still upon him. When the prospect arose of his leaving the R.A.F. in 1933, he had written to her, 'I shall be unreal & vague for ever so long, afterwards.' There are numerous similar expressions in his last notes and letters in May 1935. To Sir William Rothenstein, the painter, on 5 May: 'I just sit here in this cottage and wonder about nothing in general. Comfort is a very poor state after busyness.' To the airman poet G. W. M. Dunn on the same day: 'Something has gone dead inside me, now.' On 6 May he describes himself both to Eric Kennington and to Bruce Rogers as a leaf fallen from its tree. On 12 May, one day before the accident, he tells a friend at the Ashmolean, K. T. Parker: 'For the moment I'm sitting in my cottage and getting used to an empty life.' Other letters, by contrast, show him writing as vigorously as ever; and he was also spending much time and energy working on the improvements of his cottage. It is, however, surely a distinct possibility that after sending his telegram to Williamson – the contents

MR. T. E. SHAW GRAVELY INJURED

MOTORING ACCIDENT IN DORSET

Mr. T. E. Shaw, who recently left the Royal Air Force after serving his engagement as an aircraftman, and who during the War became famous as Colonel T. E. Lawrence, the leader of the Arab irregular forces in the Palestine campaign, was seriously injured yesterday morning through an accident while riding a motor-cycle a few miles from Wool, in Dorset. He was removed to the hospital at Bovington Camp, where it was found that his skull was fractured.

Mr. Shaw, since his discharge from the Royal Air Force, has been living in a country cottage at Moreton, in Dorset. Motor-cycling has been his chief recreation.

(Right) The Times *reports the accident.*

(Below) His home-city newspaper reports the death.

of whose letter (which incidentally has never been found) must have been somewhat disturbing – he drove back to Clouds Hill with his mind less fixed than was usually the case on the road ahead.

The funeral was at Moreton Church, not far across the fields from Clouds Hill, on 21 May. Churchill, Lady Astor, Lord Lloyd, Lionel Curtis and Augustus John were among the mourners; the bearers were Sir Ronald Storrs, the artist Eric Kennington, Colonel Newcombe, Aircraftman Bradbury, Arthur Russell of the Tank Corps, and Pat Knowles. Arnold Lawrence was the only member of the family present, as his mother and brother were still in China. The words on the headstone that was eventually placed on the grave were chosen by his mother. Curiously the one biographical detail included in the inscription is the fact that he had been a Fellow of All Souls College, Oxford.

He left behind him an acute sense of grief and loss. On the day of his funeral Sir Herbert Baker wrote to Lady Astor:

> My dear Lady who loved Him as I did;
> I was away and so got out of touch with your kindness. I should like
> to talk to you about him; the funeral would be too much for me; so
> I am here reading Shelley's *Adonais*;
>   'till the future dares
>   Forget the past, his fate and fame shall be
>   An echo and a light unto eternity.'

E. H. R. Altounyan, in Aleppo at this time, went to see Sheikh Hamoudi, who had been site foreman at Carchemish and had visited Oxford with Dahoum over twenty years before, to tell him the sad news. 'Oh, if only he had died in battle,' said Hamoudi; 'I have lost my son, but I do not grieve for him as I do for Lawrence. . . . I am counted brave, the bravest of my tribe; my heart is iron, but his was steel. . . . Tell them in England what I say. Of manhood the man, in freedom free; a mind without equal; I can see no flaw in him.' Reporting on Hamoudi's outburst, Altounyan (who himself was to write an elegy in memory of Lawrence) commented: 'Biblical all this, out of date – for the moment, yet I can only set down the words I heard and try to convey the harsh impress of their deep sincerity.'

He left behind him unanswered questions. If he had lived would he have found any notable use for his talents? In particular since he would have been only 52 at the outbreak of the Second World War would his friend and admirer Churchill have insisted that he should respond to the call of a great national emergency? Or was Sir Philip Sassoon right when he saw him as one of those beings 'who seem to have been created for one end and, having achieved it, have passed comet-like from the eyes and minds of their fellow men'?

Some months after his death Lawrence's younger brother A. W. Lawrence invited people who had been close to him from his childhood onwards to collaborate in producing a miscellany of brief memoirs about him, with the particular proviso that they should be 'candid, critical and personal'. This 'gallery of partial portraits' (A.W.L.'s phrase) appeared in 1937 as *T. E. Lawrence by His Friends*. Subsequently many of those who knew him have written or spoken about him in many contexts and on many occasions. As one sifts through this mass of material certain words or phrases stand out. He was impish; there are references to his giggle; he both loved and hated the limelight; he was vain but also ashamed of his own vanity; he was – a convenient description – a mass of contradictions. But all this was said in the knowledge that he was what would now be called a high-flyer and there were many attempts to define the quality of excellence which plainly impressed so many of his contemporaries. Altounyan wrote of his 'superlative intelligence'; former artillery officer S. H. Brodie wrote of his 'mastery'; Sir Ernest Dowson wrote of his 'extraordinary resourcefulness'; Lord Allenby wrote of his 'brilliance'. Allenby also commented on his 'will-power', and 'power' is a word that frequently occurs. Siegfried Sassoon (already quoted here in Chapter 12) thought he had 'power over life'; W. F. Stirling wrote of his 'compelling power'; Mrs Clare Sydney Smith spoke of 'this extraordinary power outside himself that made him sometimes almost afraid, because, he said, "You know, it is something which I can turn on and off like a tap".' Francis Yeats-Brown wrote in somewhat similar vein: 'He had terrific, indeed terrible energies in his small body'.

One other key word which regularly occurs is 'genius'. Apart from the two early examples of the word quoted on the title page of this book, it was used by, among others, W. F. Stirling, the M.P. Ernest Thurtle, the American Ralph Isham, the historian L. B. Namier, Lord Halifax, Winston Churchill and – a man unlikely to be lavish with such accolades – George Bernard Shaw. Perhaps the strongest affirmation in this category was by H. St. John Philby, who in 1957 (i.e. after Aldington) wrote: 'Lawrence was a genius, nothing more and nothing less, and therefore not to be judged or analysed by the standards applicable to more normal persons, however competent or distinguished.'

A later verdict more in tune with the phrase of Aubrey Herbert's from which this book takes its title, and one less likely than Philby's to cause a second wave of denigration, is that of the poet Cecil Day-Lewis, with whom Lawrence corresponded towards the end of his life. In the Preface which Day-Lewis contributed to Lawrence's *Minorities*, published in 1971, he wrote: 'Being out of sympathy with those who have sought, by diminishing him as a scholar, a writer and a military leader, to cut him down to their own size, I maintain my conviction that he was an exceptional human being.'

IN MEMORY OF T.E. LAWRENCE

FUNERAL OF E.T. SHAW
"LAWRENCE" OF ARABIA,
AT MORETON. 21.5.35.

(Above) Postcard of the funeral at Moreton, showing Mr and Mrs Winston Churchill among the mourners.

(Below) The grave at Moreton: not in the churchyard proper but in the graveyard annexe down the road.

TO THE DEAR MEMORY OF
T E LAWRENCE
FELLOW OF ALL SOULS COLLEGE
OXFORD
BORN 16 AUGUST 1888
DIED 19 MAY 1935
THE HOUR IS COMING & NOW IS
WHEN THE DEAD SHALL HEAR
THE VOICE OF THE
SON OF GOD
AND THEY THAT HEAR
SHALL LIVE

EFFIGIES OF T.E. LAWRENCE

(Right) Bust, St Paul's Cathedral: with identical copy at Jesus College, Oxford.

(Below) Recumbent crusader, St Martin's Church, Wareham. Both sculptures by Eric Kennington.

The bust was made in 1926; the crusader effigy was sculpted in the four years following Lawrence's death.

He seems to answer some sort of requirement. It's almost religious – in fact it is a religion. I had great difficulty in not allowing myself to be used as the St Paul of it. I had, I should think, something like five hundred letters after his death; the majority wanted me to take up his mantle. I suppose it was because of his disdain for worldly success. He wanted it when he was young; he got it; and despised it. . . .

(*A.W. Lawrence in* Lawrence and Arabia, *BBC*1, 18 *April* 1986)

Later, when we were often riding inland my mind used to turn me from the direct road to clear my senses by a night in Rumm, and by the ride down its dawn-lit valley towards the shining plains, or up its valley in the sunset towards that glowing square which my timid anticipation never let me reach. I would say, 'Shall I ride on this time, beyond the Khazail, and know it all?'

(*T.E. Lawrence,* Seven Pillars of Wisdom*)*

SELECT BIBLIOGRAPHY

Abdullah: *Memoirs* (Cape 1950)

Aldington, Richard: *Lawrence of Arabia: A Biographical Enquiry* (Collins 1955)

Altounyan, E. H. R.: *Ornament of Honour* (Cambridge University Press, 1937)

Antonius, George: *The Arab Awakening* (Hamish Hamilton 1938)

Boyle, Andrew: *Trenchard* (Collins, 1962)

Brown, Malcolm: *The Letters of T. E. Lawrence* (Dent, 1988)

Charmley, John: *Lord Lloyd and the Decline of the British Empire* (Weidenfeld and Nicolson 1987)

Churchill, Winston: *Great Contemporaries* (Butterworth, 1937)

Dunbar, Janet: *Mrs G.B.S. A Portrait* (Harrap, 1963, Harper & Row, 1963)

Fitzherbert, Margaret: *The Man Who Was Greenmantle: A Biography of Aubrey Herbert*, (John Murray 1983, Oxford University Press 1985)

Garnett, David: *The Letters of T. E. Lawrence* (Cape 1938, Spring Books London, 1964); *Selected Letters of T. E. Lawrence* (Cape 1938, Reprint Society 1941); *The Essential T. E. Lawrence* (Cape 1951)

Graves, Richard Perceval: *Lawrence of Arabia and His World* (Thames and Hudson, 1976)

Graves, Robert: *Lawrence and the Arabs* (Cape 1927; Doubleday, Doran 1928)

Graves, Robert & Hart, Liddell: *T. E. Lawrence to His Biographers* (Cassell 1963)

Hart, Liddell: *'T. E. Lawrence' in Arabia and After* (Cape 1934)

Herbert, Aubrey: *Mons, Anzac and Kut* (Edward Arnold 1919)

Hyde, H. Montgomery: *Solitary in the Ranks* (Constable 1977)

Kirkbride, Sir Alec: *A Crackle of Thorns* (John Murray 1956); *An Awakening* (University Press of Arabia 1971)

Knightley, Phillip and Simpson, Colin: *The Secret Lives of Lawrence of Arabia* (Nelson 1969)

Lawrence, A. W. (editor): *Letters to T. E. Lawrence* (Cape 1962); *T. E. Lawrence by His Friends* (Cape 1937; abridged version 1954)

Lawrence, M. R. (editor): *The Home Letters of T. E. Lawrence and His Brothers* (Blackwell 1954)

Lawrence T. E.: *The Mint* (Cape 1955, Penguin 1978); *The Odyssey of Homer* (translation) (Oxford University Press, 1935); *Revolt in the Desert* (Cape 1927, Doran 1927); *Secret Despatches from Arabia* (Golden Cockerell Press 1939); *Seven Pillars of Wisdom* (Cape 1935; Doubleday 1935; Penguin 1962)

Mack, John E.: *A Prince of our Disorder* (Little, Brown 1976; Weidenfeld and Nicolson 1976)

Marriott, Paul J.: *The Young Lawrence of Arabia* 1888–1910 (published by the author) c. 1978

Monroe, Elizabeth: *Britain's Moment in the Middle East* (Chatto & Windus 1963)

Mousa, Suleiman: *T. E. Lawrence: An Arab View* (Oxford University Press 1966)

Ocampo, Victoria: 338171, *T. E. Lawrence of Arabia* (translated by David Garnett, Gollancz 1963)

Philby, H. St. John: *Forty Years in the Wilderness* (Robert Hale 1957)

Richards, Vyvyan: *Portrait of T. E. Lawrence* (Cape 1936)

Smith, Clare Sydney: *The Golden Reign* (Cassell 1940)

Stewart, Desmond: *T. E. Lawrence* (Hamish Hamilton 1977)

Stirling, W. F.: *Safety Last* (Hollis and Carter 1953)

Storrs, Ronald: *Orientations* (Ivor Nicholson and Watson, 1937)

Thomas, Lowell: *With Lawrence in Arabia* (Century 1924; Hutchinson 1925)

Villars, Jean Beraud: *T. E. Lawrence or the Search for the Absolute* (Sidgwick & Jackson, 1958)

Wavell, Colonel A. P.: *The Palestine Campaigns* (Constable 1928)

Weintraub, Stanley: *Private Shaw and Public Shaw* (Cape 1963)

Weintraub, Stanley and Rodelle (editors): *Evolution of a Revolt* (Pennsylvania State University Press, 1968)

Wilson, J. M. (editor): *Minorities* (Cape, 1971)

Yardley, Michael: *Backing into the Limelight* (Harrap 1985)

INDEX

References to illustrations are given in italics.

Valentino, Rudolf 150n
Vansittart, Lord xvii
Vickery, Major Charles 75, 78

Wadi Ais 74, 83, 84
Wadi Rumm xviii, 110, *111*, 126, 223
Wadi Safra 60, 61, 67, 74, 97
Wadi Sirhan 101
Wales 3, 4, 12, 23
Wavell, Colonel A. P. 90, 109
Weizmann, Dr Chaim 145
Wejh 74, 75, 76, 77,78, 79, 83, 84, 86,
  101
Wemyss, Admiral Sir Rosslyn 53, 66
Wilderness of Zin 47
Williamson Henry xviii, 195, 196, 198,
  201, 206, 215, 216

Wilson, Colonel C. E. 59, 74, 84, 85, 148,
  195
Wilson, Woodrow 146, 147, 150
Wingate, Sir Reginald 66, 67, 88
Winterton, Lord 180
Woolley, C. L. 39, 40, 41, *41*, 42, *42*, 44,
  47, 48, 50

Yarmuk Valley 88, 105, 109
Yeats-Brown, Francis 219
Yenbo 58, 65, 66, 67, 69, 70, 71, *73*, 74
  75, 83
Young, Major Hubert 126, 127
'Young Turks' 54

Zeid, Emir 56, 61, 67, 70, 117, 120, 121,
  122, 142, 143, 161